T0161187

With a heart that yearns
for the salvation of my people Israel,
with much love, prayer and a thankful heart
I dedicate this book to those,
who are committed to the God of Israel,
who dearly love my people
and are upholding my hands
in the calling of God on my life
and to Jeff Booth,
who introduced me to the Truth.

Why Me?

I have called you by name; you are Mine
Isaiah 43

Jacob Damkani

Why Me? by Jacob Damkani

Amikam Tavor, David Smith, and Emilio Daniel Mazhindu translated the text of this book from Hebrew into English.

Why Me? is available in Hebrew, Chinese, Czech, Danish, Dutch, English, Finnish, French, German, Hungarian, Italian, Korean, Norwegian, Portuguese, Romanian, Russian, Spanish and Swedish.
More languages coming soon.

Copyright © Hebrew 1993 by Jacob Damkani,
Copyright © English 1997, 2013, 2018, 2020 by Jacob Damkani
Published by Carpenter's Son Publishing, Franklin, TN
ISBN 978-1-952025-53-2

Please contact us
Trumpet of Salvation to Israel / Jacob Damkani
P.O. Box 3565, Tel Aviv 6103402, Israel
Elisheva@TrumpetofSalvation.org
www.TrumpetofSalvation.org

Contents

Chapter 1

Trumpeldor and Other Heroes

Kiryat Shmonah (the Town of the Eight), is a small village at the foot of the Golan Heights, not far from the Lebanese border. On that day of remembrance in 1964, we students stood at attention in long, straight rows with our eyes raised toward the banner of the Jewish state as the Israeli national flag was lowered to half-mast. Today, I cannot remember all the lofty eulogies uttered by the principal and the senior class pupils on that occasion. They all spoke with pompous, austere language about the atrocities committed by the villainous Nazis against the Jews in a remote country called Germany.

When exactly did World War II break out? Ten years ago? A thousand years ago? Who knew! After all, the history of the Jewish people is inundated with accounts of atrocities. Every national and religious feast revives the memories of our enemies, who, in every generation, rose up against us to destroy us. But the Holy One, blessed be He, delivered us from their hands. In the mind of a twelve-year-old boy, all these stories were mixed up together in a confused mass of persecutions, tribulations, evil decrees, and hatred of the Jews—be it the Syrians in Hanukkah, the Persians in Purim, the Egyptians in Passover, the Romans in *Lag b'Omer* (holiday celebrated on the 33rd day of the Counting of the Omer), or the Arabs on Independence Day. What child could distinguish between these numerous enemies that punctuate our history throughout the generations, centuries, and millennia?

Strangely enough, one sentence that was spoken on this occasion remains in my memory until this very day. It was: "We shall never forget, neither shall we ever forgive!" I still recall the heavy, oppressive atmosphere of mourning and the heart-breaking shrieking of the siren, which to me resembled the wailing of a bereaved mother lamenting over her dead child. Finally, we sang the national anthem, *HaTikvah* (The Hope), to mark the end of our ceremony.

I earnestly tried to visualize what exactly did happen in Nazi Germany and hoped to feel even a tiny drop of the ocean of death at the extermination camps and in the gas chambers. Yet, in spite of my most sincere efforts, I could not revive in my spirit what had already died and been buried on foreign soil. There, among the rows of students, on the vast playground of the elementary school, I stood at attention. My eyes watched the flag, wildly rippling as it was beaten about by the Galilean morning winds. Upon hearing the familiar tune of the national anthem, my heart was flooded with a crisp sensation of pride for being a citizen of Israel. Love for my country and my willingness to run to her defense at all times overwhelmed my excited heart.

The years went by. One day a huge bulldozer appeared in the front yard of our home. We lived then on a street in the north of Kiryat Shmonah, the closest point to the Lebanese border. Goats, ducks, and chickens, which normally would roam freely in the spacious yard, fled in terror from the noisy vehicle. As I watched the bulldozer at work, digging a large hole in the ground, my mind wandered off to those accursed corpse-filled ditches in Europe—corpses of men and women, old and young alike, the remains of our people. "No one will ever dig ditches like those in our country!" I promised myself.

However, this hole, just as all the others dug in those days across the town, was designated for an entirely different purpose. Soon it was filled with wooden boards, iron bars, and a concrete casting. Eventually, this all became an air-raid shelter. The dark dirt that covered it was planted with blood-red anemones, which represented to me the blood of the Jews that were hit—and still are—by *katyusha*, missiles fired at us from across the border of Lebanon.

As I gazed at the newly built air-raid shelter, I thought to myself, "Our enemies have never concealed their hatred toward us. If and when another war breaks out, we in Kiryat Shmonah will be the first to endure their blows. The screams of the sirens will chase us like frightened rabbits into the shelters. Will I also run and hide then? Will I flee as well?"

I promised myself solemnly, "Never! I will fight back! I will never let those heathen Gentiles do us any harm again! O God, why on earth did You create those Gentiles in the first place? Wasn't it possible for You to make all of them Jews? Wouldn't it be interesting to see what this world would have looked like if all its inhabitants were Jews?"

Sabbath days and holy days were special in my family. Following the usual morning worship in the synagogue, we liked to sit together around the long festive table set by my mother and sisters. We had *kiddush*, a traditional prayer of sanctification, over the *yay'in* and *challah*, wine and Sabbath bread. In that blessed atmosphere of holiness, we ate the traditional brunch of baked potatoes, red beets, and hard-boiled eggs that had simmered all night long until they became dark and tanned. We also had slices of fried eggplant and squash and, on occasion, red spiced fish. None of us could forget the strong, sweet tea that was an inseparable part of the meal.

Afterward, while Father went to bed for his Sabbath nap and Mother fretted about everything and everybody, I would go out for my regular Sabbath afternoon stroll in the surrounding hills. There I liked to pick flowers, watch butterflies, and enjoy the wild raspberries, figs, and pomegranates that grew unattended in the valley. I refreshed myself with the cold river water and crisp air of the Upper Galilee.

Up in *Tel-Hai* (Living Hill) were the grave sites of some of the national heroes who had been laid to rest in that cemetery. All the sights and odors I absorbed on my way there in those early days of spring are still fresh in my memory, as if experienced only yesterday. I recall the huge eucalyptus trees that overshadowed the steeply meandering asphalt road, the children of the nearby *kibbutz* (a communal farm or settlement in Israel) driving their cart that was pulled by a long-eared, black mule down the road, and the weight of those baskets full of bitter olives that I would bring home for Mother to pickle.

As I ascended that "blood-stained" mound, a myriad of thoughts and emotions arose in me. Tel-Hai was where I visited my friend, Trumpeldor. With my head bowed down in deep reverence, I entered into the military graveyard. The dead, whose screams seemed to be swallowed up by the dark soil, were to me a model of patriotism, an example of love for the motherland. I could not help but think of Yosef Trumpeldor and his legendary last words, "It is good to die for our country!" He uttered those words, not with the same roar as the lion statue that overlooks his grave, but rather in a whispered, agonizing sigh from his deathbed. That whisper had begun to ring in his heart while he was still guiding the plow with his single hand in the fields of Tel-Hai, and it rings and echoes in the deep recesses of the soul of every Jew even today.

Eight heroes fell in those fields, and *Kiryat Shmonah* was named "Town of the Eight" in their honor. Am I alive today by the merit of their shed blood? If those eight heroes of Tel-Hai had not sacrificed themselves on the altar of the national resurrection, would I have been born and raised on foreign soil?

With every visit to that site came the arousal of profound thoughts and unanswerable questions: How is it to live as a Jew among anti-Semitic Gentiles? Why were the Jewish people so severely persecuted during all their exiles? Why did my forefathers forsake their homeland originally? Why were they exiled from their land for so many years, only to be returned now?

Our rabbis taught that the first seventy-year exile from our land was because of our "idolatry, incest, and bloodshed." Similarly, they told us that because of our "hatred without cause," we were driven away from our country for the last two thousand years. Was this true? How many days, weeks, and months are there in two thousand years? To whom was this "hatred without cause" directed?

Why didn't we return earlier to conquer the desert, make the wilderness blossom like a rose, and make the barren land rejoice? Why didn't we come sooner to drain the malaria-infested swamps of the Hula Valley? The land, which was given to us by God, had become the habitation of jackals, and we were dispersed and cast abroad among all the heathen. (See Isaiah 35.) Why did God decide to bring us back home right now? Is the redemption of Israel beginning to materialize right here and now, in front of our very eyes? Are we really the last generation to live in servitude and first generation to experience salvation? Are we any better or holier than our forefathers? What did we do to merit this privilege to be "the beginning of salvation," as the rabbis told us? How did I come to be part of this generation?

Why me? Of all people, why me? How is it that we were finally permitted to live in the country that, until now, was considered "a land that consumes her inhabitants"? Was it God or was it the land that abhorred us and spewed us out? Is there any other race of people on the face of this earth that has been exiled from its homeland twice, but has returned both times to revive its comatose spirit and dormant language? Who is to be thanked and praised for the return? Theodore Herzl? Lord Balfour? Chaim Weizmann? David Ben-Gurion? Or, must we rather give thanks to the Almighty God of Israel, who exiled us from our country because of our sins, and who, faithful to His ancient promises, has mercifully brought us back home?

All of these existential questions struck me with a strange power. Why, and for whom, does the stone lion at Tel-Hai roar its silent cry? Does it challenge the hatred and cruelty of our foes who look down from the Golan Heights at our young settlements, our newborn state? Does it raise its head in defiance—God forbid—against the Lord who allowed those Gentiles to drag us to their gallows like lambs led to the slaughter? Actually, what was this terrible sin of ours that caused the whole world to hate us with such passion? Who will rise up next to persecute our offspring?

I gazed at the snowcapped Mt. Hermon, dominating the distant horizon, and the green landscape around me. The contrast between the beauty of nature and the ugliness of history disturbed me. On Memorial Day, with the flag hanging low, I had stood at attention, contemplating the atrocities of the Christians and wondering where God was when the Nazis butchered us mercilessly. Here at Tel-Hai, I sat quietly, meditating on the burning hatred of the Muslim Arabs toward us. I prayed whenever I was at the synagogue, asking myself what it means to be a Jew and why on earth God ever chose us from among all the nations of the earth.

I never doubted the existence of God, but I could not understand why and how He permitted the Gentiles to persecute us with such cruelty. Why did He allow them to slaughter us? Were we chosen for this reason? What exactly does God want, and why is it so difficult to please Him?

At the center of the cemetery, on a wall of hewn stones, a large inscription is written in huge, black, iron letters:

By Blood And Fire Judah Fell;
By Blood And Fire Judah Shall Rise Again!

I once looked at that inscription and thought, "We have always had to pass through rivers of blood and fire. Even today we must fight and shed our blood in order to protect this precious country of ours. Otherwise, our land will fall into enemy hands again!" Then, a defiant, heretical thought suddenly entered my mind: "If this is what we have been chosen for, wouldn't it be better if we were uncircumcised, like all the nations around us? Isn't the *goy* (Gentile) better off than the circumcised Jew, who is always pursued to the death by the devastating sword?"

"God forbid! Put away these sacrilegious thoughts at once!" I scolded myself. "Am I not a Jew? I was born a Jew and must never defile myself with such depravity! I would rather be burned alive than follow those uncircumcised heathen, wallowing in all kinds of immorality and filth!"

From early childhood, our teachers had implanted in us the attitude of utter disgust toward the despicable "hellenizers" and "converts" throughout history—those traitors who chose lives of ease and comfort among the Gentiles, rather than to be satisfied with the sheer spirituality of Jewish life. Our teachers taught us to despise those who fearfully tried to escape the persecutions of the *goyim* (Gentiles, plural) and flee the cruel fate awaiting the hated Jews.

I reasoned that we Jews are living testimonies to the very existence of God. If we, too, were to behave as the Gentiles do, there would be no one left in this world to bear witness to the one true God! The heathen people, who wish to be rid of the Jews, in reality, are seeking to dispose of God Himself, and ultimately to become their own masters. Is this what the heathen are really trying to do—trying to remove God from His throne of glory and to usurp His authority? But, aren't we, the Jews, trying to do the very same thing?

What is it, really, that distinguishes man from beast? What makes me, the Jew, different from the rest of creation, from the trees, from the rocks and the oceans? Can the Gentile see anything special and likeable in me? Does the sign of circumcision, sealed in my flesh, encourage the Gentile to seek to know my God and to love Him above all other things? But, how can a Gentile find out that I am circumcised? After all, it isn't one of those things that one demonstrates! And, if a Gentile were to know, would it make any difference? Perhaps, the *kippah* or *yarmulke* (head covering like a beanie or a skullcap), the *tzitzith* (fringes or tassels worn on traditional garments as reminders of the commandments), and *peyot* (dreadlocks or sidecurls)—which are no longer worn by most Jews—distinguish us from the rest of humanity and indicate that we are God's chosen people. But, if this were so, would the meaning of our appearance provoke the Gentiles to jealousy and make them wish to be like us?

In spite of my national pride, I was not able to see myself as a person to be envied by anyone seeking after the God of Israel. I had to admit that I was certainly not an example of a man of God, chosen by Him to be a light to the heathen.

Perhaps, if my people would only try to be morally better than all others, the Gentiles would see the existence of God in us. But, are we any better? Even if we did manage to be the nicest and most pleasant people on earth, wouldn't the Gentiles abuse our goodness, taking advantage of our cheerful disposition? Is it better to exploit or to be exploited? And who, for heaven's sake, holds the answers to all these contradictory and confusing questions?

The hushed stillness at the cemetery reminded me of the solemn quietness of the schoolyard during the ceremony for Holocaust and Heroism Memorial Day. The long rows of graves resembled the long, straight rows of pupils standing at attention. I could not avoid the sobering thought that only young people, mere children, were buried here in the dark ground of Tel-Hai, so close to Kiryat Shmonah. But, I knew the children of Kiryat Shmonah were in no way like these stony tombs. They were vibrating with life, their hearts beating toward a better tomorrow, anticipating life in a world that knows no fear—the fear of the sudden noise of a low-flying jet or the whistle of yet another missile coming in from Lebanon.

How long will we continue to walk down this valley of the shadow of death that takes such a high, bloody toll? It is true, of course, that this precious piece of land was the possession of our fathers, and that God Himself gave it to us as an inheritance through His promises. But, does this possession justify this much sacrifice?

As for me, I would surely defend this land of mine to the bitter end. I would protect it with my own body and allow no enemy to rob me of it. When the time would come, I was certainly planning to join the army as a pilot, or at least a paratrooper. I would definitely fight for this beloved country at all cost!

The silent roaring of Trumpeldor's lion became the reverberation in my anguished heart. The stony monument had sealed its impression on my childlike heart. Then, leaving the dead behind me lying peacefully in the ground, I returned southward on the road that led back home.

The tall fir trees kissed the light blue skies, and the birds sang happily among the branches. The wind was not blowing at that hour, and it seemed to me that even the air stood still, honoring the holy Sabbath. Wildflowers decorated the roadside with splashes of color: red anemones and orange poppies, golden chrysanthemums and yellow carpets of wild mustard, all with their enchanting fragrances.

The range of the Naphtali Mountains towered on my right, and the distant Golan Heights were tinted with pale blue shades in the east, poised above the sparkling sapphire fishponds of the fertile Hula Valley. I filled my lungs with the clean air, trying to treasure these sensations in me forever: the wonder of creation, as well as the miracle of the survival of the Jewish people—my own people—during the millennia of our existence.

Suddenly, I was jerked out of my reverie back to reality with all its daily cares and worries. Despite my relative shock, I knew beyond any shadow of doubt that it was good—even if it were not easy—to be Jewish. When I arrived at home, Father was already preparing himself to go back to the synagogue. The time for the afternoon prayers had come.

Scenes from the movie "A New Spirit"

Chapter 2

At the Local Synagogue

On Sabbath mornings I liked to walk with Father to the local synagogue, which was situated about halfway between our home and the school. Together with other youngsters in the neighborhood, I ran around it, in it, and through it, always impressed afresh by its tall, narrow windows, decorated with Stars of David. In those days the synagogue seemed to me far taller and larger than all the other buildings in the area. Actually, this really was the case, because all the other houses were small indeed, while the synagogue was as tall as a two-story building. Only many years later, when I happened to come again to Kiryat Shmonah for a visit, did I realize how small it actually was.

Opposite the entrance of the synagogue, the *Aron Hakodesh* (the Holy Ark) stood. This cabinet, which holds the sacred *Torah* (the scrolls of the Pentateuch, the five books of Moses), was covered with a smooth, shining veil that was made of purple velvet and embroidered with gilded lions. The air inside was saturated with a pungent smell of snuff tobacco, which the chicken merchant from the market used to share with the worshippers—a gesture of festive courtesy—from a silver box tarnished by the passing years. I liked to help myself to it from time to time, sneezing loudly and enjoying it. The sweet fragrance of rose water and myrtle drifted over to us from the women's gallery, mingled with the scent of burnt candles. This was the intoxicating smell of *Shabbat*, the holy Sabbath.

During each *Bar Mitzvah* (the initiatory ceremony recognizing a Jewish boy as a Bar Mitzvah, a son of the divine law) or wedding celebration, a shower of colorful candies was poured down on us, all to the cheers of the children and the joyful sounds of the women. The youngsters gathered handfuls of the rare sweets, snatching them out of each other's hands, which contributed to the joyful atmosphere.

The men reverently chanted the prayers, which they knew by heart, while the ladies waved their colorful scented handkerchiefs. Our festivity reached its peak when the focus of the celebration, either the bridegroom or the Bar Mitzvah lad, was called to come up and read from the Torah. Then, he was literally stoned with candies!

About one hundred worshippers attended that synagogue, all immigrants from Iraq and Persia. Our parents spoke rather broken Hebrew, and we, their children, felt very educated in comparison. We considered it our sacred obligation to correct their speech and to teach them "good Israeli Hebrew." Yet, in spite of their broken vernacular, when it came to prayer, the adults never ceased to amaze us with their ability to read quickly. They knew their prayer books so well that it seemed to us they were coming to the synagogue just to have a speed-reading competition. Long before I knelt in honor of *Magen Avraham* (Defender of Abraham), in the middle of the silent *Amidah* (meditation) prayer, the adults had already finished and sealed the prayer with the three backward steps at the final words, *Oseh Shalom* (Maker of Peace).

When I grew older, I discovered that we, the *Sephardim* (Jews from the Mediterranean and the Middle East), are not the only ones who race through their prayers. The *Ashkenazim* (European Jews) beat us quite easily in finishing their prayers.

As a child, I found nothing extraordinary in the speed of the adults. After all, these were all devout, God-fearing people who had attended synagogue from early childhood. The prayers were an integral part of their daily routine. Obviously, every one of them had memorized his *Siddur* (prayer book) and managed to find his way through it easily, while I was only starting to get acquainted with mine. My father, who probably considered me a mature Jew from the time I was born, apparently expected me to know the siddur by heart, as if it were inherent for a Jew. He never considered it necessary to sit down with me and teach me how to use it or how to pray.

As for me, I innocently believed that it was sufficient to murmur the beautiful but seemingly meaningless sounds and syllables from the sacred book, to fulfill the duty of prayer. Prayer had become a mandatory traditional custom, which demanded three visits to the synagogue every Shabbat. It never occurred to me that prayer was meant to create a vital, direct contact with the living God. Oftentimes though, I had the urge to slow down intentionally in order to understand what the words of the prayers meant, or to stand alone before the Lord, who was hiding (as I believed in my simple naivety) in the Aron Hakodesh. Ultimately, however, group pressure prevailed, and I learned to speed along and race through my reading of the holy books as everyone else did.

I envied King David, the hero of my youth. Yet, if David were ever to visit our local synagogue, would he have joined our frantic race toward the *aleynu* (benediction) prayer? He would certainly have stood, or even knelt, before the Lord God with fear and trembling, lovingly lingering before his Maker. Unfortunately, the local synagogue worshippers reminded me of *King Shaul* (Saul) rather than David, because Shaul held onto his glorious past without realizing that the Lord had departed from him. In biblical times, worshippers would remind God of His mercies toward their forefathers, of His blessings to His people in the distant past, and about the offering of *Yitzhak* (Isaac), while they offered Him the sweet savor of their sacrifices. But now, they have almost nothing to offer Him.

I have noticed that the belief in the merits of the fathers plays a rather central role in the religious thinking of modern Judaism. Is this because we confess in our prayers that we have no good works? Most likely, the worshippers in my hometown synagogue were unaware that the God of their forefathers—the God of Abraham, Isaac, and Jacob—is a living, unchangeable God who has the power to do good to present-day believers, just as He did in ages past. They had also forgotten that the righteousness and faith of their forefathers could in no way save their disobedient, sinning children, for it is written, *"Everyone shall be put to death for his own sin"* (Deuteronomy 24:16).

In those days I did not know the Lord in the way I know Him today, but somehow, even then, I had the strange feeling that God was in no hurry and was not rushing anywhere. I felt as though God loved us and wanted us to draw closer to Him, while we in turn were going in the opposite direction, running away from Him and totally unaware of His love. It disturbed me that the synagogue worshippers did not consider God to be a loving Father at all, but rather a strict and angry boss, who needed to be appeased by their completion of a prayer quota.

I sought more than that. I wanted to express my love for God in actions, not merely in words. But, what were these actions to be? I knew the Scriptures commanded us to *"love the LORD your God with all your heart and with all your soul and with all your might"* (Deuteronomy 6:5), but how could anybody command someone else to love him? Much more, how could anyone love a distant God? Is it enough to wear *tzitzith* and a *kippah*, or to grow side curls and a long beard? Refusing to eat non-kosher foods or meticulously keeping the Sabbath—is this sufficient to satisfy the Lord's severe demands? It seemed to me that God desired to have my heart rather than my clothes, my ceremonious hand washing, or any other ritualistic custom, but I did not know yet how to give Him my heart.

Why was God so remote? Why did He hide His love from me? Why didn't He ever reveal Himself to me? These questions bothered me constantly. I would come out of the synagogue feeling frustrated and empty, as one who came a long way to meet a beloved friend who, for some reason, did not show up.

Within the walls of the synagogue, I was confronted with thoughts which I shared with no one else, because I believed they were heretical. I did not dare to share them even with my father. In spite of the holy atmosphere in the synagogue during the Shabbat services—the reading in the Torah, the priestly benediction, the singing, and the worship—I remained thirsty and hungry for God. But, no spiritual food or drink was available there, so I thought that they did not exist.

When the *hazan* (the worship leader) ascended the *bamah* (podium) and started to sell the *mitzvahs* (righteous deeds) to the highest bidder—the opening of the Aron Hakodesh, the reading in the Torah, the raising and the rolling of the Torah scroll—I felt almost insulted, as if the house of my Lord had become a den of robbers, a black market for sacred things, and of all times, on the holy Sabbath!

I longed to ask my father the weighty questions that plagued me: Why are the Torah and the mitzvahs being sold in such a manner? Couldn't the people simply leave a donation box at the entrance to the synagogue, so that the worshippers could enter on a weekday and put their gifts into it in secret, instead of demonstrating their righteousness in public? Surely, it offends those who are less fortunate. Are the poor less worthy to pray to God? Sadly, however, I kept my thoughts to myself.

My father looked down at me with sorrow in his eyes, and I felt that this auction hurt him no less than it did me. On the holidays the situation was even worse, and worst of all was *Yom Kippur* (the Day of Atonement), when the prices skyrocketed. Did God love the poor among His children any less than He did those who could afford to participate in the bidding and read the Torah at the synagogue?

However, it seemed to me that human tradition was—and always will be—the hardest thing to change and that often it was held even more sacred than the very Scriptures.

Regarding the regular Sabbath prayers, my parents were relatively tolerant with us children as far as possible, but they made no concessions and no compromises whatsoever when it came to the reading of the Torah. We boys all sat next to Father in complete silence and listened reverently to the traditional sing-song chanting of the Torah and the *Haftarah* (the Prophets), although nobody bothered to explain the Scriptures to us. The reading of the Torah was considered the most sacred part of the service, and we were taught since early childhood to listen to the reader with deep admiration and high regard.

I especially remember the Sabbath on which the Torah portion was from the book of Numbers. Here all the lodging places of Israel in the wilderness were listed, one by one, and my mind wandered away to the dispersion of the children of Israel, whichever way they went over the two thousand years. This list would be so much longer today than that mentioned in the Torah, because there is now hardly a place on the face of the earth where the Jews have not trudged and where Jews have not been persecuted. All these names could not be engraved on a table of stone to be laid near the stony lion of Tel-Hai.

What was it that dispersed us among the nations—and why? In the *tahanun* (petition, supplication) prayer we admit, "It was because of our sins that we were expelled from our land." What was this horrible sin that deported us from our own country for such a long period of time and that made us a laughingstock among the nations?

On that same Sabbath, the following Haftarah passage from the book of Jeremiah was read:

"Hear the word of the LORD, O house of Jacob,
and all the families of the house of Israel.
Thus says the LORD,
'What injustice did your fathers find in Me,
that they went far from Me
and walked after emptiness and became empty?'
And they did not say, 'Where is the LORD,
who brought us up out of the land of Egypt,
who led us through the wilderness,

through a land of deserts and of pits,
through a land of drought and of deep darkness,
through a land that no one crossed, and where no man dwelt?'
'And I brought you into the fruitful land,
to eat of its fruit and its good things.
But you came and defiled My land,
and My inheritance you made an abomination.'
The priests did not say, 'Where is the LORD?'
and those who handle the law did not know Me;
the rulers also transgressed against Me,
and the prophets prophesied by Baal
and walked after things that did not profit.
'Therefore, I will contend with you,' declares the LORD,
'and with your sons' sons I will contend.
For cross to the coastlands of Kittim and see,
and send to Kedar and observe closely,
and see if there has been such a thing as this.
Has a nation changed gods, when they were not gods?
But My people have changed their glory
for that which does not profit!
Be appalled, O heavens, at this, and shudder, be very desolate,'
declares the LORD.
'For my people have committed two evils:
they have forsaken Me, the fountain of living waters, to hew for
themselves cisterns, broken cisterns, that can hold no water.
Is Israel a slave? Or is he a homeborn servant?
Why has he become a prey?
The young lions have roared at him.
They have roared loudly...'" (Jeremiah 2:4–15)

Suddenly, this Haftarah Scripture brought to mind the roaring stone lion of Tel-Hai. "What are the worshippers thinking about as they read this?" I thought. "Do they pay any attention at all to the profound meaning of those hard words of reproval, or do they merely recite them without having the faintest idea of their meaning?"

I looked at the reader and imagined for a moment that he was the prophet Jeremiah standing before us on the platform and crying out, in his agony, his tremendous message: *"Is Israel a slave? Or is he a homeborn servant? Why has he become a prey?"* And I could not help but think, "The people of Israel must still be slaves, because, if we were truly children of the Most High God, we would have illuminated the whole world, and the peoples of the earth would have gathered to us from the four corners of the world, so that even the "secular ones" in our neighborhood would actually see that God's name is invoked by us. But then, if the prophet Jeremiah really stood in front of us today, exclaiming, *"And those who handle the law did not know Me,"* we would surely have cast him into a prison cell as our forefathers did. Are we any better than they were?"

The reader left the platform, covered with a snow-white prayer shawl, with its fringes wound around his pointing finger. He kissed them devotedly, waved them at the audience, and blessed them: "Blessed are you! Blessed are you unto the Lord!"

Again my thoughts wandered to the cemetery of Tel-Hai. I could see Yosef the Galilean (Trumpeldor) in front of me, and his friends, Yakov Toker, Benyamin Munter, and all the others with him. Somehow, I could not imagine these pioneers covered with prayer shawls or blessing the worshippers at the synagogue by saying, "Blessed are you! Blessed are you unto the Lord!" As the Sabbath ended, I was sure they did not scan the darkening sky to find three medium-sized stars to indicate they were permitted to light up their cigarettes. They were only surrounded with the scent of the black soil and the stench of the swamps, their bodies smelling like sweat and blood. What drew them? What connected them with the earth of this beloved land? What urged them to dedicate their lives to its defense and to die as martyrs for its sake? They did not die for any religious cause at all!

The worship was over. The people sang *Shir Hakavod* (Hymn of Glory) and *Adon Olam* (The Master of the Universe). While singing, they had already begun to fold their prayer shawls, putting them back into their velvet bags. Immediately an atmosphere of secular profanity overtook the synagogue. The Shabbat holiness came to an abrupt end, as if severed by a sword. Everybody was already on his way home, having locked God away in His box, so to speak—leaving Him all dressed up in a purple coat embroidered with gilded lions and decorated with silver pomegranates, imprisoned in the Holy Ark, waiting for them to return for the evening prayer. But God Almighty does not dwell in shrines made by human hands. He wants to dwell in the hearts of human beings created in His own image.

Slowly it dawned on me that the synagogue was, in fact, no more than a social club of sorts, whose members had one thing in common—religious tradition. People are inclined to indulge in secondary religious rituals or, for that matter, anything that can cause a distraction, as long as it keeps them from the reality of getting closer to God and worshipping Him in spirit and in truth. This was also the reason for the speed-reading competition at the synagogue: the worshippers were afraid to quiet their hearts, lest they might hear the still, small voice of God reproving them lovingly.

Oh, if we had only chosen to sit calmly before the Lord and listen to His voice speaking quietly to us in the secret places. If we had only prayed like King David, the sweet musician of Israel: *"Search me, O God, and know my heart; try me and know my anxious thoughts"* (Psalm 139:23). Then He would have changed our way of thinking, giving us a pure heart and renewing His Holy Spirit within us! But, frankly, we may have soon found out that we really did not have a desire to receive a pure heart and a new spirit, or that we did not at all want to serve God sincerely and to worship Him in truth. We probably preferred to do the necessary minimum by whispering prayers giving lip service to Him and by keeping ritual commandments, which are abominations in the eyes of the Lord because they do not involve the worshipper's heart at all.

Truly, the human heart is crooked and desperately wicked, for it is willing to perform any kind of religious ceremony, as long as it keeps God from taking authority over it. It was for a good reason that the prophets rebelled with all their vigor against the empty, pseudo-religious rituals, human traditions that were neither according to the will of God nor His Spirit.

"When you come to appear before Me,
who required of you this trampling of My courts?
Bring your worthless offerings no longer,
incense is an abomination to Me.
New moon and sabbath, the calling of assemblies—
I cannot endure iniquity and the solemn assembly.
I hate your new moon festivals and your appointed feasts,
they have become a burden to Me. I am weary of bearing them.
So when you spread out your hands in prayer,
I will hide My eyes from you, yes,
even though you multiply prayers,

I will not listen. Your hands are covered with blood.
Wash yourselves, make yourselves clean;
remove the evil of your deeds from My sight.
Cease to do evil, learn to do good;
seek justice, reprove the ruthless;
defend the orphan, plead for the widow.
'Come now, and let us reason together,' says the LORD,
'though your sins are as scarlet, they will be as white as snow;
though they are red like crimson, they will be like wool.'"
(Isaiah 1:12–18)

I could not help noticing that the manner of life and the morality of secular people were actually not much different from those of the supposedly religious, differing merely in their customs. The pious ones wore the *tefillin* (phylacteries or amulets, small leather boxes containing slips inscribed with scriptural passages and traditionally worn on the arm and head by Jewish men during morning weekday prayers) on the weekdays and went to the synagogues on the Sabbath, while the secular crowd traveled on the Sabbath to the beautiful nature resorts in the Upper Galilee region, or to the *Kinneret* (Sea of Galilee).

Somehow I got the feeling that true worship of God went far beyond mere religious rites. Mentally, I questioned, "Wouldn't God prefer to have the Jews abstain from coming to Him three times a day with meaningless chatter in a language that they themselves seldom understood? Wouldn't He sooner have His beloved children come to Him and speak to Him simply and spontaneously with their own words, using their own personal styles in true sincerity, rather than using the words of some obscure poet who wrote his lyrics five hundred years ago or more, in an ancient and outdated language?" I felt like shouting it out loud! But, why would anyone listen to the foolishness of a mere boy?

With the prayer over, we returned home. Father, who was an introverted but emotional man by nature, walked slowly, with his hands behind his back. Seldom did he express feelings or thoughts, but he simply observed and mused.

Above: My beloved parents
Left: Deep inside burns the question: "What am I living for?"
Right: My sister and I dressed up as "gentry".

Chapter 3

The Family Home

On our way home from the synagogue, we passed by the water spring where Mother washed our clothes on regular weekdays. This spring, which emerged from the foot of the Naphtali Mountains, was her own private school. It served as her very personal synagogue, too. Here, she learned how to cope with the problems of everyday life, and she learned this the hard way. It was here that she trod on the wet laundry with her bare feet—as one who treads grapes in a winepress—silently praying to God with sorrowful eyes but a blissful heart before Him. One could seemingly hear her soul's groanings in the tender whisper of the spring water.

Mother had eight children to care for, and I marveled at the strength she showed in bearing this heavy burden alone, while also bestowing such warmth and love on us. I helped her carry the dirty laundry down to the spring early in the morning and later return the clothes, all clean, back home at dusk. The drops of perspiration glistened on her face like diamonds in the light of the setting sun. She never complained or murmured, but worked tirelessly without attending to her own needs or wants.

Mother's eyes helped me to accept willingly whatever life might bring. Her private synagogue at the spring was altogether different from Father's large and beautiful one, but it was no less holy.

I remember those *yamim noraim* (the "ten days of awe" before Yom Kippur), during which we would go to the spring to perform the traditional custom of *tashlich* (symbolically throwing away our sins into its water). It seemed to me that Mother practiced this sacred ritual day in and day out through the entire year, rather than just for the high holy days.

Back then, my father had brought his family, which already numbered five children and a pregnant wife, from Persia (modern-day Iran) to Israel. When Mother's time arrived to have her sixth child, she was rushed to the Scottish hospital in Tiberias, which at that time was the closest maternity hospital to Kiryat Shmonah. And so it happened, that on a blazing hot July day, the first *sabra* (native

Israeli) baby boy of our family emerged into this world and was named *Yaakov* (Jacob). Later, two more girls would be born. When complete, our family totaled ten, we eight children and our parents.

Father was a tailor and a matmaker by profession, occupations he had learned in Iran. Introverted by nature, he was quite distant from us and detached from family life. When I brought his meal to him on occasion, he would accept it from my hands without a word, as something to be taken for granted. Father talked very little and seldom addressed us children.

However, he did the very best he could to provide for his family. For many years, he worked in construction, but during all these years his heart's desire was to be independent and open a business of his own. I remember the greengrocery store that he managed at the open market of Kiryat Shmonah—it was not much of a success, to say the least. The same was true of the restaurant he later managed at the Tel Aviv central bus station. Somehow, Father never did excel as a businessman. All the money that he invested to establish his dream simply paid for the many start-up expenses but never produced much income.

Thus, in spite of all his sincere efforts to provide for us, most of the burden for the housekeeping and providing for the family fell on Mother's tender shoulders. She worked days and nights as a cleaning lady in other families' homes. This neither embarrassed me, nor did I see any dishonor in it. Mother worked from dawn to dusk, and we children did our best to help her. As I think back, I only wish I could have done more. My parents lived with us eight children in a one-and-a-half bedroom flat on the northernmost street of Kiryat Shmonah. Every evening we would spread our mattresses out on the floor, until it looked like an ocean of mattresses. There we would roll, twist, and turn, snuggling against each other until we fell asleep as one large, happy crowd. Nobody ever grumbled about not having enough room. I often wonder why families today have a separate room for each child and yet are still full of complaints!

During the long, cold, winter evenings of Kiryat Shmonah, a kerosene burner stood in the center of the room. We all crowded together near it under a huge blanket. Mother sat in the center, like a hen gathering her chicks around her under her wings, and told us her stories. One of our favorites was how she and father had immigrated from Persia:

As we came down from the airplane at the Lod Airport (Ben-Gurion International Airport), the people from the Jewish Immigration Agency loaded us on large trucks, together with other new immigrants, and sent us off to our new destination. Suddenly, when we were about halfway there, your father noticed that something was wrong. The journey seemed too long to him. Although he did not know anything about the geography of Israel, he had enough common sense to realize that such a long trip carried us too far away from the center of the country. He started an uproar and banged on the walls and floor of the truck, demanding to know where they were taking us. The driver managed to calm him down with some smooth talk and then went on, bringing us all the way north to Halsah, known today as Kiryat Shmonah.

Each new family received a little tin booth to live in and a kerosene burner with a smoldering wick for cooking. This cooker was later replaced by the more modern, noisy, and far more dangerous "primus" kerosene cooker. We also received several kerosene lamps for light, several woolen blankets, and personal rationed food coupons that enabled us to purchase the basic groceries at the local grocery store. Back then, the government, overwhelmed with the flood of immigrants, stretched its meager resources to provide a minimal food allowance to all newcomers. We received an allocation of two fresh eggs per person for a week, a limited quantity of oil, flour, sugar, powdered milk, powdered eggs, *cocosine* (a white, greasy substitute for margarine, made of coconut oil), and about two hundred grams of beef per person for the month. Some time later, fish fillets imported from Scandinavia were distributed, and that was our only source of protein for a long time.

The women, who stood in the long line at the grocery store for many hours, waiting for their weekly rations, on occasion miscarried their babies due to sheer exhaustion. We lived at the end of the world, it seemed. In the distance we could see only the lights of a few Arab villages from across the Lebanese border. The Hula swamps spread down below us to the south. A narrow asphalt road meandered like a snake through them, connecting the Upper Galilee with faraway Tiberias, a city located in northern Israel, but which we viewed as distantly south.

Father and my older brothers and sisters went out to work, weeding the front yards of the *Ashkenazim*, who were greatly outnumbered by the *Sephardim* in Kiryat Shmonah. In those days we called this "relief work." After all, nobody had any money. Who needed money, anyway? Those coupons were the only means by which one could obtain food, and they were more precious than gold. In those days, one could not pay for his groceries with cash, and there were no goods to buy other than the allocated ones. The black market somehow failed to come as far north as Kiryat Shmonah, although it flourished in the big cities.

Mother would ask us, for the hundredth time, "Do you want to know how I met your father?" We all knew the story by heart, of course, but we never grew tired of hearing the tale from the more distant past of our family:

One day a young man came to Tehran, the Iranian capital, riding on his donkey. He came to the large city from a little village called Demovand, somewhere out in the high mountains of Iran. He lost his parents at a young age and had very limited opportunities for progress in the village where he lived. So he mounted his donkey and made his way to the capital to make a better future there. This was a rather unprecedented step in those days!

Well, this young man rented a room in my parents' house. Day and night, he followed me with his eyes. In the evenings he used to throw small gravel stones at my window to attract my attention. My parents did not like his courting me too much, but he persisted until he finally managed to win my heart. And this is how the young and attractive French teacher became the wife of that youthful, uneducated, audacious peasant boy. As the days went by, she became your mother, too…

More than once I detected a slight tone of wistfulness in my mother's voice. She could have married a doctor or a lawyer instead, someone with a higher education or social status, but she had to be satisfied with just a simple man like my father. Still, I thank God that she married him; otherwise I would not be myself. Frankly, I have no desire whatsoever to be somebody else!

I also remember Lupu, the village fool. He was a single, lonesome Romanian Jew, a refugee of the Holocaust. He was rather "slow of tongue," a stammerer, and lived in a tiny, dark room not far from our home. He earned his meager living by shepherding his landlord's sheep that grazed on the hills surrounding the town. Every evening at sunset, we could hear the bell on the neck of the leading sheep ringing from a distance, and all the other sheep bleating loudly behind him. We could also hear the rolling "rrrrrrrr-rrrrrrrr" sounds that Lupu would make in order to direct the flock back to its fold. Hearing the noises, we would run over to the large flock, which Lupu led as he marched in front of his sheep. Each of us caught his "own" animal and rode it as if it were a donkey. The poor shepherd hurled curses at us in juicy Romanian, at which we only laughed in sheer delight. Only many years later, we found out about his miserable past, and then we no longer laughed at him.

One night the straw in the neighbor's barn near our home caught fire. The huge flames reached up to the sky as they consumed everything that could burn, scattering terrified beasts in every direction. A field covered with thorns separated the barn from our property, and so our whole family stood in line with rubber hoses in our hands, splashing water on the burning brush to prevent the fire from spreading to our own yard.

Incidentally, on this very thorny piece of land grew several vines and a few apple trees. I remember my older brother, a natural authority figure, strictly forbidding us to pluck even one single green apple before it ripened, but he could not succeed in enforcing this prohibition.

In those days, before the age of steel doors and sophisticated locks, all the houses were wide open—and so were the hearts. Everyone could come into the house and leave it at any hour of the day or night, and we were all one large family, for better or for worse. No one had anything more than his neighbor. It was the genuine brotherhood of the poor, without envy or strife. We came to know those illnesses of human nature only many years later, when "progress" finally came.

When I was ten years old, my sister Zivah and I decided to contribute our share to the family's income. On the first day of summer vacation, we went together at sunrise to the nearby *moshav* (agricultural settlement) to work there picking apples. We worked very hard all day long. In the evening, when we went to the foreman to collect our wages, he paid us an amount that was just enough for our bus fare home. To be honest, he also allowed us to take home with us as many apples as we could carry in our hands, and then sent us on our way. Even as a child of ten, this treatment offended me deeply.

Concerning my childhood, I truly bear no hard feelings, no bitterness, and no resentment for anything that took place at that time. As a matter of fact, it is quite the other way around. We were very naive then. We did not need much and were quite satisfied with what we had. If my parents had any quarrels, they hid them from their children. They kept their problems and difficulties to themselves and allowed us to live through our childhood years as happily as possible. Looking back, if I could start my life all over again, I would not choose to live it any differently.

Wearing a hat I promise myself: "A drug addict I shall never be".

Chapter 4

Moving to the City

One evening, the familiar, noisy rattle of a motorcycle sounded in our front yard. My older brother Shmuel, who had just recently been released from the Air Force and who worked as an aircraft technician at the Lod Airport, came home with the happy news: "We are moving to Holon, to the big city!" Father was not too enthusiastic about the idea, but mother, whose top priority had always been the welfare of her family, finally managed to convince him. Of course, nobody asked me what I thought about it. After all, I was just a child, not yet a *Bar Mitzvah* (literally, "son of the law", a Jewish boy who reaches his thirteenth birthday and attains the age of religious duty and responsibility).

Again all of the family belongings were loaded on a truck. The entire family (except for my older sister, who was already married and who, with her husband, preferred to remain in Kiryat Shmonah) made its way south.

We arrived, at last, at our dream home. It was in a new, four-story building, all whitewashed and clean. With our mouths open in awe, we climbed the stairs to the third floor and entered our new mansion. First of all, there was a bell at the front door, which was an exciting novelty for us. The toilet also enchanted us in a very special way: no longer would we have to go out into the freezing, rainy nights of the Upper Galilee to use the outhouse! The large window of the front porch had shades that could be raised and lowered with a cord—another technological wonder previously unknown to us. Now we were a little less crowded, having two bedrooms and a living room at our disposal. We were a smaller family, too, since my married sister no longer lived with us.

I could be likened in those days to an ignorant, provincial country boy, who came for the first time in his life to the big city. Everything seemed so wonderful, so exciting, so different, so brand new, and so large—and here we even had a real ocean! The bloodcurdling whistles of the Mirage jets, which so often flew over Kiryat Shmonah on their way to Lebanon or Syria, gave way to the thundering roars of the large cargo and passenger planes cruising just above our heads on their way to the nearby airport. Their landing lights twinkled in the dark evening sky, creating in me a sweet sense of excitement.

At the elementary school that I now attended, I met children who were entirely different from those I knew in Kiryat Shmonah. One day as one of the youngsters thought to play a practical joke on a teacher by exploding a stink bomb in the middle of the classroom, our Bible teacher simply closed all the windows tightly, forbade us to reopen them, and left the room, leaving us to suffocate in our mischief.

As a matter of fact, I really loved that teacher, whose name was Maeir Tzubari. He knew so well how to breathe the spirit of life into the biblical stories and to make them so real to us that we could almost identify with their characters. I was absolutely sure that he knew the whole Bible by heart! Other than his classes, I did not like school too much, except perhaps for gymnastics and agriculture classes. Doing my homework was the most disagreeable part of school, but I always loved the Bible classes and could not wait for them. Since my early childhood, I had a special love for the Holy Scriptures, and even today I still love to study them thoroughly. Thank you, Mr. Tzubari.

The same year we arrived in Holon, I reached the age of thirteen and celebrated Bar Mitzvah. During that year I attended the meetings of a youth movement called *Hanoar HaOved* (Working Youth, now politically associated with the Labour Party) and a year later, those of *Hashomer HaTzair* (Young Guard, the left-wing youth movement). I loved those meetings very much. But at that time, I also started to visit the dance halls, where I watched the big senior guys from our school chasing the girls of my class. I began to acquire a taste for this way of life. The move from the closed world of the synagogue in Kiryat Shmonah to secular Holon, to the open beaches and the atmosphere of the large city, was so dramatic that finally I became secular myself. It did not matter to me much then, but I must confess that my parents did not like the change in me at all. In Holon—having no other choice—we started to attend the synagogue of the Ashkenazim, but we did not feel at home in it. We missed the Persian cantorial chanting to which we were accustomed.

Several years later, we moved from the apartment house into a little two-room flat with a little garden in front. It was located in one of the poorest sections of town. Slowly we added more rooms to it, and the tiny flat became a "train." Many Middle Eastern Jews lived in that neighborhood, and we discovered a Persian synagogue not too far from the park. However, it was not long before I stopped attending synagogue altogether. And this is how it happened.

On the morning of *Rosh Hashanah* (Jewish New Year) when I was sixteen years old, I refused to get up and go to the synagogue. This so irritated my brother that he shouted angrily at me, "If you don't feel like being a part of this family anymore, just get out of this house!" No one thought that I would take his words literally, but I did. I got up, put on my blue jeans, a red T-shirt, and a pair of tennis shoes, and left home for the first time in my life.

Without a penny to my name and without the faintest idea as to where I was going and what I was to do next, I hit the road. I stole (for the first time in my life) a watermelon from a booth, burst it open on the edge of the sidewalk, and satisfied my hunger and thirst with it. Then I hitchhiked down south to a certain kibbutz in the northern Negev, where one of my sisters lived. She had left our house some time earlier because of her failure to get along with my father; she had rebelled against his authority and his prohibitions. Of course, I could not tell her that I had run away from home! Anyway, my sister was truly happy to see me. I stayed with her overnight, and on the following morning I took a knapsack and a switchblade from her. I also "borrowed" a few food items from the kibbutz kitchen and continued my journey south.

Soon I found myself lazing around together with a bunch of long-haired, sloppily dressed hippies on the seashore of Eilat. There I learned how to smoke (until then I had not known the taste of a cigarette) and associated with folks that decent people would not care to meet in a dark alley. These bums were stretched out lazily in their hammocks day and night, stupefied with drugs, chanting endless, monotonous tunes. Being foreigners in the country and lazy by nature, they did not know how to manage their lives or how to get along in Israel, so I helped them remove some asbestos boards from deserted huts and build themselves little shacks, which looked like doghouses on the beach. As time passed, we actually built a real neighborhood in the grove near the Red Rock Hotel in Eilat.

There were nights, and also days, in which I could see the drug addicts among them suffering from withdrawal symptoms. My heart went out to them as I heard them groan desperately for hours, "Somebody, please, give me some opium." Although I tasted a little of that garbage myself, I soon came to the relatively mature conclusion—

considering the circumstances—that I would never use drugs.

One night the police raided the area in search of those responsible for a big theft that occurred on the beach. It was dark, and a policeman unexpectedly directed a bright flashlight straight into my sleepy eyes, while I was lying inside my little asbestos shack. Although I was not personally involved in the crime, I was nonetheless one of the suspects. The policeman insisted that I identify myself. When I did, several cops fell on me with shouts: "Are you Jacob Damkani, the one the whole country has been looking for? How could you do such a thing to your mother? Right now the radio is reporting you as a missing person!" Right away they took me to the detention room at the Eilat police station. The following day my parents came down all the way to Eilat to take me home with them.

This was my parents' first visit to Eilat since they came to this country, and I wished I could take them down to the seashore to show them how their son was leading his life. I told them, "Come and see the place where the children of Israel crossed the Red Sea on dry land." That event did not happen anywhere near this place, but I imagined that the biblical connection would spark their curiosity and create in them enough interest, so I was even willing to falsify the historical and geographical facts for the purpose. But, to my disappointment, they did not seem the least bit interested! They could not have cared less about sightseeing or visiting historical sites. Their only concern was their family's welfare.

"How wonderful it would be," I thought to myself, "if they stayed with me at least for one day on the beach to enjoy the quiet, the swimming, and the sun in this land of eternal summer!" But, they did not linger in Eilat for one hour more than necessary. We boarded the first bus going north, and they took me home with them, to my disgrace and utter disappointment.

Only later I found out—from other people, of course—how tormented my mother had been during those long months of my absence from home. She had roamed through the streets of the city, stricken with grief, lamenting over me as one who mourns for a dead child, "Jacob, my son, where are you? Jacob, my son, my dear child, please, please come back home!"

Back in Holon, I returned to school; this time it was the evening high school. But now, my soul was wandering in other worlds, distant and enchanting. While my body warmed the school bench, my mind was having fun on the sunny beaches of Eilat. I showed no progress in my studies, so eventually I quit school altogether. Not only did I quit school, I also stopped attending the synagogue. I divided my time between Holon, Jerusalem, and Eilat, alternately. Every now and then I would pop in to say hello at home, until my time came to join the army.

Before I had run away to Eilat, most of my friends were from the evening high school. However, when I returned home from the "Pearl of the South," I met others from our slum neighborhood, whose company definitely had an adverse effect on my attitudes. During this time I worked as an independent steel contractor, so I could arrange my own work schedule. I could choose for myself when to work and when to take a vacation.

The life I was now leading affected not only my general behavior, but also my very way of thinking, my values, and my priorities. Slowly I began to forget that exciting experience near the stone lion at Tel-Hai. I began to rebel against all authorities: first, against my parents, and later, against my teachers and rabbis. The situation deteriorated to the point where I considered a person in uniform as a possible enemy, of whom I had to be careful. I began to project this negative attitude against all authorities and uniform-wearers in general. This change in my way of thinking was so slow and gradual that, without noticing it, I eventually found myself objecting to the very idea of wearing uniforms and joining the army.

Where had the young, ardent patriot of Kiryat Shmonah gone, the one who promised so solemnly to defend his land and people as did Trumpeldor of old? Where did this "conscientious objector" come from, who stared at me from the mirror every morning? I could not explain that even to myself.

When my draft date came, I went to the military enlistment camp with a heavy mane of thick curls covering my shoulders, full of resentment and hostility toward the "establishment" that exploits the "blacks" (Sephardim). Unfortunately for me, the army was not at all impressed by my presentation of fake toughness.

I started to do everything in my power to regain my lost freedom. "I won't be any man's sucker," I decided. On the first week of my basic training, while I was still as green as a cucumber, I asked for an after-duty leave. One of the girls in our neighborhood was getting married, and I felt I just had to attend her wedding. In front of the amused eyes of the other recruits, my immediate commander mortified me with an endless string of juicy curses in the filthiest language I had ever heard. I was not going to keep silent over that! As soon as the assembly was over, I left the army camp and disappeared for seventeen days.

Then one night at three o'clock in the morning, I was sitting with one of my friends on the lawn underneath the guava tree that grew in our family's front yard. Like many other young people in our neighborhood, my friend had managed to get himself discharged from military service. Suddenly he grew tense. He already had some experience with the Military Police, and his well-trained ears heard the MPs even before they reached our house. "Run!" he barked at me, and so I ran as fast as a cat and as far as my legs could carry me. I crossed through the neighbor's yard and disappeared. My buddy stayed lying on the grass, seemingly indifferent, and calmly let the MPs cuff his hands and lead him to the police car, in order to allow me enough time to escape.

Upon hearing the noise, my father came out of the house and was alarmed by the mistaken identification. "You stupid donkeys! This is not my son at all! He must have run that way!" he shouted at them, pointing at the neighbor's house. But, of course, I was not there anymore.

On the seventeenth day of my desertion, I was caught by the Military Police on the beach of Eilat. I was brought before the judge and was sentenced to thirty-five days in a military confinement camp.

While I was still a civilian in my neighborhood, I had already learned a very important lesson: never let the authorities transfer you from the enlistment base without sending you to the psychiatrist first. In the assembly from which they sent the soldiers to the various boot camps, I refused to answer when they called out my name, until finally I managed to receive a letter ordering me to see the "shrink." Only then did I allow them to send me to the artillery drill camp in Samaria. With the help of several friends, I convinced my commander that I was not fit for military service. When I finally reached the psychiatrist, the groundwork was already prepared. After half a year of miserable army service, I was discharged from the army for "unfitness". This was, unfortunately, the end of my military career.

The situation went from bad to worse. On Yom Kippur in 1973, when the siren blasts announced the beginning of that infamous war,

I was loafing around with some of the guys in one of their flats in Holon. We did not even think of going down to the air-raid shelter. Attending the synagogue on the holiest day of the Jewish year was totally out of the question, also.

Somewhere in my conscience, my absence from the synagogue on that particular day did bother me, but I had realized long ago that the synagogue had nothing to offer me. The rebellion that I had developed against all authority was extended to the rabbis and their representatives as well. I did not know God, of course, and neither did I feel that I owed Him any account for my deeds. "Everybody is a sinner," I reasoned, "so why should I, of all people, be held responsible?" My whole world was reduced at that time to what was going on within the walls of that small flat where we were sitting and musing.

During the Yom Kippur War, I was embarrassed to be roaming around the city. No other young men were in sight; only women, children, and old people were around. All the men were on the front line, and the atmosphere of war was felt everywhere. I wholeheartedly regretted my stupid refusal to join the armed forces like everybody else. As a matter of fact, I even tried, with my brother's help, to volunteer for active service; but now the army rejected me. Nothing was left for me to do except wander aimlessly down the streets, and to answer, without words, the unasked questions directed at me by people's stares.

Pen and paper in my hand, with infantry in Samaria.

On set for the movie "A New Spirit"

Chapter 5

Into the Big, Wide World

As time progressed, I realized that I could not continue much longer in this manner. The world at large was my only chance to find fulfillment and meaning to this existence. I decided then to leave the country for a while.

My brother Shmuel, the one who had brought us to Holon, had already moved to Copenhagen, Denmark. He worked for the Scandinavian Air Service and later opened a jewelry shop in the main pedestrian zone of the city. I thought it might be nice to fly there to visit him. Thus, I found myself in Denmark's international airport on a chilly autumn day.

I planned to stay there only a few days, but my visit lasted two months. After that lengthy time, I came to the conclusion that Europe was not where I wanted to live. Compared to Israeli culture, the people were as cold as dead fish, and I did not think I would ever manage to learn the Danish language.

In those days I heard of a great construction boom in Australia. Having had some previous experience in steel works, and in building in general, I planned to go there and make a lot of money quickly. However, the good Lord had other plans for me. My brother told me that he owned a plot of land on the island of Freeport in the Bahamas. He convinced me to go there instead and to build a hotel on it.

"Get a hold of yourself, and be like the rest of the family!" my brother yelled at me angrily. "We have always been such a warm family, so closely knit; why do you need to live like a freak? You roam around like a bum and associate with dubious characters. When are you going to grow up? Go to Freeport. I am sure that if all of us join forces together and invest our money and energy in a worthy cause, we'll make history yet!"

"By the way," he added, "there is a lot of building going on there now, and you can use your skills in that area, too!"

My older brother Shmuel felt responsible for my education as well as for my conduct in a foreign country. Of course, he tried to make me change my ways. He provided me with all the documents he received when he purchased the land and sent me to Luxembourg by train, where I boarded the first plane flying to the Bahamas.

When the aircraft landed in Nassau, the immigration officer inquired how much money I had with me. With a rare outburst of honesty, I told him the plain truth—that I had no more than seventy dollars to my name. "What exactly do you intend to do with seventy bucks?" the man laughed. Then he stamped my passport, informing me of his intention to put me on the first plane going back to Luxembourg.

"What good was it to be honest?" I asked myself and walked over to the general manager of the airport. I showed him the documents that my brother had given me and introduced myself as a businessman owning a plot of land in Freeport. I also told him that I intended to invest in its development.

"There are people waiting for me in Freeport," I assured him. "You see, I was robbed on my previous visit to this island. Therefore, I prefer not to carry too much cash."

I guess the manager was impressed by my performance, because he corrected the entry in my passport. After spending the night sleeping in an open American car that was parked in the airport parking lot, I went on my way to Freeport.

Once I was in Freeport, I took a taxi and asked the dark-skinned driver to take me to a building site. He looked at me as if I had landed from a different planet—which was not altogether far from the truth—and asked me what exactly I meant.

"Take me to a building place; I am looking for job!" I told him with my broken English.

"What on earth are you talking about?" he glanced at me with a surprised look. "They have not been building anything on these islands for years. There is a depression now, and no new building is being done."

"Let me out at once!" I ordered, not willing to spend my last dollars on a useless taxi ride.

As I got out of the taxi, I looked around and saw that the island was something out of this world, a real gem. The alleys through which I strolled were decorated with palm trees and an abundance of rich tropical vegetation. Green expanses of well-groomed lawns and endless flower beds covered the roadsides and the front yards of the elegant villas. Decorative water fountains were scattered all over.

The white sands of the beach were not too far away, and behind them lay the clear, dark-blue and turquoise waters of the ocean. Everything was so impeccably clean and magnificently beautiful that I felt as if I had reached the Garden of Eden itself! I watched the huge American cars gliding silently on the well-paved highways, and all I could do was stare at the surroundings with awe and sheer delight.

I soon found myself lying on a green lawn, not far from a sparkling white hotel. I put my brown suitcase under my head, and many thoughts ran through my mind. "What a magnificent place, this tropical paradise! What kind of people am I going to meet here? What are my buddies and my family doing now in far-off Israel? How am I going to find that plot of land that belongs to my brother? Where am I going to spend the night?"

I loved the challenge and the adventure that the big, wide world provided: to land anywhere and to survive, to enjoy the unexpected, anticipating endless pleasures, just as I had done in Eilat.

Just then I noticed two dark, skinny, rather shabbily dressed men went down the hill across the street. Their faces spoke of hardship, but I also detected a certain joy of life in them. I called them over, and we started a conversation. When I told them that I was from Israel, I realized from looking at their puzzled faces that they did not have the faintest idea where on earth that was. They had not even heard of Jerusalem.

I asked them where I could find some work and a lodging place. To this, they had an answer: "Don't worry! Come with us, and everything is going to be all right!" I, of course, accepted their cordial invitation and joined them. Pretty soon we arrived at a neighborhood of small single houses, each with a tiny garden at its entrance. To my surprise, the fellows entered the house through one of the windows. The place was terribly neglected and had an obnoxious odor. My new acquaintances then told me that this neighborhood was once occupied by black people who had been forced to move out so the area could be renovated and repopulated by white residents. In the meantime, the abandoned houses stood there, empty and deserted.

I slept well through that night, and at sunrise we left the house. The two men took me to a large bakery shop that was located in an industrial area. "This bakery shop, like all the other enterprises on this island," they explained, "belongs to the white man. But, all the employees that work in them are blacks, and they will collaborate with us. Come on, then. Let's go in through the back door and take as much as we can carry out. Trust us—nobody will notice!"

We went in, and a minute later we were out again with our hands full of goodies: fresh breads, cakes, and all kinds of pastries. And truly, no one suspected anything. The owner of the place, a white man, was absent at the time, and the black workers really cooperated. This was how my new friends received their daily bread, quite literally.

On the island of Freeport was a casino for whites-only. Here, I made use of my relatively fair complexion to be allowed in—not that I had any money to gamble, but I certainly could enjoy the atmosphere. One evening, as I was leaving the gambling hall, I heard Arabic. I found three sailors who were employed on a Libyan oil tanker that was anchored in the harbor. They were going to spend three days on the island and were thrilled to meet somebody who knew how to speak Arabic, even as broken as mine was. Their attitude toward me did not change when I told them that I came from Israel. On the contrary, they were more than happy to invite me to dinner at their hotel. I joyfully accepted.

Here, for the first time, I learned about the sweet life of a five-star hotel. One of the sailors, Muhammad, invited me to his room and taught me how people live in such an opulent hotel. I'd never imagined such luxury existed. How did a simpleton like myself get from "God-forsaken" Kiryat Shmonah to such a place as this? I really felt as if I was in a fairy tale.

I joined my hosts for the meal in the hotel restaurant and was faced with a new problem. How on earth does one conduct himself at such a fancy table with endless pieces of silverware, a mountain of gorgeous china dishes, and multicolored tropical drinks served in sparkling crystal goblets? So many courses were served at each meal, and I could not even handle my knife and fork as a civilized person should!

I wondered who was going to pay for all this. But again, there was no problem. Nonchalantly, my host took a pen in his hand and scribbled an unidentifiable signature on the voucher that was handed to him. The room was automatically charged with the price of the whole meal. How extraordinary! And who would be paying that bill? I didn't need to worry, because Libya's rich government would cover my expenses, too.

I certainly liked this lifestyle. Now my imagination really ran wild. If it is this simple—if all it took was a signature on a slip of paper—why not make the most use of it?

Three days later, my Libyan hosts had to check out of the hotel and return to their ship. I pleaded with Muhammad in Arabic, mingled with broken English, "You are going to sea now. No one will be able to locate you there. For friendship's sake, why don't you tell the receptionist at the desk that you have lost the key to your room, and let me go on living here?"

Muhammad liked the idea. "God willing, the day will come when we shall meet you again, in peace, in Jerusalem!" His eyes twinkled with hope and faith for a better future.

When we bade one another farewell, almost in tears, Muhammad handed me the key to his room. I moved in and continued to charge the Libyan government with the expenses. I loved every minute of it—the delights of the swimming pool, the dining hall, and the pleasures of room service. I almost began to feel at home there.

Around that time, I saw the two black men whom I met when I first came to the island. They were still lying on the lawn where I had first met them, as if they had not been on their feet since. To my surprise, they were not at all excited at our reunion, and when I asked them to take me to the house where I had hidden my brown suitcase, they refused. They had probably "taken care" of it themselves in my absence. Until then, I still had some faith in the integrity of the human race. But now, I came to realize that faithfulness, mutual help, and the brotherhood of all men should not always be taken for granted. I had once bought them hamburgers with my meager money, but now they treated me as a stranger.

I had no choice—I had to find my suitcase. And so, using "moderate" physical pressure, I forced them to take me to the place where my belongings were hidden. I returned from there totally disillusioned and disappointed by the dishonesty of those ingrates and returned to "my" five-star hotel room, where an honest man like myself could be left in peace!

The days went by and all was well, until one evening the receptionist called me to his desk and asked me who in the world I was. "I'm Ahmed Ali," I fired back at him spontaneously, explaining that I was actually one of the crew of that particular Libyan tanker.

"But they already checked out of the hotel a week ago," he said.

"That's right," I retorted, "but the captain of that ship left me on this island to wait for the next ship, which is about to arrive. They need some professional manpower on board." I could not believe the words that I heard coming out of my own mouth. I never realized how easy it was to tell a lie. The man picked up the phone and called the harbor, but fortunately for me there was no answer at that number. I suggested that he try to call again in the morning. The poor man was so embarrassed and felt so guilty that he could not apologize enough.

As for me, I was gone before sunrise.

During my first days at the casino, I had met a young Israeli man who worked at the gambling tables. When he heard of my lodging distress, he invited me to the apartment hotel where he resided. He knew the island quite well, and I learned from him that the plot of land that my brother had purchased at top dollar did not even belong to the person who had sold it to him in the first place. Acts of deception and fraud were common in this area, just as they were in nearby Florida.

Nearby Florida? When I learned that Florida was just around the corner from the Bahamas, my eyes lit up. Until then I had no idea that America was so close. The man told me that my chances of finding any work on the islands were nil, and that if I wanted to get anywhere in life, I'd better try to make it to America.

That same week, full of aspirations, I left my dream island and boarded the plane that was to take me to the Land of Opportunity, where only the sky is the limit!

Years later...
filming "A New Spirit".

Chapter 6

New York, New York!

The wheels of the airplane kissed the landing strip of the Miami Beach Airport. I had arrived in America! If, as a boy, I thought that a two-and-a-half room apartment in Holon was a dream house, imagine my surprise in the United States! Here, everything was bigger than life—much richer, far more elaborate, and a lot more expensive. Dazzled, awestruck, and confused by what my eyes saw, I wandered along the streets of the huge city. I drank in the views, the sounds, the smells. I was taken in by the huge highway bridges that coiled like snakes into each other on several levels, emerging into multi-laned superhighways. "How can anybody find his way around here without getting lost?" I thought.

Flashing continually, the brightly colored lights that advertised a wide variety of things gradually created complete pictures, which in turn dissolved and disappeared, only to be reborn and freshly created ever anew. All this captivated my attention. It was so strange and fascinating for an ignorant country boy like me.

What does a young, Jewish Israeli of twenty-one do when he arrives in America? He looks for a job, of course! I stayed in Miami Beach for a whole week and still could not find any work. Having only one other option, I decided to visit an acquaintance of mine by the name of Michael, who lived in New York.

Previously, Michael had been sent to Israel from Brooklyn by his loving, ultraorthodox parents, who hoped that their son would eventually become a great rabbi in Israel. Of course, his wealthy parents saw to it that he had everything money could buy, and they constantly replenished his bank account whenever it grew lean. However, they never had any idea as to their beloved son's real whereabouts. Michael's mind was not altogether set on studying the holy Torah. He preferred to frequent the pubs, bars, and nightclubs of the holy city of Jerusalem rather than its rabbinical schools.

Back then, I spent my time in Tel Aviv, Jerusalem, and Eilat. Consequently, one dark night we bumped into each other at the Yellow Tea House in Jerusalem. After a rather long chat, he gave

me his home address in Brooklyn and told me that if I ever came
to America, he would be delighted to see me. I am sure he never
imagined I would actually come.

Having decided to search for Michael, I went out to the
superhighway and raised my thumb, in much the same manner as I
did when traveling from Tel Aviv to Eilat. Hitchhiking was then as
common in America as it still is in Israel, where many a soldier can
be seen on the highway. I managed to get as far north as Georgia on
the first leg of my journey. Eventually I arrived in Brooklyn, where a
policeman guided me to the subway station. Walking in the direction
shown me by the policeman, I took the elevator down to the subway
station. There I made my first mistake on American soil: I put down my
suitcase for a mere second to change a dollar bill into quarters in order
to use the pay phone. Fittingly enough, it was a Jewish passerby who
saw what I had done; she screamed at the top of her voice, "Never let
that suitcase out of your hands, even for a moment! They're all *ganuvin*
(Yiddish for thieves) here!" Later I understood how right she was and
was thankful, but at that moment, I was stunned and dumbfounded by
her thundering welcome. I have to admit that my first impression of
New York City was a rather gloomy one.

At last I ended up in front of Michael's house, only to find he
was not home. For three or four days, I managed to spend the nights
in the lobby of a worn-out hotel, where I slept behind a shabby couch.

It was in those days that I first met the phenomenon of the
"ugly Israeli." I discovered that one Israeli is like a wolf to another,
especially when abroad. It seemed to me that each one I met thought
only of himself and minded his own business, although he might
possess only a roof over his head and four walls around him that
he could share. Nobody had any regard for a fellow Israeli to offer
needed help. Although I disclosed my distress to several people and
told them that I had just arrived and had nowhere to go, no one invited
me home to stay, even temporarily. It seemed to me that the suspicion
and fear of unfamiliar faces caused our people to ignore the long-
standing customs of hospitality that they had grown up with in Israel.

I also learned that the common Israeli *yored* (emigrant) was
willing to accept almost any kind of work, even those manual jobs
that he would not think of doing back in Israel, provided they earned a
few dollars. Everyone was willing to fight like a lion for his income—
even if it meant destroying his fellowman.

Three days later, I returned to Michael's house. This time I knocked at the basement door. To my surprise, the door suddenly opened, and there stood Michael! He was occupied at that time in karate practice with a good friend of his.

He looked a little puzzled, unable to remember exactly who I was and, consequently, unable to figure out what I was doing at his door. When I showed him his own address, written in his own handwriting, and told him where and under what circumstances we had been acquainted, his face suddenly lit up in remembrance, and he gladly invited me in.

The joy of the reunion was genuine. After a short time of small talk, I learned that his whole family had moved to Jerusalem and had leased their luxurious mansion to other people. Their own son, who was left behind, had therefore nowhere else to go other than to that tiny basement of his own home.

Michael's bed occupied much of the room, but somehow a mat was spread on the floor. Apart from that, the apartment consisted of a tiny kitchen with a small gas stove and a bathroom with a shower.

I asked Michael why an ex-rabbinical student was studying karate, of all things. I received the most unexpected answer: "While I was still a young boy, I was once confronted and attacked on my way to school by a group of Gentile kids, who hit me hard, calling me a "dirty Jew" and a "Christ killer!" Right there and then, I made up my mind to see to it that nothing like that ever happened again. I swore that if in the future I, or any other Jew, should be assaulted by anti-Semites again, I would be ready and able to go on the offensive. Never again should we experience the gas chambers!"

Michael helped me to find my first job right in the center of Manhattan. However, because of my poor English, I was fired a short time later and had to look for something else. Next, I worked as an errand boy in an Italian restaurant, but since I had no legal working papers, I was badly exploited by my employers. The American "human pressure cooker" began to work.

This situation reminded me of the job I had worked in Holon when I was fourteen, at a place that manufactured iron bird cages. I was trying to make some money for myself and somehow help my family, too. I worked very hard. Even though my production was as good as that of the adults, the boss took advantage of my age, and so this unprotected minor was paid mere pennies.

In New York, I was not protected by the law either, and every potential employer considered me easy prey, so I changed jobs many times during the year. After about six months of living at Michael's place, I finally had to leave, because he had married his girlfriend and needed the space. I had to rent a flat in Brooklyn for full price. Soon I realized, however, that my total income was barely enough to cover the rent, to say nothing of my daily bread.

I moved to New Jersey, where I began to work at a building site managed by an ex-Israeli, after which I started installing private swimming pools in the homes of the American rich and famous. The luxury and splendor of their homes dazzled me. I will never forget how we once installed a large swimming pool, together with a Jacuzzi and a spacious sauna room, in one of these palaces. I found it difficult to understand how people could afford building such gorgeous mansions that were worth many millions of dollars. I wondered why they needed all those empty rooms. None of these millionaires had more than one or two children at the most, and in most cases the children were already grown and had left home. For whom was all this beauty needed—the white poodle or the Siamese cat?

In the three years that passed since I had first set foot on the "holy ground" of the United States, I achieved much. With the money I had saved from the many jobs I worked, I bought a car and a *falafel* (spicy fried patties of ground vegetables such as chick peas or fava beans) pushcart that I could pull behind my car. In Manhattan one can see hot-dog vendors at every street corner, and I was sure that in a city so full of Jews and Arabs, my falafel business would be a smashing success.

I would park my improvised stand in the middle of the Jewish market on Delancey Street, right at Washington Square. Every Sunday, when concerts were held in Central Park, I made as much as three hundred dollars—more than I could earn in a whole week of honest, hard labor!

Now I could hold my head high, but I realized that this was not the way to become really rich. I knew I had moved up somewhat when I opened a jewelry and souvenir shop in New Jersey, and now I felt like an American. My knowledge of the English language improved, and I began to prosper, both materially and socially. As far as I was concerned, the United States was my new homeland, and not even a bulldozer could have moved me out of there!

One day I received a phone call from my family in Israel, informing me that my favorite sister Frieda was about to be married. Frieda was two years younger than I, and we had always been very close. Immediately, I decided to attend her wedding. Without saying a word to anybody, I boarded the next plane to Israel. Just as the bride's car arrived at the wedding hall, I opened the door for the surprised young couple! It is difficult to describe the joy and excitement at that moment, because nobody had expected me to come. My mother almost passed out with surprise, and my brothers scolded me later: "Why didn't you tell us you were coming? Mother could have had a heart attack!"

After the wedding I stayed for three weeks with my parents at their home. The reunion with old childhood buddies and neighborhood friends was both exciting and disillusioning. On the one hand, it made me feel as if I'd never left the country at all. On the other hand, many of my old friends were in prison, and others went in and out of the detention room of the police station as if it were their second residence.

Soon, I began to feel that the place was far too small and narrow for me. Returning to a small town like Holon after a number of years in the United States was a shock for me. The difference between life in a large American city and life in an Israeli provinciality was staggering. In Israel the whole country lived and functioned like one big family; everyone knew exactly what his neighbors were cooking for dinner. I got the impression that the greatest fun the Israeli had was the joy of discussing his neighbor's daily ups and downs. However, in this visit I did not feel the sensation of warmth and closeness that I remembered in Israeli society. The filthy streets, the poorly paved roads, and the rugged houses that had known better days only oppressed me with a spirit of sadness and depression. I felt like a captured bird, imprisoned in a cage that I had created for myself. More than anything I felt like spreading my wings and flying. I could not wait for my visit to end, so I could again board the plane that would bring me back "home" to America.

As I packed my suitcase for the return trip, I found in my parents' home my old Hebrew Bible, which had served me so faithfully in my school years. Suddenly, the words of my beloved Bible teacher Maeir Tzubari, at my graduation ceremony, flashed back in my memory: "I plead with you, my friends. As long as you live, do not stop reading the books of Psalms and Proverbs."

I took that old book and put it into my new suitcase. (Being so well-off, I could at last afford to buy a new suitcase to replace the old brown one.) When the time came to depart, I boarded the plane, determined that whenever in the future I would go on a vacation, it would be to the Hawaiian Islands or to Switzerland or even to Timbuktu—but never, never again to Israel!

Left:
In Brooklyn, at Michael's wedding.

Below:
Wedding scene from the movie "A New Spirit"

Chapter 7

An Encounter with Jeff

When I returned to my shop in New Jersey, I regularly kept my old Bible on my sales counter, perhaps as a good-luck charm. Every now and then I browsed through it, mindful of my teacher's command. One bright day a tall young man came into the store. His sparkling eyes had a tender look. His soft, yet determined features were emphasized by a mustache, and his manner of talking was slow and measured. His name was Jeff.

When he saw the Hebrew Bible lying on my counter, his eyes suddenly lit up. Addressing me in Hebrew, he asked, "You believe in *Yeshua* (Jesus), don't you?"

"Of course I believe in *Yehoshua* (Joshua)!" I replied, totally misunderstanding him.

"Oh, no! I don't mean *Yehoshua Ben Nun* (Joshua, son of Nun)," he said with a smile. "No, I am talking about Yeshua, the one who is called *Yeshu* (derogatory Hebrew slang for Jesus) by those who do not know Him."

"Why Yeshu?!" I responded with a mixture of perplexity, fury, and indignation. "Are you Jewish? And if you are, what is he to you? We Jews do not believe in Yeshu! We believe in God and in God alone."

"No, I am not Jewish," answered Jeff, "but during the Yom Kippur War I spent some time in Israel as a volunteer bus driver. Before that, I worked in Israel as a volunteer in several kibbutzim, and even managed to learn some Hebrew. I love the people of Israel with all my heart, and I firmly believe that God loves them, too."

Rather rudely, I interjected, "Wait a minute! Do you really mean to tell me that you are not a Jew?" "No, unfortunately I am not Jewish," Jeff admitted honestly, "but I do love the Jews, because of Yeshua."

Now it was my turn to raise an eyebrow. "I've never heard of a Gentile who loves the Jews! And what does Yeshu have to do with all that?" Jeff did not keep me waiting for an answer. "It's because Yeshua is the Son of God and the Messiah of Israel." He made this statement with that bold assurance of a firm believer who takes his faith seriously. He probably did not consider the possibility that there might be people who thought otherwise.

"The Son of God?!" I was enraged again. "Since when does God have a Son?"

"Oh, I've got some news to tell you!" Jeff smiled. "God not only has a Son, but this Son is a perfect Jew, a Jewish King, born of the House of David!" Then, changing the subject suddenly, he asked, "Have you ever read the *Brit Hadashah* (the New Testament)?"

"Oh, no! God forbid!" I was really terrified now. "We Jews are forbidden even to hold that book in our hands! It's a Gentile book, and we must not defile our hands with it."

"It's too bad that you condemn a book that you have never even seen." Jeff changed to English. "How can you have such a fixed idea regarding something that you do not know anything about? Look, when a person is taken to court, the judge must be totally impartial and unbiased in order to weigh objectively all the allegations brought before him, both from the prosecution and the defense. The judge must not bring his own personal inclinations into consideration. He must judge honestly and righteously. How can you issue such a terrible verdict on Yeshua and on the New Covenant, when you do not have even the faintest idea about them? Don't you realize that you allow your prejudices, or worse yet, the prejudice of other people, to fix your opinion and to cause you to pass judgment without examining the facts first?"

"What are the facts, then?" My curiosity was aroused. "Since my early childhood, I've learned that Yeshu was only for the goyim, for the Gentiles! Well, I must admit that I do not know anything about Jesus or about Christianity."

It looked as if Jeff was just waiting for the opportunity to tell me more about his God. "It is possible that the things that I am going to tell you now may be entirely new for you. But, before anything else, I want you to know that the true, original Christianity—some are inclined to call it "the Messianic faith" —is quite different from the distorted image of the Christian religion as it is perceived today by most Jews.

"The Messianic faith is a way of life that a person must choose as an act of his own free will, and not a religion into which a person is born. Faith in the Messiah of Israel is the only way of salvation and of true communication with the living God, and this is true for every person, whether he is Jewish or Gentile. The Messianic faith was not designated for Gentiles only. On the contrary, it was meant first and foremost for the Jewish people. I do not want to preach Christianity to you, and I certainly do not expect you to change your religion and convert to Christianity. God forbid! As a matter of fact, although I was not born a Jew, it was only thanks to Yeshua that I've learned what true Judaism is all about."

Jeff used my embarrassed silence to go on: "There is a basic difference of opinion here, and I'm not so sure if you're aware of it. The Jews believe that only a person who was born of a Jewish mother can be regarded as a Jew. In other words, the religion of a person, or to be more precise, the faith that he must adhere to for his lifetime, is dependent upon the sexual relations that his parents had. You can claim, on this basis, that Esau was as Jewish as Jacob, because both were born at the same time and of the very same parents. In the same way, one can say that Gideon's parents were good, faithful Jews, although they served and worshipped idols. (See Judges 6:25.) The fact that a person was born into a Jewish family is by no means a guarantee of his devotion to the God of Israel. You see, if a person is born in a garage, it does not make him an automobile.

"In other words," Jeff continued, "no one can be born Messianic. In that sense, the Messianic faith is not a religion at all, as Christianity is. A person has to choose for himself whether or not he wants to become Messianic. Only one who acknowledges by faith what Yeshua has done for him, and accepts Him as Lord and Savior, may become a Messianic believer. We then say of him that he is "saved" or "born again". This does not contradict the Bible, but rather fulfills it. A Jew who accepts Yeshua becomes a Messianic Jew, while I, as a goy, who has accepted Yeshua by faith, am now a born-again Messianic believer."

I looked at him with amazement, because his words did not make any sense to me at all. "Look here," I interrupted him abruptly, "we Jews have a long and painful history of bad relations with you Christians. For two thousand years Christians have persecuted us severely in the name of that man, Yeshu. The crusaders brutally massacred us as they went forth to liberate Yeshu's tomb from the hands of the Muslims. During the Holy Inquisition, we were tormented and burned alive at the stake in Catholic Spain under the slogan, "Convert or die!" Chemelnitzki's Cossacks butchered us like hogs in Poland and Russia. Christians have come up with the infamous "blood libels", accusing us of using the blood of innocent Christian children in our Passover rituals. Possessed with infinite hatred, the enticed mobs, while singing hymns of praise to their gods Yeshu and Mary, herded whole villages of Jews into the synagogues, locked them inside, and set them on fire!

"And we do not have to go so far back in history. In this lifetime, Catholic and Protestant anti-Semitic Christians were wearing swastikas and leading our people, like sheep to the slaughter, into the gas chambers and crematoria of Nazi Europe. The blood of the victims has not dried yet and is still crying out to the heavens for revenge. And now, you come and try to preach to me, a Jew, to accept Yeshu and believe in him? I don't want anything to do with him!"

"First of all, let's get some things straight," Jeff replied. "You have simply turned to the wrong address. You place Yeshua—and by the way, His name is Yeshua and not Yeshu!—and those who believe in Him on the same level with those anti-Semites who have acted so inconsistently with the teachings of the New Testament. I am well aware of the unjust and hostile attitude that those calling themselves "Christians" have displayed toward the Jews. It was an attitude that sprang out of ignorance, sinfulness, misinterpretation of the Word of God, and a miserable misunderstanding of God's plan of salvation for Israel and for the entire world.

"You are probably aware of a certain theory prevailing in many of the Christian churches today—which is quite ancient, by the way—that says the Jews, who "once" were God's chosen people, disobeyed God when they rejected His Son, the Messiah. And so, "God" became very angry with them and "divorced" them, adopting the Christian church as His chosen people and as His new bride instead. This is not the case at all. The God of Israel—who is the Lord of the whole universe, of course, because there is only one God in existence—is a just and righteous God who never breaks His promises. Those who accept this heresy, commonly known as "replacement theology", do not realize that if the God of Israel could have broken His eternal covenant with His ancient people once, then the faith of every Christian actually hangs on nothing! What person in his right mind would believe in such a fickle God and trust Him to keep His word and save him? If these so-called Christians consider Israel as unfaithful and disobedient to God, how do they consider themselves? Are they any better?

"Many claim to be Christians," Jeff went on with determination, "but they are not faithful disciples of Yeshua at all. As a matter of fact, they are doing exactly the opposite of what their Master taught and commanded them to do. There is a tremendous difference between these nominal Christians who grew up in a Christian environment and the true Messianic believers who, at a certain point in their lives, have freely accepted Yeshua as their Lord and Savior. The former have nothing to do with the real, historical Yeshua, who was born, who died, and who rose again as the King of the Jews. Yeshua taught, and is still teaching, His followers to love God with all their hearts, all their souls, and all their minds, and to love others as they love themselves (Luke 10:27). Moreover, He even provided them with the power and the capacity to do so. He came into this world in order to forgive our sins, and to give us a new heart and to breathe in us a new Spirit!

"The Brit Hadashah (New Testament) can be understood only in the light of the *Tanach* (Old Testament). A *goy* who is born again by the Spirit of God understands very well that Yeshua was sent to the Jewish people in the first place. He also realizes that his faith in Yeshua, the divine Savior, who came into this world according to the promises God has given to His people in the Tanach, actually grafts him, the Gentile believer, into the commonwealth of Israel. That Gentile believer knows he has actually accepted a Jewish faith in the Jewish Messiah and in the God of Israel, and that he has been received into the faith of the Jews, like an adopted child or a righteous proselyte.

"Yeshua did not enter history in order to inaugurate a new religion in the world. Quite the contrary! He came here in order to fulfill the destiny of the Jewish people to be a light to the Gentiles. Yeshua came into the world in order to complete the faith of Israel and, at the same time, to open wide the gates of salvation before the non-Jews, as it is written:

"Open the gates, that the righteous nation may enter, the one that remains faithful." (Isaiah 26:2)

"When the LORD will have compassion on Jacob, and again choose Israel, and settle them in their own land, then strangers will join them and attach themselves to the house of Jacob." (Isaiah 14:1)

"The *Brit Hadashah* clearly says that God did not forsake His people," Jeff continued forcefully. "It contains, among other things, the writings of the apostle Paul. He was a Jew, born of the tribe of Benjamin in the Greek colony of Tarsus in Asia Minor, and he identified himself as a Pharisee according to his religious convictions. He violently persecuted the Jewish believers in the Messiah, until Yeshua Himself appeared to Him in a vision and completely changed his heart. In one of his God-inspired letters, the one to the believers in Rome, the people of Israel were compared to an olive tree, of which several branches had been pruned away, and onto which branches of a wild olive tree had been grafted instead. Paul then asked the Gentile believers a question: "Who supports whom? Do the branches support the root, or is it the other way around?" Paul warned the Gentile believers not to think that they are in any way better than the Jews, because it was the Jews who were the original, natural branches of the true olive tree. (See Romans 11.) Nevertheless, the Gentiles did exactly what they were clearly admonished not to do! Do you call that obedience to the Word of God?

"The judgment that is going to fall on the Gentiles who think that way will be extremely hard, because they have touched the very apple of God's eye, the Jews (Zechariah 2:8). We, the Gentiles, became Jewish through our faith in Yeshua, and not the other way around. This is why I do not challenge you to convert and become a "Christian". God forbid! I do not believe that a Jew should ever change his religion when accepting the Jewish Messiah of Israel. There is no greater absurdity than this! You must remain a true Jew when you come to your own Messiah."

"My Messiah?" I laughed bitterly. "My Messiah has not come yet! Every Jew declares three times a day that he awaits the coming of the Messiah. A Jew cannot remain a Jew and believe that the Messiah has already come."

"I'm afraid you're wrong on this point," answered Jeff. "The Messiah did come, and His true name is *Yeshua Ben David* (Jesus, son of David). Unfortunately, many of the Jews have a rather distorted mental picture of the expected Messiah. They believe that He must come as the Lion of Judah, to bring them a smashing victory over the Gentiles. Many Jews still wait for the Messiah because it is far easier to wait for the good things still to come in the distant future, than it is to accept the evils and the hardships of the present. People say, "When the Messiah comes..." and thus disregard the present. But God decided from the very beginning that, before improving the world, He would begin with the renewal of the human heart.

"The main problem lies with us, mankind. It is we who have turned away from the ways of God. It is we who have brought the wars and all their evils into the world. We have polluted the world and destroyed it, both physically and morally. Every one of us has contributed his share, with his deceitful speech, selfishness, greed, and who knows what else. These are the things that corrupt and destroy our universe!"

Jeff looked me straight in the eye as he continued: "The Messiah's first and foremost task was to solve the basic problem of mankind, our estrangement and alienation from God. Sin separated us from Him. However, God did not remain far away from us. He has always desired to draw near to us. Therefore, He came into this world to take the penalty of our sins upon Himself and to save us from our sins, so that He might cleanse and sanctify us and enable His Holy Spirit to dwell in us. This is how we can enjoy the best of God's creation together with the Creator Himself, while we are living here in this world, and can participate with Him in the renovation of His universe."

I could sense that he sincerely believed every word that came out of his mouth. Still, it did not make much sense to me, and I could not understand what all this had to do with me, or with Yeshu, and what Yeshu had to do with me.

Looking at his watch, Jeff suddenly announced that he was in a hurry, but he promised to come back, "just to polish up my Hebrew," and to show me that the Messiah had first come in order to make atonement for human sin. Jeff explained that when Yeshua came to the world for the first time, He came as the Lamb of God and was offered as a sacrifice on the altar for the sins of the whole world. However, he also assured me that when Yeshua returns, He will truly come as the Lion of Judah, and as a valiant Man of war, to conquer all the enemies of God and subdue them by the power of His love.

Jeff left, and I was alone with many confusing, contradictory thoughts racing through my mind. Messiah? Yeshu? Well, this was all I needed! Of course, I had no doubt that God existed, neither did I ever believe that the only way for the renewal of God's creation was that described by the sages of the *Zohar* and the *Kabbalah* (mystical

Jewish philosophies). But what was all this trash about Yeshu, and His method of "renovating mankind before changing the universe?" And then, I also thought, "Why renovate this world, anyway? Just let me enjoy the few more years that are allocated to me to live in it!"

Suddenly I thought of Elizabeth, a friend who once told me that I did not even know what life was all about, but immediately I expelled that bothersome memory from my mind. I reassured myself that if there were anyone who knew about enjoying life, I did. Still, I could not shake those thoughts.

I reflected on my life and began to realize how a man can manipulate his way through life, using all the right words, to get the desire of his heart. Wasn't that exactly what I had been doing? I knew what people wanted to hear and then insincerely told them those things. I had been willing to do almost anything in order to achieve my desired goals. Suddenly, this crime, though invisible, seemed terribly offensive. Ever since the world began, those words that people have been using so thoughtlessly to mislead and deceive others were the very same words that turned this world into a cruel place. The wisest of all men, King Solomon, knew well what he was saying when he wrote: *"Death and life are in the power of the tongue"* (Proverbs 18:21). As for me, how much killing and murdering had I actually done in the hearts of so many people with my evil tongue and foul language?

With a flash of spiritual understanding at that particular moment, I realized the terrible injustice we cause to one another by means of that small, wicked organ we call the tongue!

On set for the movie "A New Spirit"

Chapter 8

The Life of the Flesh is in the Blood

By now, I had already achieved several important things in my life. I had acquired my green card, opened a jewelry store of my own, and even managed to invest considerable amounts of money in Wall Street. I really felt that the sky was the limit and that I was living the American Dream. My life seemed so glamorous and successful that I began to think I was really somebody. My plans and aspirations had no ceiling. What else lay in store for me? I anticipated every increasing challenge with delight.

My highest goal at that time was to penetrate into the circle of the Jews who had come to the United States from Syria. They were famous all over the country for their tremendous wealth and controlled much of the trade in New York. It was less than a mile from my rented apartment in the slums to their luxurious mansions on the shores of the Atlantic, but we were light-years apart in our lifestyles. These people lived in the suburbs, far away from the noise and filth of downtown New York. Their villas were each worth a million dollars or more. Each one had a private beach, huge well-groomed gardens, expensive cars, drivers, and personal butlers. I hoped that, through my eloquence, I might find a nice bride at their Syrian synagogue, one who would bring with her all I needed as a dowry.

My mind was constantly scheming and plotting. If I had not been so sure of myself, I would probably have regarded the idea as altogether unattainable. However, in the meantime, I had had enough opportunity to learn that in this world, and especially in the United States, hardly anything was impossible! Apart from my endeavors to penetrate into the Syrian-Jewish community, I also considered several daring alternatives and prepared myself for them both physically and mentally. I would jog for miles across the large New Jersey lawns and swim long distances in the ocean to keep physically fit. I was determined to reach my goal no matter what, either through the Syrians or through my natural Jewish *chutzpah* (egotism, nerve), which I mistakenly regarded as courage. Although my motives were wrong and dirty, the end would finally justify them, I reasoned.

That end goal, to which I was constantly pressing forward, was crystal clear to me: a magnificent palace on the seashore with huge glass windows through which I would be able to look over the blue ocean, and then, with just a few elegant steps, board my private dream yacht. This was my American Dream, and I was determined to make it come true at all costs!

Right in the midst of all my planning and scheming to get the best possible deal out of this life, Jeff suddenly invaded my life. About a week after our first confrontation, I saw him parking his heavy motorcycle across the street from my shop. Somehow, I found it hard to imagine how such a delicate-looking fellow could ride such a huge, clumsy vehicle.

Jeff always knew to visit me just prior to the closing of the shop. As he entered my store, we greeted each other warmly. Jeff told me something about his work at a certain metallurgical factory. He was quite satisfied with his job, and especially with the fact that most of the work was performed by automatic machines, which left him only to supervise the control boards, allowing him enough free time to read the Scriptures during his shift. As he spoke without complaining about his work, he sounded like a man who was happy with his share, one who had found his place in life.

I could only pity him. Who knows how much money his boss made through Jeff's labors every hour, every day, every month, and every year! "Thank God," I thought, "that I have managed to break that snare and escape that vicious cycle."

Although Jeff spoke Hebrew fairly well, I did not have much patience for his slow, stammering speech or his constant searching for the right words. Further, I wanted to polish my English, so after some small talk in Hebrew, the conversation soon reverted to English. Jeff returned to the place where he had stopped a week earlier.

Without any previous warning, Jeff shot at me a surprise question: "Do you happen to know why people offered sacrifices in the days of the Bible?"

"Of course!" I was happy to demonstrate my thorough knowledge of the Hebrew Scriptures. "The goyim who lived in the land of Canaan used to offer sacrifices—even their own children—to their pagan deities. God could not forbid the children of Israel to participate in such obnoxious practices, so He just limited them instead, refining and sanctifying them."

Knowing I was misled, Jeff slightly rephrased his question: "Do you know who offered the first sacrifice in the Scriptures?"

"Sure, it was Abraham, our father!" I announced triumphantly.

"Sorry, wrong again!" answered Jeff with a chuckle. "Many good people preceded him. As a matter of fact, the first sacrifice was offered already in the Garden of Eden. The Torah tells us that after Adam and Eve sinned, God made garments of skins to clothe them. Now, where do you think those animal hides came from? Do you see that in order to atone for Adam and Eve's sin, God had to slay some innocent animals and use their skins as fabric? He could have created the best silk and velvet clothes for them, but He used animal skins instead. And do you know why? Well, this is how the ancient principle of *"life for life"* (Exodus 21:23) was first inaugurated and implemented. That principle of "blood for blood" goes like a crimson cord throughout the Scriptures. Lives of clean animals had to be offered ever since, as a ransom for sinful human lives, as it is written:

> *"For the life of the flesh is in the blood, and I have given it to you on the altar to make atonement for your souls; for it is the blood by reason of the life that makes atonement."* (Leviticus 17:11)

"Adam and Eve had two sons, Cain and Abel," he continued. "Cain offered to God of the fruit of his field, while Abel offered *"of the firstlings of his flock and of their fat portions"* (Genesis 4:4). How did these boys know they should offer sacrifices to God in the first place? I cannot tell you for sure whether their parents taught them about it or if they heard about it directly from God. One thing is certain, however: there is a deeply rooted, built-in consciousness of sin and failure within the human nature, as well as a profound awareness of the need for an atonement. Even the most primitive idol worshippers among the pagans offered sacrifices to their deities in order to appease the feared evil spirits. They were even willing to hurt themselves physically in order to punish themselves for their sins and somehow ease their consciences.

"In spite of all that, Cain freely decided to offer something else instead, some of the crops that had been produced by his labor. This was actually the first recorded case of a man-made religion, because here we find for the first time a man who is trying to justify himself before God by the merit of his good works. Since then, practically all the religions of the world have been based on that same principle, which says that man must do something, or refrain from doing something else, in order to find favor in the sight of his god.

"Abel, on the other hand, chose not to try to fool God, but instead obeyed Him literally. He offered an animal; consequently, God accepted his gift. This principle of the atonement achieved through animal sacrifices was passed down from generation to generation. It is God's appointed way for the forgiveness of man's sin. The realm of effectiveness of these sacrifices grew wider and larger through the years."

As Jeff went on with his explanations, I had to admit that this goy, who had a far better knowledge of my Jewish Bible than I had, began to intrigue me.

"You see, after Adam and Eve fell in sin, God provided a sacrifice for each one of them, by clothing them with garments of animal skins. Abel also offered God a sacrifice that was sufficient for himself only. Many years later, the blood of the Passover lamb, when smeared on the doorposts, provided shelter and protection for the whole family from the angel of destruction—one sacrifice for each household. On the Day of Atonement, the high priest offered a sacrifice for the whole nation of Israel, and that sacrifice was sufficient for a whole year. Later, the once-and-for-all sacrifice of Yeshua, the Messiah, was offered for the sin of the entire world and had an eternal value. This offering put an abrupt end to all the animal sacrifices at the Temple.

"By the way, have you noticed the fact that exactly one generation after the crucifixion of Yeshua, the Temple was destroyed and all the sacrifices ceased? This happened because there was no longer a need for sacrifice from then on, since the one eternal sacrifice had been made!"

All of this was entirely new to me. Although I liked to study the Scriptures in school, I could not remember my teacher Maeir Tzubari speaking to us about these things even once. My curiosity was definitely aroused, and I let him continue without any further interruptions—for a few moments, anyway.

"Come on, let's talk a little more about these sacrifices," Jeff said. "The clear, definite instructions Moses gave in the Torah were that the sacrificial animal had to be blameless and without any physical blemish, since that would symbolize imperfection or sin. All men are regarded as sinners in the eyes of God. The trouble is that no sinful person can offer himself for the sins of somebody else, but instead each has to pay the penalty for his own sins. It may be humiliating to think about it that way, but the fact is that a bull, a lamb, and even a dove are worthier to be offered as sacrifices on God's altar than a sinful man, since sin defiles us and renders us unclean."

"Hey, wait a minute!" I interrupted him. "You're talking all the time about sin, taking for granted that every human being is a sinner by nature. I have to disagree with you on this point. What about all the great and righteous sages who never committed a sin in their lives? Isn't it written in the Tanach about the people of Israel: *"All your people [are] righteous; they will possess the land forever"* (Isaiah 60:21)? And what about the thirty-six legendary "righteous people" upon whom, according to Jewish tradition, the whole universe is standing?"

Jeff's eyes were filled with sincere sorrow, and he chose his words very carefully: "Well, here we have a case in which a man-made tradition stands in conflict with a clear biblical statement. Every individual has been granted the free choice either to believe the Word of God or to follow the traditions of men. The context of the verse in Isaiah that you have just quoted speaks about the time when Israel will turn to King Messiah and will be glorified at that future time. Then, *"all your people will be righteous..."* You have to admit that today they are not yet altogether righteous, are they? Well, throughout the Bible we see that in the eyes of God,

> *"Indeed, there is not a righteous man on earth who continually does good and who never sins."* (Ecclesiastes 7:20)

> *"When they sin against Thee*
> *(for there is no man who does not sin)..."* (1 Kings 8:46)

> *"God has looked down from heaven upon the sons of men,*
> *to see if there is anyone who understands, who seeks after God.*
> *Every one of them has turned aside;*
> *together they have become corrupt;*
> *there is no one who does good, not even one."* (Psalm 53:2–3)

"According to these Scriptures, and many more for that matter, sin is a universal phenomenon that entered the world soon after the first man moved on the face of this earth. Now, I want to make myself very clear, because I know it is a very delicate subject that has often been misunderstood by Jews and Christians alike, as well as by the rest of the world's religions. You see, sin is not so much a matter of what man does or does not do, but rather of what the human nature is. In other words, you do not have to wait until you begin to commit sin in order to be a sinner. In fact, it is exactly the other way around; you commit sin because you are already a sinner by nature.

"We may perhaps look at sin as a malignant disease that destroys your body from within and that causes the external symptoms to appear on the outside. The symptoms do not make the sickness, but it is the disease that creates the symptoms. You see, we were all born with the germs of that horrible disease already in us. We were conceived as sinners, even as King David wrote: *"Behold, I was brought forth in iniquity, and in sin my mother conceived me"* (Psalm 51:5)."

I contended defiantly, "Do you mean to tell me that a baby, who cannot distinguish his right hand from his left, is already a sinner?"

"I did not say it—the Bible did—but you can see it for yourself in everyday life. Our educational system is designated only to make our social lives as bearable as possible. Come to think of it, one of the first words any baby utters, no matter in what language, is usually "No!" You never have to teach a baby how to be disobedient or rebellious; he already knows that by his very nature. Through education we try to tame him and break that evil inclination of his, which is built into his character from the very beginning. This is one of the first principles that the Torah sets forth, near the beginning of the book of Genesis:

> *"Then the LORD saw that the wickedness of man was great on the earth, and that every intent of the thoughts of his heart was only evil continually."* (Genesis 6:5)

"The original sin in the Garden of Eden was not only the horrible crime of tasting the forbidden fruit. When you look at it, it was not such a terrible thing at all, certainly not worth expulsion from the Garden! But rather, it was Adam's disobedience to God's clear prohibition that made the Lord so angry. And until this very day, all the human sin put together is nothing but rebellion and defiance against God's will. Whenever you do something that contradicts the will of God, you sin. Since there was not even one single soul on the face of the earth who did God's will continually and without failing even once, the Scriptures regard the whole human race as sinful.

"We know that Adam was created in the image of God, but that was true only for the first human couple on earth, and only at the stage of their innocence, before they fell into sin. That image of God, in which the first man was created, was terribly marred and corrupted beyond recognition as the result of sin.

"Now, within the framework of Moses' Torah, whenever a person wanted, or rather had to, offer a sacrifice to God, he was to bring a clean, *kosher* (ritually fit for use) animal to the priest. Then he laid his hands on the head of the animal as a sign of identification and confessed his sin, thus transferring his sin and guilt to the sinless beast. Only then was the animal slain by the priest and offered on the altar. The life of the animal had to be terminated for the guilty person's sake, and the latter was from that moment on regarded by God as though he had not sinned—until the next time, of course."

I asked, "But what did the poor, innocent lamb or the sinless bull do to deserve that terrible fate of being slain in my stead and to pay the penalty of my sin? Why shouldn't I pay the price of my own sin myself?"

"Oh, you do pay for it, all right! Do you realize what the penalty of sin is? Somebody once said that sin is like a cruel taskmaster; actually, it is the worst tyrant of them all! All the days of your life it enslaves and exploits you, causing you nothing but guilt, shame, damage, and misfortune—and you serve it faithfully like a bond slave. But then, on your last day, when you come to collect your wages, it laughs in your face and pays you for your diligent and faithful service with death, because *"the wages of sin is death"* (Romans 6:23)!

"Tell me the truth, are you really willing to pay this awful wage of sin, which is death, by yourself? Aren't you glad that somebody else has already paid it for you in full? Believe me, paying for your sin is not a good deal at all!"

"But we all finally die one day, don't we? Why is it so terrible, then?" I inquired.

"The Scriptures talk of two different kinds of death," Jeff explained patiently. "On the one hand, there is what we call "physical death", the kind of death of which you have just spoken. This is the termination of the physical activities of the living organism. In this respect, there is a resemblance between the human race and the rest of animal life on this planet of ours. But, on the other hand, there is another kind of death, the *"second death"* (Revelation 20:14) as the Bible calls it, which is spiritual death, the eternal and final separation of man from the living God, who is the ultimate Source of life. All men, being sinners, must pay for their sin with eternal, spiritual death unless they have accepted God's means of salvation, His atonement and forgiveness of their sin through the sacrifice of Yeshua, the Messiah. When the Holy Scriptures describe this eternal death, they use very strong images indeed, such as *Gehenna* (hell), *"the lake that burns with fire and brimstone, which is the second death"* (Revelation 21:8), where *"their worm shall not die, and their fire shall not be quenched"* (Isaiah 66:24), and *"the outer [external] darkness; in that place there shall weeping and gnashing of teeth"* (Matthew 22:13).

"It is true that the clean animal is not guilty of your crime," Jeff went on from the spot where I interrupted him earlier. "You are the only one who is guilty of it. But God, in His infinite mercy, wanted to show you how terrible sin is in His eyes by demonstrating to you that only a perfectly beautiful, blameless, innocent (and very expensive) creature—just as you should and would have been if you had not sinned—can take your place and die in your stead."

"But today we have neither a temple nor sacrifices," I insisted stubbornly. "Our rabbis have taught us that ever since the destruction of the Temple, all the sacrifices ceased, and that God has since changed His method of atonement. Since the time of the destruction of the second Temple until today, it is "Prayer, repentance, and alms that remove the evil decree". Today the verse, *"Take away all iniquity, and receive us graciously: so will we render the calves [sacrifices] of our lips"* (Hosea 14:2 KJV), applies to us as a means of salvation."

"Here you are both right and wrong, in a sense," Jeff replied. "It is true that today we have neither a temple nor sacrifices. It is also true that the sacrifices were terminated at the destruction of the Temple in Jerusalem. However, it is wrong to think that God would change the system and that today fasting and prayers are sufficient means for salvation. If that is the case, why did we need the sacrifices to begin with? If prayer and fasting alone could save the soul of man, why did He bother to demand the loss of so many innocent animal lives in the first place? No, God has never changed, nor will He ever change. He is eternal, and He has no alternative plan for the salvation of mankind.

"I repeat what I said before: this is exactly why God had to send the Messiah. Yeshua is the perfect and eternal sacrifice who, by His atoning death, has put an end to all animal sacrifices once and for all!"

"But it wasn't Yeshu who put an end to the sacrifices!" I was irritated again. "You, the Gentiles, were the ones who terminated our sacrifices by destroying and burning our Temple."

Jeff looked at me as if he could read my thoughts. "Do you really think that the Almighty God is so weak and incompetent that He could not prevent that from happening? In other words, if God had refused to allow the heathen Romans to destroy the Temple, could they have removed even one stone? You probably know the book of Amos tells us that God has never done anything without first revealing it through His servants, the prophets, informing them in advance whatever He intends to do."

I nodded in agreement. I knew it alright. But I had a strange feeling as if everything I knew and believed in until that hour was seemingly floating in the air without any solid basis, while Jeff had everything well established, grounded, and anchored in the firm and stable Word of God. Yes, I had also noticed that his entire faith was based solely on the Bible.

"Even in this case," he said, "as in all others, God revealed to His servants, the prophets, that the Messiah's first and foremost task was to atone for the sins of the human race. Putting an end to the sacrificial system was, in a way, only a by-product of that all-important task.

"Oh, my, I have to go now!" Jeff exclaimed suddenly, after a quick look at his watch. "But I'll come back soon and show you some of the prophecies that reveal several things concerning the people of Israel, and about Yeshua, that I'm sure you have never dreamed about!"

I had to agree that I had never heard anything like that in my whole life! I wondered what else that man would show me in the Bible.

I locked the shop and went out to take a walk on the promenade overlooking the Atlantic. My head was dizzy with contradictory thoughts. That night I could not help thinking of my aging father. I could actually see him practicing the traditional cleansing ritual of tashlich by the spring, symbolically ridding himself of all his sins on *Rosh Hashanah*. I pitied him, because that was obviously not the way to get rid of sin.

Suddenly, I saw Father slaying the atonement rooster on the eve of Yom Kippur. I watched him carefully waving the bleeding and resisting white fowl, as he held it firmly. He waved it above our heads in circular movements, while he murmured the traditional chant: "This is my atonement, this is my substitution, this is my replacement; this rooster will go forth to death, and we shall enter into good life and peace!" Mother later used the slain fowl as she prepared the traditional chicken soup for the last meal before the Yom Kippur fast. I thought to myself that if all our sins were really transferred onto that poor creature, it did not take us very long to receive them back by way of eating!

Was this truly the meaning of the sacrifice? Where, by the way, is the rooster sacrifice mentioned in the Bible? The Torah speaks of bulls, of rams and lambs, of goats, doves, and even birds, but where is the rooster or the chicken mentioned in this context? I can still remember that at the end of every Yom Kippur, I was never quite sure whether or not my sins had truly been forgiven. Oh, yes, we congratulated each other with the traditional blessing of *"Gemar hatimah tovah"* (May your name be inscribed in the Book of Life), but even this beautiful blessing became no more than a routine.

Could it be that Jeff was right when he said that the central thing about the Day of Atonement was really the sacrifice, and that since we have no scapegoat today, we cannot have any assurance that our sins have been forgiven? I reflected for a moment on the Talmudic story concerning Rabbi Yohanan Ben Zakkai, who on his deathbed confessed to his grieving disciples that he was not at all certain where the angels were leading him—to paradise or, alas, to hell!

Could it be that Jeff was correct in saying that the need to offer sacrifices was built into the very nature of man and that this need was as old as sin itself?

Along with my confused embarrassment, I became so intrigued and curious that I could hardly wait to meet my new friend again. Jeff loved the Lord as a child loves his father. He also knew God in a very personal and intimate manner, while I hardly knew anything about Him. For Jeff, God was not just a supreme force, strange and remote, who moves the wheels of the universe from afar. Rather, God was to him a loving Father, who knew His children through and through, and still loved them in spite of all their human weaknesses and failures. I seemed to know the God of the Jewish tradition. I loved the feasts of Israel and even enjoyed reading the Tanach occasionally. But for Jeff, the Tanach was the living Word of the living God. He read it as one would read a love letter from someone very precious and dear to him.

Jeff had complete confidence that his sins were forgiven, while all I knew was that my life was full of lechery and fornication. Jeff knew that when his time came, the gates of heaven would open wide for him and that he was going to be forever with his beloved Lord in heaven. By comparison, I did not have the faintest idea where I was going to find myself at the end. Jeff spoke about this life as merely a corridor that led to the banquet hall of everlasting life. I wondered how I could prepare myself while in the corridor. If I didn't, was there any banquet hall for me in eternity?

Wherever I turned, I realized that Jeff had a clear advantage over me. He knew something that I was supposed to know. He had something that I suspected was originally mine, but that I had somehow miserably forfeited. I could have given all the treasures of the world just to find out what that "something" was. Yet, I was scared to death and was not sure at all whether I wanted to find the answer, because I knew that the answer involved both a responsibility and a commitment, something that I was not willing to accept at that point.

Ceremony of slaughtering chicken on Yom Kippur.

Who is the sacrifice?

Scene from the movie "A New Spirit"

Chapter 9

Who Is the Sacrifice?

A few days passed before I saw Jeff again through my shop window. It seemed that he came with new ammunition, ready to drop several more "Yeshua bombs" on me. I was willing to agree with him, at least on one point: the rotten religious establishment was nothing but a huge fig leaf to cover the bare nakedness of politics. Jeff did not tell me anything that I did not already know about the existence of God. I had known that all too well since childhood.

During my wanderings through the world, I had met all sorts of people, but I had never come across anyone who had such a cheerful approach to life. During our first meeting I noticed that Jeff was gifted with a very special kind of wisdom, and I really enjoyed the way he presented his case. I also appreciated the way he so patiently withstood all my vicious attacks against his faith. Although this issue of Yeshua was as far removed from me as the east is from the west, I was nonetheless happy to see him, because I felt that he still had a lot he could teach me. I truly desired to hear the information about the Bible that I had never heard at synagogue, in my parents' home, or at school.

When Jeff entered the shop, he went straight to the point, picking up the conversation exactly at the place where we had stopped it last time. I really admired his perseverance.

"The prophets prophesied, but only about the coming of the Messiah," Jeff quoted from the sayings of the Jewish sages with his typical enthusiasm. "I promised to show you several prophecies concerning Yeshua mentioned in the Bible. Do you want me to show you Yeshua in your own Hebrew Bible, or in mine?"

When I offered mine to him, he responded, "Find Isaiah 52:13, and read from there to the end of chapter 53, will you?"

This was an irresistible challenge. I opened my Bible and started reading, and I could not believe my own eyes!

"Behold, My servant will prosper,
He will be high and lifted up, and greatly exalted.

Just as many were astonished at you, My people,
so His appearance was marred more than any man,
and His form more than the sons of men.
Thus He will sprinkle many nations,
kings will shut their mouths on account of Him;
for what had not been told them they will see,
and what they had not heard they will understand.
Who has believed our message?
And to whom has the arm of the LORD been revealed?
For He grew up before Him like a tender shoot,
and like a root out of parched ground;
He has no stately form or majesty that we should look upon Him,
nor appearance that we should be attracted to Him.
He was despised and forsaken of men,
a man of sorrows, and acquainted with grief;
and like one from whom men hide their face,
He was despised, and we did not esteem Him.
Surely our griefs He Himself bore, and our sorrows He carried;
yet we ourselves esteemed Him stricken,
smitten of God, and afflicted.
But He was pierced through for our transgressions,
He was crushed for our iniquities;
the chastening for our well-being fell upon Him, a
nd by His scourging we are healed.
All of us like sheep have gone astray,
each of us has turned to his own way;
but the LORD has caused the iniquity of us all to fall on Him.
He was oppressed and He was afflicted,
yet He did not open His mouth;
like a lamb that is led to slaughter,
and like a sheep that is silent before its shearers,
so He did not open His mouth.
By oppression and judgment He was taken away;
and as for His generation,
*who considered that He was **cut off out of the land of the living**,*
for the transgression of my people to whom the stroke was due?
His grave was assigned with wicked men,
yet He was with a rich man in His death,
because He had done no violence,

nor was there any deceit in His mouth.
But the LORD was pleased to crush Him, putting Him to grief;
if He would render Himself as a guilt offering,
He will see His offspring, He will prolong His days,
and the good pleasure of the LORD will prosper in His hand.
As a result of the anguish of His soul, He will see it and be
satisfied; by His knowledge the Righteous One, My Servant,
will justify the many, as He will bear their iniquities.
Therefore, I will allot Him a portion with the great,
and He will divide the booty with the strong;
because He poured out Himself to death,
and was numbered with the transgressors;
*yet **He Himself bore the sin of many**,*
and interceded for the transgressors."
(Isaiah 52:13–53:12, emphasis added)

In spite of the education I had received and all the nationalistic history lessons I had studied in school, and despite all the prejudice that I'd absorbed with my mother's milk (according to which it was always the innocent, blameless people of Israel who had to suffer atrocities at the hands of the evil, depraved Gentiles), I had to admit that the portion I had just read in my Hebrew Bible clearly described an innocent, guiltless individual who suffered terrible treatment, even death, from the hands of others who were called "his people," although he himself committed no wrong! At this point, I really could not ignore Jeff's explanations.

Jeff continued, "The prophet started with a rhetorical question: *"Who has believed our message?"* He well knew that the people of Israel could never accept or believe in a King who was *"just and endowed with salvation, humble, and mounted on a donkey, even on a colt, a foal of a donkey"* (Zechariah 9:9).

Isaiah the prophet saw with his spiritual eyes how Israel would despise and reject their Messiah, because when He came, He was not going to fulfill their expectations regarding the victorious and militant leader who would conquer all the heathen kingdoms, subdue all the nations under His feet, and rule over the whole world out of Jerusalem. On the contrary, Isaiah saw that *"He was despised and forsaken of men... and we did not esteem Him."*

God was not taken by surprise by the fact that Israel rejected the Messiah. On the contrary, He even foretold it, saying, *"But the LORD was pleased to crush Him, putting Him to grief; if He would render Himself as a guilt offering, He will see His offspring, He will prolong His days, and the good pleasure of the LORD will prosper in His hand."* In other words, Yeshua was predestined to be the sin offering for the whole world, so *"the good pleasure of the LORD will prosper."*

I was speechless as I read the descriptions that needed no explanation: *"But the LORD has caused the iniquity of us all to fall on Him." "The Righteous One, My Servant, will justify the many, as He will bear their iniquities."*

Moreover, I realized that this Gentile Jeff, who according to our Jewish sages did not possess any *neshamah* (soul or spirit), stood right here in front of me with a soul far cleaner and purer than my own—although I was Jewish—because I lived in sin. "Which of the two of us should be stoned to death now?" I thought.

Immediately I confronted him with another question, hoping for the usual answer: "Who, then, killed Yeshu?" It was a trick question, because I was sure he was going to blame us Jews for that hideous crime, as all Christians did.

"The Romans did it, and so did the Jews; you and I are to blame for it. The whole of mankind is equally guilty," said Jeff.

That was a strange answer! "What do you mean by that?" I marveled. "How could you and I kill Yeshu? Didn't He live two thousand years ago?"

"Yes, He did. Historically speaking, it was the Jews who delivered Yeshua to the Romans, because they did not have the authority to sentence anybody to death, being subject to Roman rule. However, the Romans performed the actual execution by crucifixion, because that was a common way of putting convicts to death in those days. God foreordained it that way, so that the whole world, Jews and Gentiles alike, would be found guilty in the eyes of God and would be equally privileged to partake of His salvation. God delivered them all to rebellion, so that He might be able to grant all of them His pardon. No one today can claim that he had no share in the crucifixion of Yeshua. Accusing one part of humanity only does injustice to historical and spiritual truth.

"Furthermore, if Yeshua had not been crucified, the Hebrew

prophets would have been wrong, since they foresaw His death on the cross many years in advance. But, on the other hand, it was neither the Jews nor the Gentiles who were totally responsible for Yeshua's death. Human sin is to blame for that. Aside from your being a Jew and my being a Gentile, we are both sinners, and as such, we stand equally guilty before the holy and righteous God. It was sin, both yours and mine, that sent Yeshua to the cross. More importantly, if He were not willing to accept this death penalty and to die for you and me, no power in the universe could have made Him do it! It was because of His love for sinners that He died as the eternal sacrifice, to grant us remission of sins."

"What on earth are you talking about?" I was infuriated again. "We don't have sacrifices anymore! You Gentiles saw to it that we have neither temple nor sacrifices! And, generally speaking, the people of Israel had offered enough sacrifices throughout history, don't you think? I believe that it was the people of Israel who were this sacrifice described by Isaiah."

"The fifty-third chapter of Isaiah cannot possibly refer to the people of Israel," Jeff replied patiently. "Don't the Jews confess twice a week, every Monday and Thursday, at the tahanun prayer: 'It was because of our sins that we were driven out of our land'? You see, the people of Israel had to pay for their own sins and thus could not atone for the sins of the Gentiles by any means. The Scriptures repeatedly counted the multiple sins of Israel, listing them one by one. Read, for example, what Isaiah had to say about it in the first chapter of his book:

"Alas, sinful nation, people weighed down with iniquity,
offspring of evildoers, sons who act corruptly!
They have abandoned the LORD,
they have despised the Holy One of Israel,
they have turned away from Him...
From the sole of the foot even to the head
there is nothing sound in it,
only bruises, welts, and raw wounds, not pressed out or bandaged,
nor softened with oil...
Unless the LORD of hosts had left us a few survivors,
we would be like Sodom, we would be like Gomorrah."
(Isaiah 1:4, 6, 9)

"It would be difficult to say that God flattered the people of Israel in those verses! God never flattered or complimented His children when He had to chastise and discipline them or reprove them for their sins. The people of Israel could not atone, therefore, for the sins of the nations, because they were guilty of sin themselves. It is a biblical principle that no sinner can atone for the sins of another. This is why God had to send the Messiah!"

Once again, I was surprised by that Gentile, who knew the Bible and who could even quote from our Jewish prayer book. I was really embarrassed for neglecting my study of the Bible so much that I could not find even one sound "Jewish" answer to his interpretations. Jeff must have noticed my embarrassment, because he quickly changed the subject, and by doing so he just threw another bomb into the room: "Do you happen to know when exactly the Messiah had to come?"

"I'm sure there are many Jews—including the Rabbi of Lubavitch himself—who would be willing to pay you a lot of money for that piece of information!" I joked.

"And I'm willing to show it to you free of charge, here in your Hebrew Bible!" Jeff retorted.

"Oh my, this Gentile has certainly gotten my attention!" I thought. I handed him my Bible, and he opened it with expertise. Here came the inevitable comparison again: although I loved to read my Bible, I could hardly even remember the order of its books.

Jeff quickly flipped through the pages in my Bible until he came to the ninth chapter of Daniel, and then he asked me to start reading aloud at the twenty-fourth verse:

"Seventy weeks have been decreed
for your people and your holy city,
to finish the transgression, to make an end of sin,
to make atonement for iniquity, to bring in everlasting righteousness, to seal up vision and prophecy, and to anoint the most holy place.
So you are to know and discern that from the issuing of a decree to restore and rebuild Jerusalem until Messiah the Prince
there will be seven weeks and sixty-two weeks;
it will be built again, with plaza and moat, even in times of distress.
*Then after the sixty-two weeks **the Messiah will be cut off** and have nothing,*

*and the people of the prince who is to come
will destroy the city and the sanctuary.
And its end will come with a flood;
even to the end there will be war; desolations are determined.
And he will make a firm covenant with the many for one week,
but in the middle of the week
he will put a stop to sacrifice and grain offering;
and on the wing of abominations
will come one who makes desolate,
even until a complete destruction,
one that is decreed, is poured out on the one who makes desolate. "*
(Daniel 9:24–27, emphasis added)

"I admit that the language of that passage is especially rough," Jeff commented. "Do you understand it properly?"

I read the passage again from beginning to end and had to confess that I found it really difficult to comprehend. I had never read this chapter before, and to be more accurate, I barely knew that there was a book called "Daniel."

One little phrase bothered me the most. I always knew that the Messiah was supposed to come "at the end of days" to redeem and save Israel from all its adversaries, to conquer all of God's enemies, and to establish His everlasting and true peace. In His reign the wolf would dwell together with the lamb, and the leopard would live in harmony with the kid. (See Isaiah 11:6.) Then, the people of Israel will live in perfect security, everyone under his vine and fig tree (see Micah 4:4), with all the Gentiles subdued under their feet.

But here, in this passage, I read that *"Messiah will be cut off. "* What does "cut off" really mean? I knew that "*karet*" meant in Hebrew "death by heaven". Are we actually wasting our time waiting for a kingly Messiah, when He will eventually be *"cut off"?* I thought of what I read before, *"Like a lamb that is led to slaughter... His grave was assigned with wicked men... Because He poured out Himself to death. "* Did the Messiah really have to come and die? God forbid! In that case, was it possible that those Christians were right after all in ascribing that death to their Yeshu?

Trying to help me out, Jeff said, "Let's first consider the general background of this story. Daniel was a young boy when he was exiled by Nebuchadnezzar from Jerusalem to Babylon. He had to work in the service of several kings during his long lifetime, first in Babylon, and later, after the Persian conquest, also in Persia. One day he came across an ancient scroll, in which he read an old prophecy of Jeremiah. According to this prophecy, the exile to Babylon would take seventy years. A simple calculation made it clear to him that this period was just about to expire. He began to fast and pray, confessing his people's sin and trying to understand why the end was lingering. After a period of prayer and fasting, an angel appeared to him in a vision' and revealed to him what the future held in store for his nation."

"I see that the word *Messiah* appears twice in this passage, but how can one conclude from that when the Messiah was scheduled to come?" I asked.

Jeff replied, "Here you must have some knowledge in linguistics, history, astronomy, and it will do you no harm to know some math, too. Once I read a rather comprehensive study on that prophecy, and I want to share it with you and explain it accordingly. We have here some very important clues in each of these areas.

"First of all, let's examine this paragraph from the linguistic point of view. Today we speak of a week as a time unit that holds seven twenty-four-hour days. But in biblical days the word week had an additional meaning. We read, for example, in the book of Genesis, that Laban, the sly and scheming uncle, after deceiving his nephew Jacob regarding Rachel and Leah, proposed this to him: *"Complete the week of this one, and we will give you the other also for the service which you shall serve me for another seven years"* (Genesis 29:27).

In other words, a *week* can also mean a period of seven years. Here in Daniel, we also have the obscure plural form *shavuim*, which we may explain as periods of seven years each, while the regular plural form of *shavuah* (Hebrew for a week) is *shavuot*, and that usually indicates regular seven-day weeks.

Let us consider now the historical aspect. We know from secular history that the King Artaxerxes-Longimanus of Persia ascended the throne in the year 465 B.C. In Nehemiah 2:1–5, we read that in the twentieth year of his reign, Artaxerxes issued a decree that permitted the rebuilding of Jerusalem. That means that this decree described by Daniel was issued by Artaxerxes in 445 B.C.—our starting point for the calculation of this prophecy."

"Now, how about your math?" Jeff went on. "It is only a matter of simple arithmetic. This chapter speaks of 70 "sevens" or 490 years. This period is subdivided into three unequal periods: seven "weeks," which are one jubilee or 49 years, 62 "weeks," which are 434 years, and another "week," which is in turn divided into two "half-weeks." According to this passage, the Messiah was supposed to be cut off some time after the first two periods. Now, if we add 434 and 49, we get 483 years.

"In the ancient world, the year was calculated according to a lunar year of 360 days. Therefore, the Messiah had to be killed a short while after 173,880 days (483 times 360) passed from the time King Artaxerxes' decree was issued.

"Now, Nehemiah 2:1 also tells us that the decree was issued in the month of Nisan. The first of Nisan was the Jewish New Year for the kings, which means that the years of their reign were calculated from Nisan to Nisan. On this occasion, various official events and festivals were celebrated, which leads us to assume that this royal declaration was also issued on the first day of Nisan.

"Let's consider the astronomical point of view now. According to the Royal Planetarium in Greenwich, England, it was determined that the first of Nisan, 445 B.C., fell on the fourteenth day of March of that year. Now we have a starting date in common calendar terms.

"From this it is possible to compute exactly on which day Yeshua entered Jerusalem, riding on a donkey, several days prior to His crucifixion. The Gospel according to Luke tells us that Yeshua's public ministry began in the fifteenth year of the reign of Caesar Tiberius, who came to power in A.D. 14. Most of the scholars agree that Yeshua's public ministry lasted approximately three years, which now brings us to the year A.D. 32, the year when He was crucified.

"In John 12:1, we are told that Yeshua went to Bethany six days before the Passover and, in verse twelve, that He entered Jerusalem on the following day. The Passover always falls on the fourteenth day of Nisan, which, according to the Astronomy Center's calculations, fell on the tenth of April, A.D. 32. Yeshua came to Bethany on the fourth of April, then, which was on a Friday. The meal that he ate there must have been the Sabbath meal, whereas the 'following day' was obviously not the Sabbath, on which Yeshua and His disciples rested, but rather Sunday, the sixth of April, A.D. 32.

"Now, did the sixth of April, A.D. 32, fall exactly 173,880 days after the king of Persia issued the decree to rebuild Jerusalem, namely on the fourteenth of March, 445 B.C.? According to the *Julian calendar* it is obvious that between the two dates there is a time span of 477 years and 24 days. But, as you probably know, there is no such thing as "year zero" between 1 B.C. and A.D. 1. One year should therefore be omitted, and now we have 476 years and 24 days, which are 173,764 days (365 times 476 plus 24). To that we have to add another 119 days, because the Jewish calendar has a leap year with an additional day every fourth year (476 divided by 4 equals 119), and so we come up to 173,883 days—very close to the number of days according to the prophecy, 173,880!

"However, this is not good enough for biblical prophecy—we have to be one hundred percent accurate and reach the exact day. We know that the Julian calendar deviated slightly from the actual solar year: its year is 1/128 day longer than the solar year. In order to correct this deviation, we must subtract one day for every 128 years; thus, for the period of 483 years (Daniel's 69 "weeks"), we have to subtract 3 days, which brings us exactly to 173,880 days!"

Now I really had a problem: Whom should I believe? Should I trust the synagogue and the Jewish traditions in which I was raised, which described an ideal Messiah designated for Israel only, leaving the rest of the world out of the picture? Or, should I instead accept the Bible that was open right in front of my eyes, which told me something entirely different: that the Messiah was going to come before the destruction of the second Temple and be "cut off"?

But, if the Bible is right, how is it possible that our rabbis' eyes were so blind as to neglect such obvious truth? I was sure that there must be a satisfying answer to this puzzle. I had to find out all I could about it.

Jeff seemed to have read my thoughts again, because he answered my unasked question even before I had the opportunity to express it: "Oh, I've read the rabbinical interpretations about this issue. Most of the traditional commentaries concerning this passage, as well as other Messianic passages in the Scriptures, are generally divided into two main categories: the more ancient ones, which date before the first century A.D., and the later ones, which were in most cases arguments that endeavored to refute the claims of the *minim* (apostates, and also the initials of the Hebrew phrase for "believers in Jesus of Nazareth"). Most of the ancient commentaries, like that of Yonatan Ben Uzziel, ascribe these prophecies to King Messiah; while the more recent ones, like Rashi's, for example, tend to negate such a possibility, inventing rather tenuous alternatives that bear a very strong anti-Messianic bias.

"Let's see what the Bible, the pure Word of God, has to say; it certainly can speak for itself! The sages of Israel are still unable to see these things. You cannot blame them for it, any more than you can blame a blind man for not being able to see. It's not that they are too stupid, because they aren't. Because of their sin, God has shut their eyes temporarily, in order to enable the Gentiles to accept the Jewish Messiah and be saved. For the time being, God has set the children of Israel on the shelf, so to speak, but He did not forsake them completely. God forbid! The day will soon come when He will remove that veil from their eyes, and then they will repent, as Jews, and look on Him whom they pierced."

"What do you mean by 'whom they pierced'? Does the Tanach say that, too?" I asked. I had come to the stage where nothing could surprise or shock me anymore. At this point I was ready and able, if not willing, to accept anything. Somehow I got the point that this Bible of mine had much more in it than I had ever imagined!

"Yes, this is a verse from the book of Zechariah," Jeff said matter-of-factly. "Go ahead and read it."

He opened the Bible and let me read it for myself. The passage spoke of a terrible war that was going on in Judea and Jerusalem. From the context I could not tell for sure whether it described a war that had already taken place in the past, or one that was still due to happen in the future, heaven forbid! And then I read the following verses:

> *"And it will come about in that day that I will set about to destroy all the nations that come against Jerusalem.*
> *And I will pour out on the house of David and on the inhabitants of Jerusalem the Spirit of grace and of supplication,*
> *so that they will look on Me whom they have pierced;*
> *and they will mourn for Him, as one mourns for an only son,*
> *and they will weep bitterly over Him,*
> *like the bitter weeping over a firstborn."*
> (Zechariah 12:9–10, emphasis added)

I liked the idea that God planned to destroy all the nations that come against Jerusalem. It agreed with the way I understood the Messiah's character. Now, however, I was told that the Messiah would not only be killed and cut off, but, according to this verse, He would be pierced, and the whole nation of Israel will behold Him when God opens their spiritual eyes and pours His Spirit of grace and supplication on them! Somehow, this seemed to be in perfect harmony with the rest of Scripture.

"Oh my! Is God opening my eyes right now?" I was deathly terrified at the very thought of it!

Jeff knew exactly what to say and how to say it: "You see," he proceeded, as if taking for granted that I knew it all simply because I was Jewish, "Isaiah spoke about the Lamb who will atone for the sin of mankind by His death. Daniel foretold the time, accurately to the day, when the Messiah would be killed. Zechariah prophesied that a day will come when the whole nation of Israel will look upon Him who was pierced, which referred to the circumstances of His death, and that they will mourn for Him. Now I want to show you yet another prophecy that will shed some more light on the day of Yeshua's return:

> *"I kept looking in the night visions, and behold,*
> *with the clouds of heaven One like a Son of Man was coming,*
> *and He came up to the Ancient of Days*
> *and was presented before Him.*
> *And to Him was given dominion, glory and a kingdom,*
> *that all the peoples, nations,*
> *and men of every language might serve Him.*
> *His dominion is an everlasting dominion which will not pass*
> *away; and His kingdom is one which will not be destroyed."*
> (Daniel 7:13–14)

"Do you see?" Jeff pointed out to me. "Every prophet gave us still another piece, or even several other pieces, of the same large jigsaw puzzle or of the mosaic picture, if you please, that portrays the Messiah. Daniel described Him coming in the clouds of heaven, while Zechariah pictured Him as the One who was pierced. You will have to agree that He was not pierced in heaven!

"Do you want me to show you what the Bible says about the place where the Messiah had to be born?" That was another stunning blow!

Again I was astonished at Jeff's thorough knowledge of Scripture. He opened the Bible and read the prophecy in fluent Hebrew, though with a heavy American accent:

"But as for you, Bethlehem Ephrathah,
too little to be among the clans of Judah, from you One will
go forth for Me to be ruler in Israel. His goings forth are from
long ago, from the days of eternity." (Micah 5:2)

"Most of the Jewish commentators agree regarding this verse that the Messiah's birthplace should be Bethlehem in Judea, the royal city of David. But the ruler of whom Micah is speaking must be a very special person; otherwise, we might be tempted to conclude that he spoke of a regular, flesh-and-blood king just like David, the son of Jesse, who was also born in Bethlehem. However, Micah said that His going forth was from long ago, *"from the days of eternity",* and Daniel also spoke of Him as a ruler of an everlasting dominion. And this is truly so, because Yeshua was not just another ordinary man. Only Yeshua could atone for our sins and breathe a new Spirit into us.

"When we meet again I'll be glad to show you, straight from the Scriptures, that God truly has a Son. You must realize that you would never be able to obtain by yourself all those things that the Son of God can and wants to give you. Isn't it a terrible waste of time and energy to look in vain for the true meaning of life in places where it cannot be found, in broken cisterns that hold no water?" (See Jeremiah 2:13.) Jeff pronounced these words with such authority that it sounded as if they came to me straight from heaven. He seemed to know me thoroughly, including all those empty wells that I frequented in a futile search for the waters of life!

I smiled at him from ear to ear, but I still ridiculed what I had labeled his "fanaticism" in my heart. How stubborn and perverted the human heart can be! We talked a little about Israel, which we both missed very much, and then he left.

I closed the shop and went again to my favorite place, the promenade that overlooked the Atlantic Ocean. I loved to go down to the wharf, sit on one of the rocks, and watch the fishermen rowing in the distance, as I gazed blankly at the horizon, thinking and planning my next moves.

The ocean was quiet that evening, but my heart was in turmoil. The things that I had just seen in the Bible bothered me. Deep inside

I felt that they really referred to Yeshua. Abruptly, I thought of a tract about Jesus that I once received somewhere in Manhattan. I remembered how repulsive it had been to me then, but when I thought about it again, I did so with fascination. As I was staring at the stars of heaven and the sand on the seashore, two of the typical scriptural symbols of my ancient and beloved people, I could not escape the nagging thought that Israel might have missed the mark after all. I did not hold any accusations against the Judaism of the rabbis, or against the Christian church, for that matter. Rather, all I wanted was to find out the truth about that Man!

On set for the movie "A New Spirit".   Below: Main camera man.

Chapter 10

A Hunger for the Truth

Several days went by, and Jeff did not return to the store. At first, I regretted the fact that I had not asked him for his telephone number, but the storm that raged within me slowly subsided. Time ran its course, and the long, philosophical debates I'd held with Jeff eventually began to fade from my mind. The whole world was out there, twinkling with its many pleasures, and I was ready to partake of them as if nothing had ever happened.

I particularly liked to spend my nights in a certain nightclub in Asbury Park, New Jersey, called the Stone Pony. At that time, a relatively unknown rock singer was just taking his first steps into the show business arena. He demonstrated a rather captivating masculinity with his dark sunglasses, his cowboy hat, and his warm, sandpapery voice. His name was Bruce Springsteen.

Nightclub entertainment was not anything new to me. As a teenager I would frequent, together with my pals, all the nightclubs and discotheques in Jaffa and Tel Aviv, where we smoked, drank, and dated the girls, because that was what everybody did. Then I was just a boy, but now I was a man—at least, I fit my concept of what a man was.

More and more, my life revolved around that person who looked at me from the mirror every morning. Sin was offered to me, so to speak, as a poisonous pill coated with a thick layer of sugar, and I had no problem swallowing it, just like a fish that swallows the hook along with the bait. The deeper I plunged into the swamp of sin, the less attention I paid to the lifeline that Jeff was trying to throw down to me from the high and solid Rock on which He was standing, Yeshua the Messiah. Of course, I never noticed my deteriorating condition because it happened so smoothly and pleasantly.

One evening, again prior to closing time, Jeff marched into the shop, just as if he had never left. He beamed with his familiar, bright smile and continued our conversation as if he had paused only for a moment. By this time, I already had mixed feelings toward him. On one hand, I liked to listen to what he had to say about the Bible;

on the other hand, the sin that resided within me resented his words passionately, because they presented a hidden threat to my corrupt way of living.

With all my heart, I resisted and rebelled against this new teaching, which attacked my Jewish pride as well as my natural vanity. I vowed that I would never accept the idea that modern Judaism had missed the mark. After all, how could I ever show my face in my country again if I accepted his words as truth and "converted"? God forbid! I was not even willing to think of the possibility of repenting in the way Jeff presented the term to me, and the idea of accepting the yoke of God's kingdom on my neck was repulsive.

"Do you remember how angry you became when I first told you that God had a Son?" Jeff just voiced my innermost thoughts aloud.

I nodded in the affirmative.

"God knew that no fallen man could ever save himself and that a sacrifice was necessary for that purpose. But an animal, no matter how pure, can never be equivalent to man. Man alone can be equal to another man in worth. Therefore, God decided to enter into this world in the form of a man in order to take the penalty of human sin upon Himself and to die for the sins of the whole world.

"Yeshua, being God in human flesh, was the only Man who ever lived on this earth without falling into sin. He alone could therefore be the innocent and pure Lamb of God, the perfect sacrifice! You see, Yeshua was not just an ordinary man; He was the incarnated God, the Deity who came into the world. How was that possible? Only God Almighty could have the answer to this, because God stands outside the cycle of human sin. He loved us sinners so much that His righteousness would not be perfectly vindicated had He not provided, by His grace, salvation for the fallen human race. For that purpose, God sent His Son into the world, so that whosoever believes in Him should not perish, but could have everlasting life (John 3:16). And this Son of His was the Messiah!"

"What does this have to do with the Messiah?" I questioned. "I know that Christians have idolized Jesus and made a god out of him, but this is sheer blasphemy! No Jew can ever believe that God has a Son!"

"Wrong again," Jeff smiled. "Christians did not take a human being and deify him—it was exactly the other way around! It was God who humbly took on human flesh in order to save sinners and to bring them back to Himself. Besides, why couldn't God have a Son? The Bible speaks many times about the Son of God. As examples, we find these Scriptures in the Tanach:

> *"Why are the nations in an uproar,*
> *and the peoples devising a vain thing?*
> *The kings of the earth take their stand,*
> *and the rulers take counsel together against the LORD*
> *and against His Anointed...*
> *I will surely tell of the decree of the LORD:*
> *He said to Me 'Thou art My Son; today I have begotten Thee.*
> *Ask of me, and I will surely give the nations as Thine inheritance,*
> *and the very ends of the earth as Thy possession.'...*
> *Now therefore, O kings, show discernment;*
> *take warning, O judges of the earth...*
> *Do homage to the Son, lest He become angry,*
> *and you perish in the way..."* (Psalm 2:1–2, 7–8, 10, 12)

> *"Who has ascended into heaven and [reigned]?*
> *Who has gathered the wind in His fists?*
> *Who has wrapped the waters in His garment?*
> *Who has established all the ends of the earth?*
> *What is His name or His son's name? Surely you know!"*
> (Proverbs 30:4)

> *"Then King Nebuchadnezzar was astonished;*
> *and he rose in haste and spoke, saying to his counselors, '*
> *Did we not cast three men bound into the midst of the fire?'*
> *They answered and said to the king, 'True, O king.'*
> *'Look!' he answered,*
> *'I see four men loose, walking in the midst of the fire;*
> *and they are not hurt,*
> *and the form of the fourth is like the Son of God.'"*
> (Daniel 3:24–25 NKJV)

Jeff explained further: "You see, the Bible does not have any problem whatsoever with the term *"Son of God"*. The rabbinical controversy began only much later. It started with the theological debates that the rabbis conducted with the Messianic Jews. Messianic Jews used these same Scriptures to support their conviction that

Yeshua was truly the Son of God. This is also why Yeshua had to be born of a virgin."

"Oh, give me a break!" I retorted in disgust. "Every child knows that children are not born of virgins. Christians talk about the virgin birth of Jesus and expect enlightened twentieth-century people to swallow that superstition. This is a blatant insult to our intelligence!" Jeff smiled at me with that grin of his that said, "Oh, I've heard that argument before."

"Actually, I was expecting you to react that way!" He waited patiently until I calmed down, and then he said, "It really strikes me as funny to think that weak-minded and incompetent people like ourselves dare to tell God what He can and cannot do! God is the Creator. He made this whole universe with just the word of His mouth. He did not need to have sex with anybody at all in order to create Adam and his wife, did He? He gave Abraham and Sarah a son when they were far too old to have children by natural means; He gave Isaac to them supernaturally, in order to show them, and us too, that He was all-powerful in this realm also. Tell me, Jacob, is God Almighty, the Creator of heaven and earth, unable to create new life in the womb of a virgin without using male sperm for it?"

Shocked, I was unable to respond to this question that confronted every traditional, prejudiced belief I had held.

Jeff continued: "But let me tell you frankly, the question of God's technical ability or inability to plant the seed of life in a virgin is not relevant. The fact is that the Messiah had to be born of a virgin and of the Spirit of God. Otherwise, how could He be *"the Ancient of Days"* (Daniel 7:9), whose *"goings forth are from long ago, from the days of eternity"* (Micah 5:2)? And let me tell you something else, even this idea of the Virgin Birth is not totally strange to the Bible. Isaiah already hinted at such a possibility, when he said, *"Behold, the virgin shall conceive and bear a Son, and shall call His name Immanuel"* (Isaiah 7:14 NKJV). And in another place, Isaiah wrote this about that unique child:

> *"For unto us a Child is born, unto us a Son is given;*
> *and the government will be upon His shoulder.*
> *And His name will be called Wonderful, Counselor, Mighty God,*
> *Everlasting Father, Prince of Peace.*
> *Of the increase of His government and peace there will be no*
> *end, upon the throne of David and over His kingdom,*

to order it and establish it with judgment and justice
from that time forward, even forever.
The zeal of the LORD of hosts will perform this. "
(Isaiah 9:6–7 NKJV)

"The Messiah, this marvelous Child who was born of a virgin, the Possessor of the divine titles and the eternal kingdom, had to be born outside the sinful human dynasty, which started with Adam. He had to come into this world free of the heredity of sin, in order to be the pure, sacrificial Lamb of God, who could be offered in atonement for the sin of mankind.

"You said before that Christians took Yeshua and made a god out of Him. But, as you can see now, just the opposite was true. Yeshua was not a man who evolved and became God, but rather He was God who came into this world in human form for a short while and then went through a temporary death. Three days later He rose from the dead, in order to conquer the last enemy, which is the second death. Only in this way could He pay the price of our sin and fully satisfy God's holiness and the demands of His righteousness. By doing so, He fulfilled all the most demanding requirements of the Torah and overcame death, once and for all, for the whole human race."

"But," I tried to understand, "if the Messiah truly came into the world to save and redeem humanity with His blood, why do we look today the way we do? Didn't the Messiah come to establish a kingdom of peace here on this earth, a kingdom in which the lion will live peacefully with the lamb?"

"He certainly did," Jeff agreed. "However, if He had inaugurated that kingdom of peace and justice in the world without first preparing the hearts of sinful men to accept it, they would have immediately spoiled and corrupted it, just as Adam and Eve did to the Garden of Eden. Right now, God is preparing for Himself a little flock of saints, people who know Him and love Him and who want to obey His commandments above all else. This is His congregation, composed of Jewish and Gentile believers alike. Only when Yeshua finally completes His work will He return to this earth with all His saints to establish that glorious kingdom, about which Isaiah spoke in his wonderful prophecy."

"That makes sense," I dared to admit for the first time, "although I find it too difficult to believe. I realize I am a sinner alright. I also know that I cannot pull myself up by my bootstraps to get myself out of the mud, but I just cannot accept the idea that somebody else had to die in my place and that I am not required to do anything about it in return. It sounds too cheap to me."

"I understand very well how you feel. We all have that natural desire to atone for our sins, either by tormenting ourselves through fasting, or even harming ourselves physically to appease our anguished consciences. The Jews overloaded themselves with thousands of positive and negative laws, with all kinds of *dos* and *don'ts*, far beyond the plain instructions of the Torah. They insist that 'the more you study it, the better you are,' in spite of the fact that they are unable to keep even one single commandment properly!"

"What do you mean by that?" I became upset again. "We had so many holy and righteous rabbis, men of God. How can you say that they failed to please God? Didn't they keep all of God's commandments?"

"No, Jacob, unfortunately they didn't. They did not keep the Torah, but not because they did not want to—I'm sure they did. They simply couldn't keep it, because the Torah wasn't given in order to be kept at all!"

Now, I was really confused and puzzled. "You must be joking!" I cried out. "Do you mean to tell me that God gave us the Torah when He knew from the beginning that it was impossible to keep it? Then, why did He give it to us in the first place?"

"He did it to show us His standards and to prove to us that, because of the sin that rules over us, we would never be able to meet His requirements. God gave us the Torah for us to check ourselves in its light and see how utterly inadequate we are and how desperately we need His salvation. This is also the reason He gave us the sacrificial system as the center of the Torah.

"Let me give you an example. An average person can jump, let's say, as far as two meters. A well-trained athlete may jump, perhaps, five meters. If he is an Olympic champion, he might even reach a record distance of nine meters, but this is about the most that a human being can achieve in our generation. Now, let's suppose that we are standing on the edge of a chasm, and the distance to the opposite side is two hundred meters. There is no one among us who is able to jump over to the other side, is there?

"Now, let's consider this example as a parable and that God is on the other side of that chasm, beyond the abyss we call "sin". He looked at us poor grasshoppers, as it were, and had mercy on us. He knew that we were absolutely incapable of reaching Him with our own efforts. This is why He sent Yeshua, His Son, to us as a heavenly Bridge. Yeshua is the Mediator between man and God. We can walk with Him safely, because He is, according to His own words, *"the way, and the truth, and the life"* (John 14:6). I know that there are many people who reject this divine solution as too easy. They would rather do something in their own strength to save themselves. But human effort will never bring us to God, only straight into the depths of hell!"

"I like the story," I said, "but what about all those people who are still trying to keep the Torah to the best of their abilities? What about all the martyrs who died for God's holy name? How can a righteous, loving God allow so many millions of people to perish, just because they did not believe in Yeshua?"

"Here you touch a very delicate subject. We live in the age of humanism, in which man is idolized and set as the central point of interest. In the common mindset today, everything revolves around man, his natural right for self-expression, man's achievements, his conquering the universe and taming the forces of nature, and the magnitude and wonders of the marvelous human mind. But, as noble as this humanistic approach may sound, it opposes the Scriptures, because the Bible is God-centered, rather than man-centered. In other words, it is God, the Creator, who is at the center of the universe, and not man, His creation. We did not create God in our own image, as many modern-day theologians would have us believe, nor did we create ourselves. Instead, God created us for His glory!

"It was no problem at all for God to destroy by flood the whole known world, with all the people and animals that lived at that time on the face of the earth, and to save just eight human beings and samples of all the animals, only because men had so miserably failed and corrupted their ways before Him. God could get along much better without sinful, fallen man. The fact is that every man who rejects God's salvation will eventually have to give an account of his sins before his Creator and to pay the whole penalty, which is eternal death. It is not God who lies in wait for us around the corner to catch man red-handed in order to punish him. It is the sinner who is constantly on the run, always escaping from his loving, compassionate

God and chasing wildly after corrupt, sinful pleasures because they give him some temporary fun. Eventually, however, every person will be required to give an account for the way he spent or wasted his life.

"There are people who blame God for being cruel and inconsiderate, letting so many billions of people go to hell, only because they have never had the opportunity to hear about the Messiah and to accept Him. But, believe me, God is a just and holy God. He did not create hell, that horrible lake burning with unquenchable fire and brimstone, for man at all. It was made as an eternal punishment for Satan and for his fallen angels, the demons. Those people who fail to repent and turn to God, all those who rebel against Him and refuse to accept Him as Savior, those who prefer following their own lusts and sinful desires instead of doing the will of God for their lives—they will inevitably join Satan and his fallen angels and partake of their eternal destiny.

"But, if we do agree to come to God and accept Him, we think we're being so nice! We still put millions of conditions before Him: 'If You do this and that for me, then I may perhaps consider the possibility of accepting You!' We tend to forget that God is the sovereign Lord who created heaven and earth, and that it is He who invites us to come to Him unconditionally and to accept His gift of eternal salvation – free! He gave it to us as a free gift, not because it was so cheap, but rather because God's grace was so costly and precious that no man on earth could ever afford to pay for it. It cost God nothing less than the blood of His beloved Son! Only if we accept this sacrifice by faith is God willing to accept us as if we have never sinned. God has paid the wages of sin with the blood of Yeshua."

"Now I understand you Christians!" I exclaimed. "It's so easy and clear to me! All you have to do is just ask for God's forgiveness, and you're off the hook, so to speak. This way everyone can go on sinning, taking for granted that eventually he will be forgiven. This theology enables you to sin as freely as you like. As long as you go to church and confess your sin to the priest, you're guaranteed exoneration."

Jeff shook his head sadly. "Unfortunately, there are too many people who think just like that—or at least they act like that. However, this isn't what the Bible teaches. Yeshua the Messiah did not come to the world to give us the right to sin and then to be automatically forgiven. Instead, He came to conquer sin and to give us new life, not to be enslaved by sin anymore."

I angrily responded, "Do you mean to tell me that all those Christians who butchered my people for the last two thousand years were innocent people who were not enslaved by sin—or isn't the murder of Jews a serious enough crime in your eyes?"

"Of course it is, Jacob. I'm not justifying the hideous atrocities of any criminals, whether Christians or others, committed either in the name of religion or in any other name. God Himself does not vindicate them! You see, many pagans accepted the external forms of Christianity but failed miserably to repent of their sins. They have called themselves Christians, but their unrepentant and ungodly behavior shows that they are not what they claim to be. Moreover, the mainstream "Christian" church, even in the early stages of her existence, developed very strong anti-Semitic feelings that accelerated and intensified as the number of Messianic Jews in her ranks decreased. The need for a scapegoat, which could be blamed for the sins of commission and omission of the church, brought about the abuse of the Jews, who were accused of the worst of all crimes— *deicide*, or the murder of God!

"Remember, though, that neither Yeshua nor His disciples ever intended to establish a new religion that would rebel against its Jewish roots. They lived and operated within the framework of first-century Judaism. Moreover, Yeshua came not only to forgive the sin of mankind, but also to give us a new beginning and to break the power of sin. The Tanach, which promised us all these things, regards the change in a person who has accepted them for himself, as such a dramatic revolution in his life that the Scriptures describe it in the strong terms of receiving a *"new heart"* and a *"new spirit"* (Ezekiel 36:26) from God. Yeshua gives us eternal, spiritual life, which begins at the moment of that regeneration or new birth and never ends."

"And what exactly is this "new birth"?" I asked. "What do you mean by that?"

"It makes no difference what I mean by that," Jeff grinned at me. "Let's see what the Tanach has to say about it. Both Jeremiah and Ezekiel spoke about that tremendous, revolutionary event in the human life. Let's read what they wrote about the future of Israel as a nation, because that also refers to every one of us as individuals:

"Therefore, say to the house of Israel: Thus says the Lord GOD,
'It is not for your sake, O house of Israel, that I am about to act,
but for My holy name,
which you have profaned among the nations where you went.
Then the nations will know that I am the LORD,'
declares the Lord GOD,
'when I prove Myself holy among you in their sight.
For I will take you from among the nations,
gather you from all the lands, and bring you into your own land.
Then I will sprinkle clean water on you, and you will be clean;
I will cleanse you from all your filthiness and from all your idols.
*Moreover, I will give you a **new heart**,*
*and put a **new spirit** within you;*
and I will remove the heart of stone from your flesh
and give you a heart of flesh.
*And **I will put My Spirit within you***
and cause you to walk in My statutes,
and you will be careful to observe My ordinances.'"
(Ezekiel 36:22–27, emphasis added)

"Here we see the impassable gulf that separates true faith and man's religion: in other words, the gulf between truth and lies, life and death!"

"Now, what does all of that mean?" I wondered aloud.

"Pure faith claims, and rightly so, that God alone can make a move toward man, cleanse him, and give him a new heart and a new spirit. According to Ezekiel, it is up to God to reach for fallen man and take the initiative to save him. Even earlier in Scripture, however, through Moses, God not only commanded us, *"Circumcise then your heart, and stiffen your neck no more"* (Deuteronomy 10:16),

but He pledged,

"Moreover, the LORD your God will circumcise your heart
and the heart of your descendants,
to love the LORD your God
with all your heart and with all your soul,
in order that you may live." (Deuteronomy 30:6)

"All the religions of this world, on the contrary, demand that man should improve himself by working to the best of his abilities, to add commandment upon commandment, work upon work, and to abstain from sin as far as possible. This is the only way religions can offer a person to be able to cleanse himself and to please the deity. That each religion has its own particular set of rules explains why there are so many religions in the world.

"In the long run, man does not wish to submit to God's truth, nor does he really wish to obey His will. Man would prefer to be his own little god and take upon himself divine authority and glory, although not always the responsibility involved. This is why he created his gods after his own image.

"The Jewish people were the only nation in the world who received the divine truth directly from God Himself by His revelation, but even they twisted it into a man-made religion of *dos* and *don'ts*, which is a far cry from the original truth of God. You see, even the divine truth can be easily perverted and distorted if one injects human ideas into it that were not originally there and then ascribes divine authority to them. In this context, let's read the prophecy of Jeremiah:

> "'Behold, days are coming,' declares the LORD,
> 'when **I will make a new covenant**
> with the house of Israel and with the house of Judah,
> Not like the covenant which I made with their fathers in the day
> I took them by the hand to bring them out of the land of Egypt,
> My covenant which they broke,
> although I was a husband to them,'
> declares the LORD.
> 'But this is the covenant which I will make
> with the house of Israel
> after those days,' declares the LORD,
> 'I will put my law within them, and on their heart I will write it;
> and I will be their God, and they shall be My people.
> And they shall not teach again,
> each man his neighbor and each man his brother, saying,
> 'Know the LORD,' for they shall all know Me,
> from the least of them to the greatest of them,'
> declares the LORD,
> 'for **I will forgive their iniquity,
> and their sin I will remember no more.**'"
> (Jeremiah 31:31–34, emphasis added)

"Jacob, you must have noticed," Jeff explained, "that God speaks in these verses of something that He Himself intends to do with the people of Israel, to cleanse them from their sins, to implant a new, tender heart in them, and to fill them with His Holy Spirit. In other words, He is making with them a new covenant of forgiveness after bringing them back into their land."

"Hey, wait a minute!" I cried triumphantly. "What if you're taking all these Scriptures out of context and giving them a false interpretation that suits your own philosophy? You can read into the Bible practically anything you want to. I know that most of the cults and the false religions base some of their claims on the Bible, but they twist it and interpret it as they wish. How can I know for sure that all those passages really speak about Yeshu?"

"Excuse me, Jacob," said Jeff, as if changing the subject. "May I have your home address in Israel, please?"

"Do you really want it?" I hesitated for a moment.

"Yes, I do!" Jeff sounded determined.

"Well," I complied, "my address is: Jacob Damkani, 42 Hanevi'im Street, Holon, Israel."

Jeff wrote down the address in Hebrew and then asked, "Did you notice how many identifying details you have here?"

I gazed at the written address, not having the faintest idea where his reasoning was headed.

"Let's suppose that I live here in America and that I want to write a letter to you, when you are living in Israel. If I wrote this address on an envelope, put a stamp on it, and mailed it to you, it would be sorted out at the American central post office and put into a postal sack that goes by plane to Israel. This way all the other countries of the world are eliminated. Later, at the main sorting station in Israel, this letter would be put into the sack that should go to Holon and not to any other settlement in Israel. When in Holon, the letter would be allocated to the mailman who works in your area. There are many houses on your street, but the mailman would bring the letter to house number 42, right to your own mailbox. Do you see? All one needs is to have four or five identifying details in order to locate one particular person from among over five billion people who presently live on the face of this earth.

"And do you know how many identifying details of the Messiah there are in the Bible? Somebody once counted 333 different clues, hints, and references in the Tanach alone, some of which are already fulfilled prophecies, and others are yet to be fulfilled in the future! So, even if you were mistaken concerning one or two of them, or even about ten—which is impossible when it comes to the infallible word of God—you really cannot fail to identify this one Person, since there are so many identifying signs given to you regarding Him.

"Now, let's consider another aspect. Suppose you make an appointment with someone whom you have never met before, to meet him at a certain place downtown. You tell him that you will be wearing a blue jacket, a white hat, and black shoes, that you are about six feet tall and heavy set, that you have a full, brown beard and curly hair, and that you wear glasses. I don't suppose that there would be many people right on that spot who would fit so detailed a description. Now, the Bible provides us with an identity card of a Man who has 333 identifying marks, describing Him to the last detail. It tells exactly where and when He would be born, the manner of His birth, the purpose of His coming, what exactly He was going to do during His lifetime, how He was going to be betrayed, tortured, killed, buried, and finally raised from the dead, after which He would ascend to heaven. It even clarifies that He will return to earth as a conquering King and as the Judge of the living and the dead. How many people do you know who can meet all these descriptions?"

I scratched my head with embarrassment and did not know what to say. The simple logic of his answers rendered me speechless. After a while and with some hesitation, I asked, "Suppose Yeshua knew all these biblical prophecies; couldn't He have planned His life in such a way that it might be in harmony with them? There is, for example, the tradition that the Messiah must come riding on a white donkey, and there is even a prophecy about it in the book of Zechariah, if I'm not mistaken. Now, Yeshua knew that the Messiah should enter Jerusalem riding on a donkey, and so He fulfilled this prophecy."

"You are absolutely right about this prophecy, but not about all of them. That was one of the few prophecies that was dependent on Yeshua's will. Most prophecies couldn't have been determinedly fulfilled by Him, because even with the strongest willpower, no man can actually choose his birthplace, the exact date of his birth, and certainly not the details of his execution, his burial, and his resurrection from the dead!

"Yet, Daniel foretold that Yeshua would appear and be cut off shortly before the destruction of the second Temple in Jerusalem. Micah told us that He was going to be born in Bethlehem and have an eternal nature. Isaiah, who was known as the "Messianic prophet", told us of His virgin birth, His ministry, His death, and His coming kingdom. All these events, and many others, were not dependent on Yeshua's will at all. But if they were all literally fulfilled in Him, one would have to be blind not to see that He was truly the One He claimed to be!"

"But, I find it hard to understand," I insisted stubbornly, "how all the sages of Israel in the last two thousand years read the Bible and still failed to understand it, while you, who are not Jewish at all and much younger and less experienced than they are, can see all these things so clearly."

Jeff was a little embarrassed by that remark. He hesitated for a moment and then took the Bible, opened it up, and handed it to me. Although he had already shown me so many wonderful things in it, he managed to surprise me again:

"For the LORD has poured over you a spirit of deep sleep,
He has shut your eyes, the prophets;
and He has covered your heads, the seers.
And the entire vision shall be to you
like the words of a sealed book,
which when they give it to the one who is literate, saying,
'Please, read this,' he will say, 'I cannot, for it is sealed!'
Then the book will be given to the one who is illiterate, saying,
'Please read this,' and he will say, 'I cannot read.'
Then the Lord said,
'Because this people draw near with their words
and honor me with their lip service,
but they remove their hearts far from Me,
and their reverence for Me consists of traditions learned by rote,
Therefore, behold, I will once again
deal marvelously with this people, wondrously marvelous;
and the wisdom of their wise men shall perish,
and the discernment of their discerning men shall be concealed.'"
(Isaiah 29:10–14)

I was devastated and shocked! I felt as if God Himself were forcing me to lie down on His operating table, putting me to sleep, so to speak, and trying to perform on me open heart surgery, removing the stony heart out of my bosom, and replacing it with a heart of flesh; but I still resisted Him with all my might. What would people say? What should happen to me, if…?

We were both silent. Jeff certainly had given me much to consider. It turned my stomach to think that the entire nation of Israel had gone wrong and that up until now I had lived all my life in terrible error. Was it really possible that all our rabbis and wise men were mistaken, and that only Jeff, this goy, knew the truth? The very thought of it made me jittery.

It was altogether clear to me that if God were real—which I had never doubted for a moment—then there must also be one divine, absolute truth that was not dependent on any particular religion or way of thinking. Yet, for me, it was impossible that both the Jewish people and the "Christian" Jeff, or the "Messianic" Jeff as he preferred to be called, were both saying the same absolute truth; there was too much contradiction. And, as a Jew, I could not accept the idea that my people had gone astray and followed a false teaching, while those ruthless, bloodthirsty Christians were right.

Jeff sensed the inner turmoil I was experiencing. He realized that words could no longer help in this situation, but only the Spirit of God could. There comes a time when a person has to cope with the truth by himself and struggle with the Angel of God at his personal ford of Jabbok, as Jacob of old did, and emerge from it victoriously at his own Peniel. (See Genesis 32:22–30)

Jeff must have felt that I had reached that point. He bowed his head in silent prayer. Then he said softly, "If you find out that all I have said to you until now is the truth, would you be willing to surrender and give yourself to the truth? If you should ever be convinced that Yeshua is truly the promised Messiah of Israel, would you accept Him as your Lord and Savior?"

I shrank back with terror as if bitten by a snake. How on earth could he know what was going on in my mind and the depths of my heart? I looked at him without saying a word.

Jeff looked at me compassionately and said, "I will pray for you, that the God of Israel will open your spiritual eyes and show you the truth. It is not enough that you understand my words, accept them as truth, and give them your mental consent; you must also receive them into your heart. I'll also pray that God will not give you any rest until you do accept Him! Will you allow me to pray with you?"

Somehow, I expected Jeff to pull out a prayer book from his pocket and read a prayer, but nothing of that sort happened. He just sat down beside me, held both my hands in his, closed his eyes, and bowed his head. Puzzled, I looked at him and did not know what to do next. And then, Jeff spoke to God as a man speaks to his best friend who stands right in front of him. His prayer came straight from his heart, and so it touched mine.

> Father in heaven,
> Please look down at Jacob and open his spiritual eyes to see the truth that he already has begun to grasp with his mind. Let Your Holy Spirit speak to his heart and show him his desperate need for the forgiveness of his sins, which You so graciously provided and offered to him through Yeshua the Messiah. Lord, stir up the desire in his heart to receive a new heart and a new spirit from You. I now commit him into Your hands. Please do with him whatever You desire! I ask this in the name of *Yeshua HaMashiach.* Amen

Jeff looked at me lovingly, as a father looks at his son, and asked, "Do you mind praying with me? I will lead you in a short prayer, and if it speaks to your heart, repeat it aloud after me."

Before I had time to object, he bowed his head, closed his eyes, and prayed once more.

> O God of Abraham, Isaac, and Jacob,
> I do believe that You have given Yeshua, Your Son, as an atonement for my sins. Thank You, Yeshua, for coming to wake me up to a new and holy life, to the glory of God. Amen

To this day, I have no idea why I repeated that prayer after him. I did not believe the words that came out of my mouth. They did not have any echo in my heart at all. But Jeff was very happy that I said this prayer with him and asked, "Will you permit me to leave this copy of the Hebrew Brit Hadashah with you? Read it, and ask God to reveal the truth to you as you do. I'm sure you will find in it answers to many of your questions, those which you have already asked, and those which you have not."

Jeff said goodbye and left the shop. The room grew dark, and it was time to close up and leave. As I went out, a strange sensation of heaviness mixed with deep expectancy overwhelmed me, as if something great and wonderful were about to happen—something crucial, which was about to change my entire life. I also had that odd feeling that somehow this wonderful thing had something to do with Yeshua and that this gift from Jeff was the key to that mystery.

What was hidden in that book?

Pictures from the movie set "A New Spirit".

Our Jaffa House - with a large sitting area in the garden, as well as on the roof. There is a grave yard behind the house where Jeff is buried.

Here, the saints from Israel and the nations come to study the Word and go out to reach Israel with the Good News.

Chapter 11

What Is Hidden in this Book?

When I came home, I took out the small blue book from my coat pocket, turned on the light, and opened it. I was amazed to find this prayer on the first page:

O God of Abraham, Isaac, and Jacob,
Show me the truth as I read this book, and help me follow the light that You show me. Amen

I read this short prayer and moved on to the first chapter. The very first verse hit me like an electric shock.

*"The book of the genealogy of Jesus Christ,
the son of David, the son of Abraham."* (Matthew 1:1)

So, Jeff was right after all that Yeshua really was a Jew! Jeff was also right that those whom I had previously defined as Christians knew nothing of Christ (Messiah). How, then, could the "Christians" claim that they love Yeshua and at the same time hate the Jews, Yeshua's own flesh and blood?

I continued reading. Immediately following this amazing declaration came a long list with many of the biblical heroes I knew so well from school days: Abraham, Isaac, and Jacob, Judah and his brothers, King David and the kings of Judah who followed him, and all of them were good, kosher Jews! Do the Christians who read this book understand at all what they are reading? What can be more Jewish than that? I saw Yeshua in the synagogue, and in the Temple. He was celebrating the Sabbath, the Passover, and the Feasts of Pentecost and Tabernacles. I could not find anything about the Christmas trees or Easter eggs.

Suddenly, a terrible suspicion arose in my heart: How many of these Christians really read their Bibles? If the answer is about the same percentage as Jews who read the Tanach, then both Jews and Christians alike are nurtured only by man-made traditions, which falsify and distort the truth beyond recognition.

As I went on reading, I felt as if I had stepped into the page of the book and was back in my beloved Israel. Along with John the Baptist, I wandered in the dark caves of the Judean Desert and walked with him on the shores of the Jordan River. I joined Yeshua and His disciples in their journey along the shores of the Sea of Galilee and among the Galilean mountains. Together we walked about the narrow streets of Jerusalem. Everything was right there: The Temple and the synagogue, the Pharisees and the Sadducees, the righteous people and the self-righteous ones. I saw the shepherds tending their flocks in the fields of Bethlehem and observed the old scholars of the Torah bending over their sacred scrolls at the rabbinical school. I saw the golden wheat fields that were already white-ripe for the harvest, and I watched the wildflowers and the birds that were sold two for a farthing and five for two. I spent some time with the hardworking fishermen on the seashores, and I could actually smell the intoxicating fragrance of the fruit orchards and the pure olive oil. I felt as if I were physically there!

But, what did all this have to do with what I had considered to be Christianity? I did not hear any church bells ringing, nor did I see there any brown-robed monks making the sign of the cross on their breasts and kissing icons. No one was worshipping crosses made of gold and silver in gorgeous cathedrals to the strains of a pipe organ.

Everything was so Israeli that tears came to my eyes. I never felt so homesick in my life! The United States, with her glittering neon lights, her broad superhighways, and her frightening skyscrapers, was suddenly left far behind me. I was in my well-known rural Land of Israel again, which was crisp and bright in my vision.

Suddenly, I wondered how it was at all possible to pray to God in English, or in any other language for that matter, except Hebrew. Yeshua was "one of us." This was a tremendous revelation for me!

I continued my reading and could not believe my own eyes: *"I was sent only to the lost sheep of the house of Israel"* (Matthew 15:24). Did Yeshua really say those words? What do the Gentiles think when they read them? What do they have to do with Him in the first place? And, on the other hand, why don't the Jews follow Him? Is the blindness of the sinful human race really so great?

Then I understood what Jeff had been trying so hard to get across to me all along, but with so little success: the difference between a man-made religion and a God-given faith, between anti-Semitic "churchianity" and the true Messianic faith. I realized that all those Jew-haters, who persecuted our people throughout history, just took the name of Yeshua in vain and killed His own people, the Jews. They did not know the New Testament, which I was holding in my hands, nor did they hear and obey their Lord and Master. The warning words of Yeshua suddenly flashed through my mind like a mighty bolt of lightning and penetrated my understanding:

> *"Not everyone who says to Me 'Lord, Lord'*
> *will enter the kingdom of heaven;*
> *but he who does the will of My Father who is in heaven.*
> *Many will say to Me on that day,*
> *'Lord, Lord, did we not prophesy in Your name,*
> *and in Your name cast out demons,*
> *and in Your name perform many miracles?'*
> *And then I will declare to them,*
> *'I never knew you; depart from Me,*
> *you who practice lawlessness.'"* (Matthew 7:21–23)

As I continued reading, I could finally see why the rabbis of that time had rejected Yeshua and had hated Him with such passion. With the words of His mouth, which were sharper than a two-edged sword, He pierced through the distortions of their religious bias and nationalistic pride. He scolded them sharply for their moral hypocrisy and corruption, although He never challenged their spiritual authority. He answered them wisely and publicly confounded their self-righteous pretenses.

If the same Yeshua who is described in the New Testament would visit today a Jewish synagogue, or even a Christian church, would He be recognized and accepted there? I thought of the religious symbols I had seen in many Catholic shrines, the images of Baby Jesus in the arms of His mother, the Virgin Mary, as well as those sculptures of Jesus hanging on the cross, and I understood that it was an entirely different "Jesus" that the European artists had imagined, creating Him in their own image and likeness with blonde hair and blue eyes. This was not the Son of the humble carpenter who was born in Bethlehem and raised in Nazareth, who walked across the country healing the sick, cleansing the lepers, opening the eyes of the blind and the ears of the deaf, and raising the dead from their graves! They definitely were not portraying the humble Jewish Teacher who taught that the most important commandment of all:

> *"And He said to him,*
> *'You shall love the Lord your God with all your heart,*
> *and with all your soul, and with all your mind.'*
> *This is the great and foremost commandment.*
> *The second is like it,*
> *'You shall love your neighbor as yourself.'*
> *On these two commandments depend the whole Law*
> *and the Prophets."* (Matthew 22:37–40)

I was really embarrassed now, because in spite of all his efforts, Jeff did not manage until now to make me call Yeshua by His real name. He had explained to me the meaning of His name, from the root word *Yeshu'ah*, which means "salvation". Yeshu, however, is a degrading curse word, composed of the initials of the Hebrew phrase, "May his name and memory be blotted out!"

"What other man could perform all the works that Yeshua did, without making even one mistake?" I thought with amazement. Was there any other person in the whole world besides Him who fulfilled so perfectly all the words of the Scriptures that refer to Messiah? I found the New Testament full of quotations from the Tanach that revealed that what the prophets had foretold was fulfilled in Yeshua.

Obviously, Yeshua was not just an ordinary man. Wisdom and goodness that were not of this world emanated from Him. All the heroes of my childhood—Moses, King David, Isaiah, and all the others—sinned at one time or another; the Bible never attempts to conceal their failures and transgressions. Only Yeshua alone had never fallen into any sin, only Messiah could speak with such authority. It is no wonder that the Pharisees, the teachers of the Torah in those days, considered Him a constant menace and a threat to their self-created righteousness!

In spite of my inner resistance, I suddenly felt an urge to turn to God in prayer. I remembered something that Jeff had said in one of our previous meetings: "God is a living Lord, and even as He revealed Himself to different people in the Tanach, He can reveal Himself also to you. He does not always do it in a physical manner, using an audible voice or by means of a vision. But let me assure you that when God eventually opens your spiritual eyes, you will see Him, you will be cleansed of all your sin and be born of God's Spirit, I have no doubt about it!"

When Jeff once told me that God had revealed Himself to him on several occasions, I looked at him as if he had lost his sanity. I could understand that God could reveal Himself to some righteous Jews like Abraham or Moses, but why would the God of Israel bother to communicate with a goy like Jeff? I must confess now, that although I appreciated and even admired Jeff for his love of the Bible and his dedication to God, at certain times I was convinced that he needed to be committed to an asylum!

But now, as I read the New Testament for the first time, I knew I had nothing to lose if I turned to God and asked Him for a revelation, at least in the same way He revealed Himself to Jeff. And so, I prayed:

O God of Israel, the God of Abraham, Isaac, and Jacob,
If You are really God, and if Yeshua is truly the Messiah,
I want to know it for sure. If everything that Jeff told me about You is true, I want to accept it, even if the whole world is in error. I promise to follow You and to be Your faithful servant. You know me thoroughly,
and You know how I was brought up and taught
since my early youth to reject Yeshua with all my heart.
But if He is really *"the way, and the truth, and the life"* as Jeff read to me from the Scriptures, then I am willing to relinquish all my resistance and follow in Your footsteps, even if I am the only Jew on earth to do so!

I hesitated a little, and then sealed the prayer with "Amen!" I felt I was making an eternal covenant with the God of Israel, even as my forefathers did before me. This was a holy hour indeed.

After that, every day when I returned from work, I read several chapters from the New Testament, admiring the love and wisdom of Yeshua. Then I would kneel and pray to God to reveal Himself to me. Two weeks passed, and the expected revelation did not come. However, I persisted, not giving up my daily reading of the Scriptures and my prayer. I really fell in love with Yeshua and read His words as if they were personal love letters to me. Still, I was not convinced with all my heart that I had to surrender myself to Him and to give

Him my life totally. The New Testament became my favorite book to read, but it was nothing more than that.

And then, one night at about three o'clock in the morning, I suddenly woke up from a deep sleep with a sensation of a strange presence in my room. I was neither scared nor tense; on the contrary, it was a rather pleasant feeling. I felt as if a spring of clear, living water burst open within me, flowing in and through me, cleansing me thoroughly and pouring out through my heart and soul. It flooded the whole world and then returned and filled me again to the brim. I did not know how to explain that experience in words. A strong, yet pleasant shiver went down my spine and through my whole body. I thought that if that presence were visible to my eye, I would not have been able to bear it but would have fallen dead before it instead. This stream cleansed and purified me from within and from without at the same time.

I sat up in bed and said, as Jeff had taught me, "O Lord, speak to me. Here I am!" I neither saw anything with my eyes nor heard anything with my ears, but an overwhelmingly pleasant feeling filled my heart and washed me with the sensation of water flowing in and out of me and flooding my whole being with its power. This experience lasted only for a few minutes, but it seemed to me to last for an eternity. Then everything gradually subsided, and I was left alone again. I knew that something wonderful had happened to me, but I could not define it or tell exactly what it was. I lay awake, marveling about this wonderful experience, until I finally drifted back to sleep.

As I woke in the morning, I automatically stretched out my hand to the right corner of the window sill. Every evening, before I went to sleep, I would lay my New Testament there, face down but open to the page I had been reading. However, that morning I groped along the sill to the left corner, where it lay open to an entirely different place, much closer to the end of the book. Curiously, I saw the location was between the fourth and fifth chapters of 1 John, and I started reading there with genuine thirst. The words pierced my heart like a sharp sword. I felt as if God Almighty had said those words to me Himself, right from heaven. God, who knew me so well, also knew exactly what I was supposed to read on that particular morning. I burst into tears as the light of God shone in my heart. I wept and wept and wept more, until all the burden of my sin that lay so heavily upon me (although I was totally unaware of its existence before) was lifted away!

I felt like a newborn baby, light as a feather floating in the breeze. The Bible, which until that day had been a wonderful but sealed book to me, suddenly became as clear as the midday sun. I now understood why Israel was chosen by God from among all the nations and why Yeshua came into this sinful world. The eternal, perfect truth of the Lord God of Israel brought me out from servitude to liberty, from the darkness of sin to the great light of God's forgiveness. Suddenly I saw and regretted how I had wasted the best twenty-five years of my life in vanity, chasing after the delusions of this world, while the treasures of heaven had been at my disposal all the time.

I realized that God had kept His part of the covenant and that He had proved His existence and authority to me in a most tangible way. Now, it was up to me to keep my part. Only later did I realize that the experience that I had is called the "new birth," of which Yeshua so emphatically spoke:

"Jesus answered,
'Truly, truly, I say to you, unless one is born of water and the
Spirit, he cannot enter into the kingdom of God.'" (John 3:5)

This was the first time in my life that I had experienced an answer to prayer. Now I finally understood what Jeff had tried to explain to me about the new heart and the new spirit, and about the promised new covenant. For the first time in my life, I was filled with joy that was totally independent of external circumstances. I felt like a person who had received a million-dollar inheritance from an unknown relative. All at once, I realized how true the imagery of the new birth was. It was an indescribable joy. It was perhaps what the sweet musician of Israel, King David, meant when he wrote,

"How blessed is he whose transgression is forgiven,
whose sin is covered!
How blessed is the man
to whom the LORD does not impute iniquity,
and in whose spirit there is no deceit!" (Psalm 32:1–2)

The tears of joy that flowed from my eyes washed all the filth and the scum out of my life. I wept uncontrollably. Then I realized that God does speak. I did not hear any voice with my physical ears, but within my soul I knew that I had heard His voice, calling me home, to my homeland and His—and more than anything else, to my own people. I recalled my past vow never to tread the soil of Israel again, and I was all too happy to break it. God called me, and I must go, to bring His good news *"to the lost sheep of the house of Israel"* (Matthew 10:6).

The Jews must be shown the difference between the distorted Yeshu and the true Yeshua, between man-made religion and God-given faith.

At that time, I thought I was the only Jew in the world who believed that Yeshua was the Messiah of Israel. I could not imagine that there was another Messianic Jew in the world, whose heart's desire was to behold the salvation of Israel. I had the strong conviction that the spreading of the Good News of God was the reason for which I was created.

That was how I went to work that morning, armed with a strong, noble resolution to serve the Lord at any cost.

On the left the actor, who played Jeff in "A New Spirit"
and on the right my friend Jeff,
who for months faithfully shared the Gospel with me.

Chapter 12

Growing Pains

During those first happy days of infatuation, I was not aware of the fact that the true struggle had only begun. I was sure that from that day on I would never fall into sin again; that the Lord, who lived in me, would take care of all my needs; and that the problem of temptation would never bother me again. In a way, I lived with my Redeemer in the heavenlies, high above the clouds. As far as I was concerned, the whole world with all its vanity could go straight to hell. Only later did I understand how wrong I was.

Immediately I grasped what it meant for me to be Jewish and what this life was all about. Before I was born again, I had been willing to take any risk to discover this meaning. Previously, I thought that if only I could lay my hands on enough money to last my whole life, I would finally begin to live. Romance and other adventures did not satisfy me. Nevertheless , I was determined to reach all the goals that I had set, although there was little chance of that. In contrast, I now found in Yeshua everything I hoped to find in my rosiest dreams. I found life in all its fullness.

Theological questions such as the existence of Satan, or sin and its consequences, were not too clear to me, and I preferred to ignore them altogether. The sting of sin in my life was slightly weakened due to my closeness to Yeshua but certainly remained in my flesh, just waiting for the right opportunity to raise its ugly serpent's head again.

During the ensuing period, all I wanted was to share with everyone about the wonderful Messiah whom I had just met, Yeshua HaMashiach. I told Michael and my other Jewish friends from Brooklyn about Yeshua, but they acted as if I had lost my mind. I had quickly forgotten all of the questions and arguments I had before my eyes were opened to see the truth. I could not understand how my friends were unable to see something so self-evident and clear. I was like a blind man whose eyes had been opened to see the light of the world, and who then tried to explain to his blind friends what he saw. I just could not comprehend their inability to see.

Even the non-Jews among my acquaintances, "Christians" by birth, who went to church on occasion, were not so willing to listen to my speaking about Yeshua. They did not understand the tremendous change that had occurred in me and my way of thinking. I could only remember Jeff's words, that not every churchgoer is necessarily also a Messianic believer, and that one could only become a true believer through one's personal choice to be born again.

There was a reason that Yeshua called Himself *"the living bread that came down out of heaven"* (John 6:51). Since I was born again, I felt a deep and ever-growing hunger in me for the Word of God. I read the Scriptures and meditated on them day and night, and I could not get enough. Slowly the Word became an integral part of me, just as the physical food we eat is digested and absorbed in our bodies until it actually becomes a part of us. No longer were the Scriptures just dead words printed with black ink on white paper. Instead, the Bible had become the Word of the living God, alive and active in my life.

Another magnificent change took place. Whenever I needed the loving care of my heavenly Father or His protection, I began to cry out to Him and to seek Him in prayer. My new prayers were not at all like those prayers that I used to recite back in the synagogue. I understood that God wanted to hear the anguish of my soul and the gratitude of my spirit every minute, not just three times a day. I also knew that my loving Father would listen to my prayers even if they were as coarse and unsophisticated as the baby talk of an infant, whose every sound makes his mother happy and excited.

One of the major issues I encountered as a new believer was recognizing and accepting the fact that I, just like a newborn baby, was totally helpless and incompetent on my own and that I could not do anything for myself or for others, let alone anything for God. Later I came to understand that this was not only my position as a new believer, but that it was, and should be, the believer's experience throughout his whole life. It is as Yeshua said: *"Apart from Me you can do nothing"* (John 15:5).

In modern society, sin is so widely accepted that a person who tries to keep himself clean and pure is considered to be eccentric or even perverted. However, since I had been born anew, the Holy Spirit of God came to dwell in me and turned my body into His temple. The Spirit cleansed me and gave me a sharper sensitivity toward sin.

Even things that until then had seemed so normal, so accepted and innocent to me, suddenly were like rotting, stinking carcasses that I tried to get rid of as soon as I possibly could.

If I had known ahead of time everything that I would so willingly relinquish after being born of God's Spirit, I doubt that I would have accepted *"the way, and the truth, and the life"* (John 14:6) at all! But, since the Truth, Yeshua, had revealed Himself to me with all His glory, I felt a strong urge to give up all those things that until then had occupied my whole being. I started to discover how vain the things of this world are: money, possessions, success, and the filthy life of sin in which I had so lustfully wallowed like a pig rolling in the mud. I found myself shaking off the very things that, until then, had seemed to me the spice of life.

I continued to open my shop every morning, but soon I lost interest in it. Pursuing money and women seemed to me so silly and tasteless. I gave up the Stone Pony nightclub because I did not need it any longer, since I found in God the source of all happiness and joy. About the same time, I also lost a large amount of money on the stock market. I marveled at myself, because I was totally indifferent to it at this time, while before I probably would have considered suicide! I no longer recognized myself. Yeshua's words meant everything to me:

"Do not lay up for yourselves treasures upon earth,
where moth and rust destroy,
and where thieves break in and steal.
But lay up for yourselves treasures in heaven,
where neither moth nor rust destroys,
and where thieves do not break in or steal;
For where your treasure is, there will your heart be also."
(Matthew 6:19–21)

I was actually happy about my unexpected disinterest in material things and about the lack of anxiety, because they proved to me that I was on the right track now. Money lost all importance to me. Before it had been a very cruel master, but now it was my servant. I controlled it, not the other way around.

My home and the neighborhood where I lived began to oppress me like prison walls. The unruly life, which I had lived until then, lost its glamour and charm. The proud godlessness of my former friends and drinking partners, with all of their dancing and chasing women, stood in absolute contrast to my burning love and zeal for God, who revealed Himself to me with His grace. Through my dissatisfaction and uneasiness, I knew I needed to move on.

So, one clear day, without any regrets, I closed the shop for good, leaving all the valuable articles at Michael's home. (In the meantime, he had moved from the asphalt jungle of Brooklyn to rural New Jersey.) I packed all my personal belongings in one medium-sized suitcase, took all the money I had to my name, and headed west in my car.

It seemed to me that only yesterday I had stood on the roadside with my thumb up, hitchhiking north to New York—or maybe an eternity had passed since then. Now the tables were turned, and I was the one picking up hitchhikers in my car and sharing with them the most wonderful thing that had ever happened in my life.

What a tremendous change had occurred in me since I came to this city! This time I was leaving with the Gospel of Yeshua the Messiah in my mouth, and the most wonderful thing about it was that I was not responsible for that change at all. To the Lord God of Israel belongs all the glory, the praise, and the honor!

Baptism.   Then I will sprinkle clean water on you, and you will be clean; I will cleanse you from all your filthiness and from all your idols.
(Ezekiel 36:25)

Brethren, my heart's desire and my prayer to God for them is for their salvation.

...How then will they call on Him in whom they have not believed? How will they believe in Him whom they have not heard? And how will they hear without a preacher? How will they preach unless they are sent?

Just as it is written, "How beautiful are the feet of those who bring good news...!"

... So faith comes from hearing, and hearing by the word of Christ. (Romans 10)

A new believer destroys his worldly music before the Lord.

...and so all Israel
will be saved;
just as it is written,
'The Deliverer
will come from Zion,
He will remove
ungodliness from Jacob.
This is My covenant with
them, when I take away
their sins.'
(Romans 11:26-27)

"You shall be
My people,
And I will be your God."
(Jeremiah 30:22)

"But this is the covenant
which I will make with
the house of Israel after
those days,"
declares the Lord,
"I will put My law within
them and on their heart
I will write it; and I will
be their God, and they
shall be My people."
(Jeremiah 31:33)

Chapter 13

General Direction: West

It was a hot summer day when I started out on my trek away from this vast, extended metropolitan area. I stopped at a filling station and bought a detailed road map. I crossed the state line of New Jersey. Driving on the United States superhighway system was an unforgettable experience for me as a novice Israeli. I took US 95, and there, for the first time, I came to a tollgate. I was fascinated that I had to pay a toll for the right to use the road!

During my complete sojourn south and westward, I crossed mountains covered with endless forests and drove by miles of wheat fields, green meadows, and cattle ranches. At every interchange there were bridges that coiled and wound into each other. When I thought of our poorly paved roads back in Israel and of the aggressive, impatient Israeli drivers, I really admired the wonderful American roads. One can drive on the highways for days without stopping, without getting tired, and even without being tense. Compared to Israelis, the Americans were more relaxed, patient, helpful, and kind—or was this only the first, misleading impression of a naive Israeli boy?

Several hours after starting, I arrived in Washington, D.C., and went to see Rebecca, a girl whom I had met a year earlier. She was a college student, and she introduced me to her friends and colleagues. In the scholarly, dignified atmosphere that prevailed there, I felt very uncomfortable. I knew that I possessed a wisdom far more precious and valuable than the sum of the combined knowledge of all these learned students and professors. I was not impressed by the unbridled participation in sex and drugs. I could sense the pervasive immoral corruption and secular perversion, materialism and atheism.

Rebecca and I did not take very long to discover that we did not have anything in common. We had nothing to talk about, since I wanted only to speak about Yeshua, while she was not even willing to hear about Him. After a week, I knew that it was time for me to leave.

I cannot go on without mentioning, with shame, the problem that bothered me the most in those days and the scars that I still carry today, namely, my relationships with the opposite sex.

Ever since my adolescence, I had learned to treat women as objects for fun, human beings who were destined at best to be pregnant and bear children. Along with the rest of the guys in our poverty-stricken neighborhood, I used to brag about my conquests, both real and imagined. Everybody wanted to be near me when it came to picking up girls, because they believed that I knew more about it than anyone else did. Soon enough, I began to believe this hoax myself. As a result, I became certain that a real man had to act like that with women. Just like my rebellion against the "establishment" and my defiance of the law, I believed it proved my masculinity. Unfortunately, this is a distorted view of reality that I had created for myself, due to the circumstances and the culture in which I was raised.

When I became a believer in Yeshua and my eyes were opened to see things as they really were, I sat down to write a letter of confession, asking forgiveness from a girl who had been offended by me in a very serious manner:

Dear ...,
You must be surprised to hear from me again after such a long time. Maybe it is not the right time or place to go into detail and relate everything that happened to me in recent years, but I do want to tell you about a very extraordinary experience I had with God. I hope someday I'll have the opportunity to tell you more about it, perhaps to talk to you about it face-to-face, when I come back home to Israel.
In the light of all that has happened to me recently, I feel obliged to ask your forgiveness for the terrible injustice that I did to you, when you became pregnant because of me and were forced to abort the baby. It was not only that I used you as a tool to gratify my lust, but I added a crime upon that sin by causing you to murder our child, who could otherwise be alive today.
I can see it all in a different light today, and I am totally against abortion of any kind and for any reason. We do not give life to our children, nor do we have the right to take life away from them. I pray from the bottom of my heart that the abortion you had to go through because of me will not harm you in the future, whenever you get married and wish to have children.
I know that it might seem strange to you, but since that extraordinary experience I previously spoke of, I really was born

anew. I am no longer the same Jacob you used to know. Now I feel I must make all wrongs right as much as I can. I beg you to forgive me for the criminal offense that I committed against you. Words are insufficient to tell how it hurts me to know that I hurt you so much. I do hope that you will find the power and the grace to forgive me.

Yours cordially,
Jacob Damkani

I left Washington, D.C., on my way south to Florida. I cannot remember how many hitchhikers I picked up on my way, but one thing is certain: no one left my car without hearing something about Yeshua the Messiah. Most of the people who took the ride with me were long-haired, tattered hippies. Foul odors usually emanated from them, and some were high on dope. Some of them worked sporadically where they could and then generously shared their income with their friends.

I could see that many of them came from wealthy families, had rebelled against their well-off parents, and had left their comfortable homes as a protest against the "materialistic capitalism that had ruined society," to use their own words. They wanted to be different, special, unique individuals, and for this reason, they all looked so much alike. Others rebelled against the "oppressive establishment," and would not listen to the Good News about Yeshua because they used to hear about Him in Sunday school while they were children. They marveled how a guy more or less their own age, and a Jew, could be so narrow-minded and limited as to believe all that religious stuff.

Several of them told me about their involvement in the occult and Hindu mysticism, which had just arrived in the United States, proclaiming the inauguration of the worldwide New Age. They were fascinated by different gurus and followed their esoteric doctrines, practicing witchcraft, yoga, transcendental meditation, voodoo, and spiritism, while studying astrological charts and horoscopes.

Generally speaking, they believed that the age of Christianity, symbolized in astrology by the zodiac sign Pisces, was almost completed and was ushering in the new world order of the occult, called the age of Aquarius. They read palms, tarot cards, and tea sediments. In their séances they made spiritualistic connections with spirit guides and other departed spirits, which were none other than demons in disguise. I was too young a believer then to know how to approach them correctly, but their very presence sent strange chills of fear up and down my spine and made me truly concerned about their eternal destiny.

In the South, I drove through ghost towns that looked as if they were taken out of old black-and-white movies. After miles of scenery that I had never seen before, I came to New Orleans, the hometown of the blues, a musical style that seemed to me to have originated out of deep heartache. Here I could again breathe the well-known salty, fresh smell of the ocean.

As I went on my way, rejoicing over the wonderful miracle of the new birth, I soon reached Houston, Texas. There I visited an Israeli acquaintance by the name of Uri, who had been a friend of my brother while in the army and later at the Hebrew University in Jerusalem. At Uri's, I started to write a diary that recorded my experiences, hoping secretly to publish it one day as a book, so that my kinsmen, the children of Israel, would read it and come to know the Messiah whom I loved so much. I had no idea how many years would go by until that dream would be realized.

Some time later, I drove northward to Dallas, Texas. I was invited to visit the campus of the famous Messianic Bible school, Christ for the Nations. For them, the excitement of meeting a young Messianic Jewish believer from Israel was immense. Not every day did they have the opportunity to meet such a rare individual! They invited me to tell my testimony to a huge crowd of believers who gathered in a giant auditorium. It was the first time that I had stood in front of such a large audience, and I publicly related my favorite story about the wonderful Messiah who loved me so much!

There I met Messianic Gentiles who, like Jeff, loved Israel with all their hearts and who prayed daily for her safety, as the Scriptures commanded them to *"pray for the peace of Jerusalem"* (Psalm 122:6). These people fasted and prayed whenever any danger threatened the welfare of Israel. Until then I did not know that there were Gentiles who loved Israel and the Jewish people so much. Since then, however, I have met many more like these beautiful believers, for whom I am eternally thankful.

At Christ for the Nations, I met a young man from India who was studying in the States. While I was there, an elderly acquaintance of his had joined him, someone who had lived all his life in a remote village somewhere in the mountains of northern India. They planned to drive to Oklahoma for Christmas and invited me to join them.

I will never forget that dear old man who stood in speechless awe at the sight of the technical achievements of the West. He marveled at the wonders of the big cities. When we reached Oklahoma City and our wealthy host invited us into his mansion, the poor man just could not get his mouth to shut. He was especially impressed by things that were operated by remote control, such as the Cadillac windows that went up and down "all by themselves," or the garage door that was opened as if by an invisible servant. As he was gaping at the huge refrigerator filling his glass with ice cubes, I had to smile, remembering that young lad from Kiryat Shmonah coming into a two-and-a-half room "luxury" apartment in Holon and seeing an indoor bathroom for the first time!

Here in Oklahoma City, I had the opportunity to express my obedience to the Messiah by keeping His commandment of immersion in water. Contrary to what the prevalent Jewish thought is about it, immersion in water, or water baptism, is not a Gentile practice. On the contrary, the practice of immersion is very common among observant, orthodox Jews and serves as ritual purification. No pious Jewess would ever dare to renew sexual relations with her husband after her menstrual period before cleansing herself by immersing in a kosher *mikveh* (a ritual bath). Every Friday night, some ultraorthodox Jewish men go to the mikveh to purify their bodies by immersion, for which even the cleanest and most fragrant bath water is insufficient. These customs were derived directly from Scripture.

As the years went by, another dimension was added to baptism by Jewish tradition: it was made a necessary step in the process of proselytization, or conversion to Judaism, in which it was (and still is) understood that the convert comes up out of the water as a "new" person, whose old Gentile life has been washed away.

To the Jews, water baptism historically symbolized true repentance and cleansing from the defilement of sin. This is evident from the ministry of the Jewish prophet, John the Baptist, as he preached *"a baptism of repentance for the forgiveness of sins"* (Mark 1:4) to the Jewish people and then *"baptized [them] in the Jordan River, as they confessed their sins"* (Matthew 3:6).

After the Messiah's death and resurrection, another meaning was added to this one: identification with the Redeemer's death and resurrection. A believer testifies by his immersion in water that he, too, has died to sin with the Messiah and is raised with Him into newness of life. (See Romans 6:3–7.)

Thus, the immersion in water has always been a Jewish practice and symbol, even in its most distinguished Messianic contexts.

When the pastor of that Oklahoma City congregation asked me during a midweek prayer meeting whether or not I had been baptized in water, I had to answer in the negative. Then he explained to me what baptism was all about and asked me whether I wanted to obey the Lord by identifying with His death and resurrection through baptism. This time I answered in the affirmative without any hesitation.

Arrangements were made for me to be immersed in water on the following Sunday. In the presence of his entire congregation, the pastor and I, both of us dressed in special robes, descended into the water-filled mikveh that was right in the center of the platform. When he heard my declaration of faith in Yeshua, he announced, "I baptize you, therefore, in the name of the Father, in the name of the Son, Jesus Christ, and in the name of the Holy Spirit. Amen." I was bent backward and was totally immersed in the water. I was so joyful and elated that I repeated the act three times!

The meeting itself was wonderful. The choir, the singing of the hymns, the prayers, the sermon, and then the baptismal service, all left a tremendous impression on me. What a blessed way to serve the Lord in the midst of His saints! How delightful it was to worship God together with other brothers and sisters who love the Savior and one another! But, like all other good things, this meeting came to an end, too.

After two unforgettable weeks, my Indian friends and I returned to Dallas. From there, I headed west on the superhighway. Again, I traveled long distances and had some interesting experiences. With all my heart, I am thankful for the way in which the Lord has guided me, and will continue to do so, even until His coming.

On one of the Indian reservations, I met a Native American from whom I learned something about the white man's attitude toward the members of his tribe and race. I also met Doris, an elderly Messianic believer from Las Vegas who managed a Bible school for young believers, whom she taught how to follow in the footsteps of the

Messiah. These wonderful people and others added interest to my travels, which continued for several months.

After a seemingly endless trip in the scourging hot desert, I finally arrived in Los Angeles. Before leaving New York, Jeff had given me the address of Gideon Miller, a Messianic believer who resided there, and made me promise to pay him a visit if I ever reached the West Coast. I called Gideon, who gave me detailed instructions about how to get to his place. Exhausted and worn out, I finally parked my dusty car in front of his gate.

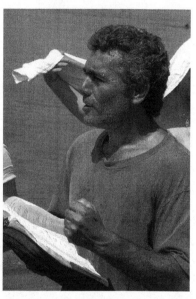

"I will cleanse you from all your filthiness and from all your idols."
(Ezekiel 36:25)

"You shall be my people and I will be your God."
(Jeremiah 30:22)

"And this is my covenant with them, when I take away their sins."
(Romans 11:27)

Scenes from from the movie set "A New Spirit"

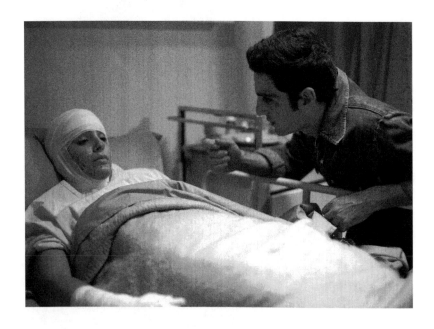

Chapter 14

California Greens

Gideon received me gladly and invited me to stay in his home for a few days. He was a man in his sixties who, like Jeff, knew some Hebrew, which he had picked up while living in Jerusalem for several years. He suggested that I join a certain community called "Last Days Ministries", which was managed by a most extraordinary person, Keith Green. The more Gideon told me about this man, the more I was intrigued. Two days later, Gideon took me to the Greens' commune in a Los Angeles suburb.

Keith Green had begun a promising musical career in Los Angeles bars, but when he became a believer in Yeshua, his life changed completely. As a born-again Messianic Jew, he roamed the streets of the metropolis, telling every person he met about his new-found Savior. He turned to the outcasts who lived on the margins of society, as he spoke with drug addicts, perverts, prostitutes, and all those people whom Yeshua Himself had addressed and loved unto death. Keith would invite these people to his home, where they could eat and sleep. On several occasions he found that valuables, money, and other things disappeared, but this did not deter him. His house soon became too small for the ever growing number of guests who stayed in it, and he was forced to rent a nearby building. By the time I met him, he already had six such rented houses, in which he rehabilitated all those people who showed interest in the Gospel.

Keith was a tall, bearded man with curly hair and blue eyes that were tender and firm at the same time. His wife, Melody, supported her husband's enterprise with all her heart. She managed the household economics, did the shopping, supervised the cleaning of the premises, and even found enough time to join her husband in composing the songs that later made him so famous. They had adopted an Indian girl who was twelve years old when I first saw her. Later, they also had several children of their own.

Keith received us in his humble residence, and after Gideon introduced me, he turned to me and asked, "Jacob, tell me something about yourself. Who are you?" I began to tell him my life story, intentionally omitting all those details I'd decided to ignore. After all, nobody wants to give a bad first impression!

"If you wish to join us, you must know that we do not laze around here. We have a fixed daily schedule, and not everyone who comes to us is able or willing to abide by it, at least not at the beginning. Are you willing to try?" Keith asked. "Tell me, please, what exactly do you do here?" I answered with a question.

"Well, wake-up time is at 6 A.M., followed by a quiet time for personal prayer and reading the Scriptures until 7:00. At 7:00 sharp we have a communal breakfast, and at 8:00 everybody goes out to work. At 1:00 we have lunch, and then we go out to the streets to proclaim the Gospel of Messiah, telling people about the Lord Jesus. Sometimes we go out in pairs from door to door, or to the beaches, the streets, the shopping malls, and other public places. Other times several people join me at the recording studio and pray for me while I record my songs. We come home for the evening meal at 6:30 P.M., followed by a period of Bible study, singing, and prayer together. Bedtime is at 11:00 sharp. What do you think—will you be able to keep up with that kind of schedule?"

"No problem," I said, "I've been used to hard work since I was little. When I was fourteen, I helped support my family back in Israel." "That's good," said Keith. "I tend to overemphasize the difficulties, because some of the youngsters who live here were spoiled ones from wealthy homes, who left their families and turned to the drug subculture in protest. They have never worked a day in their lives, and if you let them, they would simply turn over in their beds and do nothing. They have no work habits at all, and as a matter of fact, the only habits they do have are those we want them to kick. We try to teach them what discipline is all about, to educate them, and to turn them into productive citizens, besides the evangelistic work that constitutes a major part of our daily schedule."

"How many people live here in each room? How do they get along with each other?" I asked. "It seems to me almost like living in a monastery."

"A monastery?" Keith laughed heartily. "Quite the opposite! We have to go and preach to the priests and monks, telling them that they have to repent and be born again!

"In every flat six people live together, two in a room," Keith explained. "You will see for yourself that they are not too tidy, but the cleanliness and the order in your room depends on you, first of all. We will not pamper and spoil you, nor will we do anything for you that you can do for yourself.

"We teach everyone here how to lead a Messianic way of life according to the Scriptures, but it is up to the individual to apply what he has learned in his own life. If you have any problems with your believing brothers, you must first go to them and talk to them about it." I thought to myself, "Why shouldn't I try it for a few days, to see if it suits me?" Aloud, I said to Keith, "You see, I've been a believer for less than a year. I am looking for a place where I can learn the Scriptures in an orderly manner and live the life of faith with other brothers who are in a similar situation. I think this place might be good for me at this stage, and I am willing to try and participate without any commitment."

"No! I insist you make a commitment! If you're not willing to join us for at least three months, you'd better not start at all. True spiritual growth takes time and real commitment."

"Well, I realize it is a serious matter," I said. "I am willing to try it for a period of three months, and then we'll see."

To be honest, I was a little scared, although I was afraid to express my apprehension in words. I knew what life in a kibbutz was like, and I also knew that not everyone was able to adjust to it. I knew that I was not fit for kibbutz life at all. It is true that when I lived as a youth on the shores of Eilat, I learned something about communal life, but there it had been absolute anarchy where *"everyone did what was right in his own eyes"* (Judges 21:25). Here, on the contrary, we had to submit to a fixed schedule and abide by the rules. I had not obeyed orders and kept up with other people since I had left my parents' home in rebellion. This was a serious challenge for me.

However, living with others polished me well. The constant rubbing with brothers and sisters, the profound spiritual fellowship, the study and prayer together, the work and active evangelism—all developed discipline in me and a commitment to the Lord and to other people, which helped me to grow in faith in a way I could not imagine otherwise. At times we found ourselves making each other's beds and taking turns to clean our rooms in the morning, thus learning to cooperate and help each other. Yeshua was our living example.

Every evening about thirty of us gathered together, with many sitting on the floor, to study the Word of God. I loved those lessons very much, because they provided me with the opportunity to express my own opinions on many issues. Since I was already familiar with the Tanach, it was not too difficult for me to understand the New Testament in its light. Every day I grew more and more in holiness and love, while God was slowly and gradually changing me into His likeness.

The classes that Keith led helped me to understand, for the first time in my life, the true meaning of the Cross. I had thought that this Christian symbol had caused my people so much trouble and persecution in ages past. I now understood that the Cross was not merely two pieces of wood joined together, displayed in churches to be worshipped and kissed by "Christians," and neither was the Cross a piece of jewelry that Gentiles casually wore. Rather, I knew the Cross is a way of life.

By His own life, Yeshua gave us all an example of self-denial, of crucifying the flesh with all its desires and lusts. He also challenged all true believers to take up their crosses and follow Him (Matthew 16:24). The sinful nature opposes the will of God, but the one who is born again really seeks to live and to act in harmony with God's divine will. But, in order to live according to the will of God, one has to "crucify" his flesh, which means to relinquish his own will, desires, and wishes, and not to be affected by their influence to act against God's standards and desires. This process can take place only in the life of a person whose way of thinking God has changed:

"Now those who belong to Christ Jesus have crucified the flesh with its passions and desires." (Galatians 5:24)

"I have been crucified with Christ; and it is no longer I who live, but Christ lives in me." (Galatians 2:20)

I was so glad that Yeshua, who now lived in me, changed my selfish attitude toward women and helped me to honor them as human beings in their own right. Now I began to consider them as sisters and a magnificent creation of God. That was a real achievement for me, for which I am thankful from the bottom of my heart. Again I was convinced that it was no longer I who lived, but Yeshua lived His life through me.

Sabbath nights were my favorite. We had common, open-air Sabbath meals in the front yard and invited the people to whom we preached the Gospel during the past week to join us as our guests.

Other believers from the surrounding neighborhoods would also come, because our reputation spread like wildfire. All of our guests brought along some delicacy for those potluck gatherings, making the meals varied and interesting. This was our weekly treat. We ate more than usual; we prayed and sang, while Keith accompanied us on his guitar. Although he became world-famous as a gifted pianist, he always avoided drawing too much attention to himself. After the meal he gave a sermon, in which he led interested unbelievers to the Messiah.

On one of these Sabbath evenings, a man named Martin came to us. As a son of a wealthy pilot, his life had been a bed of roses. But, he quit his studies at the university when he found out that one day he would have to stand before the throne of God and give an account of his life in this world. He said, "It is important that we do whatever we do in faith, because whatever we do without faith is sin (Romans 14:23); and I do not believe that God wants me here at this university!" Martin was already a Messianic believer when he came to us, and I detected in him true humility and a special measure of God's love. The Holy Spirit worked in him and showed him that there is more to life than making lots of money and having a high status in society.

On that particular evening, I sat beside him during supper and handed him a slice of watermelon, having removed the rind previously, as is the custom in Israel. Later he told me that it was this simple gesture that spoke to his heart and convinced him to join us. For some reason or another, it was very meaningful to him.

Martin became my closest friend from that moment on. We made a very special prayer team. God revealed to him the need for prayer for the salvation of Israel, and we carried that common burden together in unity. We poured out rivers of tears for the welfare and safety of Israel and, of course, for her redemption. In those days, I could feel the presence of God in a way that cannot be described in words.

Gradually the desire awakened in me to establish a Messianic-Jewish kibbutz in Israel, in which we would go to work on the farm in the mornings, and in the evenings we would reach out into the towns and cities to tell the people about God's power to change human lives. "It is high time for God to circumcise the hearts of His people Israel," I said, and I wished with all my heart to take an active part in that process.

I spoke to Keith about it more than once. He liked the idea, but he said to me repeatedly, "Patience, Jacob, have some patience. The Bible says that the Israelis' hearts will be changed, but you must allow God to perform it in His own good time!"

One day Martin invited me to his home after prayer. He had in his room a huge collection of about three hundred rock and roll, blues, and pop albums that he had accumulated over the years. This collection had once been the most precious thing he possessed, but now he could not wait to get rid of it, having realized that it was not the Spirit of God that inspired these songwriters and performers, but that their inspiration came from satanic sources. He knew that he could not build a true, solid spiritual life with this music as part of the foundation. He felt he could no longer serve God with all his heart while having that kind of music in the background.

Until then he had been addicted to that secular music, but now he had only one desire occupying his heart—to serve one Master only, the Lord Yeshua, and Him alone. His younger brother begged and pleaded with him to give him that magnificent collection, but Martin would not even listen to him. With a sense of urgency and determination, we took this expensive collection to the garbage dump and broke every single record into pieces. With every broken record, Martin's face shone brighter and brighter with unspeakable joy, until the whole burden was rolled away from his heart. I could only admire him for the sacrifice he offered, and I was sure that Yeshua must have smiled at him with satisfaction at that hour.

After a six-month sojourn at Keith and Melody's, I knew I had to keep on going. Keith thought I needed to stay with them longer, but I stubbornly insisted on having my own way. Thus, we parted with dissonance. Several months later, I received a letter from him in which he apologized for being angry with me. In retrospect I could understand him, because he was genuinely concerned about my spiritual well-being, even though I had originally misinterpreted his intentions. I am sorry for my arrogant attitude toward him, but unfortunately there is no way I can make up for it now, because he died a short time later in a plane accident.

When I left the community, I decided to visit my friend Bill in Topanga Canyon. We had met at one of those Sabbath evening potluck gatherings at the Greens' home. Bill shepherded a flock of thirty goats, and his place reminded me of Mount Carmel in Israel.

The land belonged to a well-known sculptor who had placed his strange-looking sculptures throughout his extensive property. In the open areas between the metal forms, grass sprouted and weeds abounded.

The beauty of the ocean, the clean-smelling air, the vineyard with its grapes, the goats grazing in the fields, and the sky filled with stars, all made me feel as if I were in Israel or the Garden of Eden. On this mountaintop, I really fell in love with the new life in Christ. Situated on a slab of concrete was a tabernacle that was made of a vine-covered frame of latticework. We often ate our meals there. Not far from our outdoor dining room was the milking area. I loved to milk the goats at early dawn and then shepherd them into the open fields.

While I tended to the flock, I played my harmonica and composed worship music to the Lord. As I basked in God's Word and in the light of His Son, I tried to imagine King David in his youth. During those blessed days, I gave thanks to God that no one else was in the area, because not everyone can hear my singing and enjoy it.

After three months, I felt an urge to return to Oklahoma City to the congregation where I had been baptized. It was as if a secret voice called me back home. Somehow I considered this church to be my "spiritual home," although I had attended it only for a very short while. Without a second thought, I loaded my car and drove east again.

A scene from the movie set "A New Spirit".

Pictures from the movie set "A New Spirit".

Chapter 15

Heading Back East

Arizona—120 degrees in the shade. I took a dirt road into the mountains in order to visit a group of Messianic believers that called itself "Hallelujah." I reached them after a long drive on a desert road in the blazing hot wilderness.

That place holds very special memories for me. Shortly after my arrival, one of the wooden structures, which served as the children's dormitory, suddenly caught fire. One of the men instinctively jumped into the flames and, several seconds later, emerged with three of the children, bringing them to safety. Three other children (two of them brothers) remained inside. The fire rapidly consumed the entire building as if it were made of kindling.

I cannot describe the horror of this calamity in words. Men and women cried out for help, but there was no way to rescue the three little ones left inside. The tragedy lasted only several minutes. We were all petrified with shock and terror, unable to move or react.

I was very angry at myself for not daring to help in such a crucial moment, for not jumping into the fire and trying to rescue the children while it was still possible. Within a few seconds, however, the blazing fire did not allow anyone to come near. When the flames subsided, nothing was left except a smoldering heap of coals. I was really ashamed. In the past I could perform daring acts without even blinking, but here, when I had a once-in-a-lifetime opportunity to save little children from sure death, I did nothing about it in trying to save myself. I found out I was not much of a hero after all.

Friends from all over the area came to share the grief of the bereaved families and to offer them their condolences. I will never forget the funeral service as long as I live. Over the open grave, the mother of the dead brothers said the following:

> "We all know that it was God who gave us this life. I received these two precious children as a deposit from God, and now He wanted me to return this deposit to Him. Yeshua said:
> *"Let the little children come to Me, and do not forbid them; for of such is the kingdom of heaven"* (Matthew 19:14 NKJV).

I believe that God, whose love for us is stronger than death, and who willingly died for our salvation, sees death in a different way than we do. In His eyes the death of little children may not be such a terrible tragedy at all.

He, who knows in advance how this evil world might still deteriorate, has chosen in His infinite wisdom and love to save these little ones, who believed in Him with all their hearts, from those horrible tribulations that He is going to bring upon this earth, and to take them directly into His kingdom.

It hurts me. I miss my little children so much! But I am neither bitter nor am I angry with God for taking my dear ones from me. I love Him, and I will continue to love Him in spite of everything, and with no connection to my grief. He knows what is best for them and for us all, and He has chosen the very best for them.

If there is anybody among you who does not know Yeshua the Messiah, who suffered the most terrible death for us on the cross, I hope that this tragedy of mine might draw you to Him.

As she concluded, the grieving mother turned and spoke to the freshly opened grave, "My dear children, wait for me patiently. The day will come when we shall meet again, and then we will never part—I promise! Yeshua told me that, and He is always right."

At the end of the funeral service, the whole excited but pained gathering stood and sang God's praises for His love and grace. I could not believe my own ears. How powerful must this Messiah be, who has conquered death and swept away the tears of bereaved mothers on the open graves of their loved ones!

I had attended many funerals in my life. I had seen the highly emotional funerals of the Sephardi Jews, with their shrieks of grief and screams of agony, with their bitter laments, and with all their face scratching and hair pulling. I had also attended the quiet, restrained funerals of the Ashkenazi Jews, who keep all the pain deep within. I had seen military funerals in which tough, sturdy soldiers collapsed in tears over the grave of their friend who had fallen in the line of duty. But never in my life had I heard a grieving mother mourn in such manner over her children who were lying dead at her feet. The world does not know anything of that divine peace!

Later, the mother of the other child who had died in the fire sang a song of praise to God. Her clear voice soared up like a lark, high above the blinding desert sun, and shattered into myriads of diamonds at the foot of the throne of glory. Such singing one hears only once in a lifetime! She poured out her pain-filled heart before the Lord in public.

With the funeral over, all the participants gathered in the open and spoke freely and naturally, as if they had not come to a burial service at all, but just to say goodbye to some friends who had gone away for a while, knowing that they will meet again soon, at the feet of the beloved Redeemer.

After several more days in that amazing place, with the impressions of that extraordinary experience still fresh in my mind, I got into my car and launched eastward again to Oklahoma. The trip to Oklahoma City passed without incident, and I arrived there safely. I stayed in Oklahoma City for three years, where I lived in the church complex and attended the meetings regularly.

It seemed that I led a kind of life that may have looked outwardly holy, very much like that which a true believer should lead. But, without my noticing it, my first love for Yeshua gradually grew cold. Of course, I did not commit any atrocious or contemptible crime, but I sank into a complacent routine. I did not seem any different from the rest of the church members, and now I thought it was time for me to settle down and get myself economically established.

At one of the church meetings, I met Woody, who bought buildings at bargain prices to renovate and resell at a good profit. He agreed to employ me, and together we worked around the clock, renovating and reconstructing old ruins.

Later, Woody introduced me to his brother Keith, who, in addition to his law practice, owned a farm that produced carpets of sod for lawns. Keith suggested that I come to manage the farm. I liked the offer very much, because I loved to work hard. From sunrise to sunset I mowed the lawn, cut the sod into long strips, rolled them and loaded them onto the company trucks, and delivered them to the clients, where I planted them. As time went by, I managed to purchase a house and a truck of my own, and my business grew and prospered.

All too soon I invested more and more of my time and energy in my work, and I dedicated less and less of it to God and His kingdom, to prayer and the reading of the Word. The close intimacy that I used to enjoy with Yeshua was gradually forgotten. Outwardly, I was still keeping the facade of holiness, not because of my closeness to the

Lord, but rather because I wanted to do what seemed right in God's eyes with my own energy and strength. This motive was exactly the opposite of what I knew to be right at the beginning of my walk with the Lord. At the start, it was He who worked within me, and I followed Him out of obedience, happiness, and joy. I had now become a pious, religious, *"Messianic Jew"*, trying to overcome the works of the flesh by carnal means.

The new spirit that the Lord had breathed into my life did not leave me, of course, but it had been lulled into a sleep because I neglected my reading and praying—and even the very Bread of Life Himself. Additionally, the new heart that He implanted in me began to rust and rot a little. I kept on singing to the Lord at work, but obviously it was not enough, and I did not realize that calamity was right at my door.

One morning I woke up with a severe toothache. I had not been to the dentist for quite a while, and now I had more cavities than I had teeth. Mary, the sweet dental assistant who treated me, attracted my attention a little too much. Soon enough, I found myself in embarrassing intimacy with her. Temptation and sin caught me totally unaware!

In those days I was renovating a house that I had purchased for myself, and so I found a good excuse to move into Mary's home— temporarily, of course. Although I was living in sin, I could not think of hiding my religious convictions from her. As I told her about the Messiah, suddenly reality slapped me right in my face. How on earth could I, so unclean and defiled in my filthy sin, preach to others and tell them about a Messiah who came to redeem them from their sins? I was suddenly so embarrassed, so despicable and dirty in my own eyes, having caught myself red-handed. I realized that my desire for a woman had made me forfeit the wonderful love of my best Friend, Yeshua HaMashiach. When I fell, I lost everything—the security of His everlasting love, the deep inner peace that I had enjoyed so much, the joy of my salvation, the confidence that He was with me and I in Him—in short, I lost His abiding presence. To be accurate, He did not remove His grace from me even for one single moment. He never stopped loving me. He only withheld the sensation of His love from me. He let me feel that my sins separated me from Him. I was devastated, lonely, lost, and miserable, as if the whole world lay in ruins before me.

Right then, with bitter tears of remorse, I got down on my knees and asked God to forgive me—and He did! After repenting from my sins, I could speak to Mary earnestly and seriously, to confess my sin due to the weakness of my flesh, and to ask for her forgiveness, too. The result was very impressive. Several days later, I found out that Mary received the Lord as her personal Savior. Of course, I immediately moved back into my own house, where I lived during the last stages of its renovation. We continue even to this day to be friends. I praise God for her commitment to Yeshua as she continues to serve Him in various ways, leading others into a personal relationship with our Lord.

My broken relationship with the Lord, the loss of His presence and peace, and the true awareness of His love have all been restored to me. All along I had understood the importance of a holy walk with a holy God, but now I had experienced the cost of rebellion. I discovered that nothing is this world is worth having if it is outside of God's will. The house that I had built for myself in Oklahoma City on a small plot of land took an important place in my heart, while the rest of my heart was occupied by the truck, the car, and the growing bank account. My life went on peacefully, the realization of the American Dream! I thought that the child from the one-and-a-half-room flat in Kiryat Shmonah had come quite a long way to the luxurious mansions of Oklahoma City. And this time, it was all achieved through honest, hard work, for a change! I had no intentions whatsoever of giving up my little fortune or my well-earned earthly possessions.

Eretz Yisrael (Land of Israel) seemed as far from me as the east is from the west! On occasion, God's calling to return to my people to tell them about Yeshua came to mind; but this calling, including all the prayers and burning tears offered together with Martin for the salvation of Israel, had faded from my memory. I removed them gently by promising myself that someday I would certainly go back to my people, but now I had something more important to do in the United States. I became a man of the world and enjoyed every minute of it. Gradually, my willingness to obey the prompting of the Spirit disappeared altogether.

Then, one Sunday morning, right in the middle of the service, the Spirit of God came upon me mightily, and I heard the Lord's voice rebuking me sternly and earnestly, "Jacob, My son, where are you? Have you completely forgotten My commission to you, to go forth and preach My salvation to My people, Israel? What happened to you, that you sit in the fleshpots of Egypt, instead of going up to the Promised Land? Arise and go now!"

I cannot remember at all what the preacher spoke about that morning, but I knew that the words of the Lord had penetrated my heart like a sharp, two-edged sword. God then overwhelmed me with His love in such a majestic way that my eyes became like two fountains of water. Really, how could I live a life of ease and comfort in a strange land, while the divine truth concerning the Messiah was still hidden from the eyes of my people, my own flesh and blood?

On the following morning, I began to make arrangements to leave everything and go back home. I liquidated the business and leased the house, which was just about finished. Truly, the Lord must have a unique sense of humor. For three long years I had worked like a slave, investing all my money and energy in building my dream house. Just as the time came when I could finally sit back and enjoy the fruits of my labor, He required me to forsake everything willingly, lease the house for the mortgage price only, and follow Him to our homeland. Those who know the joy and happiness that can be found only in obedience to God will understand what I mean!

That same week, I went east to New York, with my mind set to fly back to Israel as soon as possible. But, I still did not know all the tricks of Satan, and all the sly, crafty methods he uses to spread a net at the feet of the believer in order to trap him in the snare of sin.

"Now, while I'm in the East," I thought, "why shouldn't I hop over to visit Michael, Aryeh, and Yisrael, my old buddies, whom I haven't seen since I left for the West?" Truly, as the famous proverb says, "the road to hell is paved with good intentions." Without thinking twice, I shelved my original plan to return immediately to Israel, just to be able to say hello and goodbye to old friends before leaving the States.

In those days, I did not know yet the biblical principle that if God calls someone to perform a certain task, he must get down to business and do what he was commissioned to do, without even greeting anyone along the way. Every delay of that kind might be disastrous.

As I came to New York City, my friends introduced me to some acquaintances who had just purchased a summer resort in the Catskill Mountains in upstate New York. When they learned of my skills in renovating old buildings, they asked me to come over and help them rebuild the camp buildings, the foundations of which had sunk. On the spot I accepted, postponing God's calling for my life once again. We had agreed about my wages, and I went to work diligently. "After all, what do I have to lose?" I thought. On the contrary, I would return to Israel with a substantial sum of money to build the kibbutz of my dreams and to preach the Gospel.

My job was to dig underneath the buildings and to deepen their foundations, until they reached the solid rock down below. "But," I said to myself, "why bother to pour a meter and a half of concrete into the ground, when half that depth will do?" It was a clever calculation; that way I would be saving on materials. The only problem was that I did not bother to share this ingenious plan of mine with my employers. Finally, the houses stood in their places, their bases perfectly horizontal, looking as stable and firm as anything, and nobody could imagine that their foundations were not deep enough.

Here I discovered for the thousandth time that the old, crooked Jacob who still dwelt within me was alive and well, not at all dead with Yeshua on the cross. He was only dormant under the influence of God's Spirit, lying in wait to cause me to fall into sin once again. The work seemed perfect, and my employers were satisfied with it. I received the full amount we had agreed upon, and I went on my way rejoicing. But this time, unlike in the past, the Spirit of God gave me no rest: *"Cursed be the one who does the LORD's work negligently"* (Jeremiah 48:10). My conscience, the new heart and spirit that I received from the Lord Yeshua when I was born again, pricked me so much because of the deceitful act I had just committed against my employers' trust. The reproach I brought on the name of the Messiah, as a consequence, made me feel so rotten that I turned my car around, went back to them in shame, returned their money in full, apologized for my deception, asked their forgiveness earnestly, and refused to receive any payment for my long and tiring work at their place.

What did I get from all this? My assets did not increase, and the time for my flight to Israel according to God's timetable was late, so much time having been wasted for practically nothing. Still, I knew that I had done the right thing by returning the money. The oppression, which was a heavy burden on my heart, lifted, and I was free again to do the Lord's will. I wonder if the prophet Jonah might have felt the same way when the great fish threw him up on the dry land (Jonah 2:10).

Scenes from the movie set "A New Spirit"

Chapter 16

At My Brother's Open Grave

Although time was passing by and I had experienced on more than one occasion that still, small voice of God giving His instructions to return to Israel, I had not even bought a plane ticket. However, I found out that God cannot be mocked.

I will probably never remember how I learned that the funeral of my older brother, who died under tragic circumstances, was going to take place on August 16 in Holon. Shmuel, who had lived in Copenhagen for many years, had wanted to return to Israel for a long time. It was his wife's stern opposition that stopped him, but that had broken his heart.

Now, I really had no choice. It seemed that God was grabbing me and putting me forcefully on the plane. More than anything, I was upset by the fact that my brother had passed away before we had the opportunity to make things right between us, and that we parted for good without my knowing if he had ever changed his hostile attitude toward Yeshua. I could remember the harsh letters he wrote to me as a response to the news regarding my salvation. "You have betrayed Judaism and converted to Christianity," he wrote angrily. "Have you forgotten all about the Inquisition, the Crusades, and everything that these Christians have done to Jews in the name of Jesus? How dare you convert like all those who destroyed their own souls!"

Although his response hurt me deeply, I could understand it. After all, how can one ask a blind man to describe the different colors of the rainbow? All the other members of my family, despite their pain and disgust because of my "defection," did not react so strongly. Was it because of those long years Shmuel had spent abroad that the question of our Jewish identity was so sharpened in him? Was that what drove his attitude toward the Christian Gentiles to such an extreme?

After receiving Yeshua HaMashiach as my Savior, I wrote to my relatives and friends many long letters, which were full of quotations from the Tanach and detailed explanations. I sent those letters with much love and prayer, trying my best to make it as clear as possible that God expects all men to believe in the Messiah whom He sent. But, unfortunately, my words fell on uncircumcised ears and hearts that do not know the difference between man-made religion and God-given faith.

In my letters I described the revolutionary turnabout that had occurred in my life. I expressed deep remorse and regret for the sins that I had committed, first of all against my parents, but especially against my mother. From the bottom of my heart, I asked for her forgiveness for the heartbreak I had caused her when I ran away and disappeared to Eilat. I also asked my brother to forgive me. He was truly concerned about my future, but I never treated him seriously enough. In retrospect, I feel so sorry for the wrong attitude I had toward him, especially for the crooked part in me that laughed at his conventionalism because he considered his studies the purpose and goal of his life, while I thought I knew what real life was because I did not submit to authority. What an ugly distortion of the truth had been in me!

Now, looking back, I have no doubt whatsoever that God worked all of my past experiences together to get me to this position. I received God's salvation by His grace alone, and I would not trade it for any title or social status. All I want is to do the will of my Creator wholeheartedly. For that reason I was born, and for that purpose I came into this world. I have life with all its fullness in this world, and I have the Holy Spirit's witness within my spirit that I will be raised from the dead to eternal life in the world to come.

I wrote to my sister, who was two years older than I, and asked for her forgiveness for breaking her jaw with a blow of my fist. And last but not least, I apologized to my younger sisters, Carmelah and Frieda. I had always compelled them to make my bed, fold my clothes, wash my dishes, and shine my shoes. Every now and then, I paid them a little something for their services, but I had done to them what I did not want others to do to me. I had exploited them the way others did me. I also asked their forgiveness when I became a believer, and they did forgive me, although they could not really understand what exactly happened to me.

I was excited to return home after nine years of self-imposed exile. I almost fell prostrate on the concrete at the Ben-Gurion Airport in my desire to kiss the precious soil of the land where I was born and to which I was now bound. Now I was ready, willing, and prepared to follow my beloved Lord and Master, to give myself completely to my people so that they, too, might be privileged to see the salvation of God and find their way home to the eternal Father.

Nobody understood the true meaning of the tears that streamed from my eyes. The people who looked at me thought perhaps that these were tears of happiness and homesickness for my family or for the homeland. Instead, my thoughts carried me all the way back to the prophets and the apostles. Except for several brief periods in the days of Joshua, David, and Nehemiah, the spiritual life of my people had always degenerated into gross idolatry and immorality. God poured on us His just, righteous judgments, while we pointed our accusing fingers at the Gentiles around us and blamed them for all the evil that had beset us, instead of turning back to the Lord. God always knew when to bring the armies of Ammon and Moab, Assyria and Babylon, Greece and Rome, against us. The farther we wandered from Him, the harder were the wars waged against us. And who knows what the future has in store for Israel?

I shed tears of both sadness and joy—grief for our people's desperate spiritual condition and a profound happiness springing out of the faith that my people have reached the point in history where they are ready to accept Yeshua as Lord. I had a big dream—or perhaps I may call it a vision from God—to establish a Messianic kibbutz and raise an army of evangelists.

Among those lofty thoughts, I kept thinking of my dead brother. I asked myself whether he would have died if I had not delayed in the States. Finally I did come home, but at what a price! This time my return was not for a joyful wedding, but for a sad funeral and to sit *shivah* (the traditional seven-day period of mourning for the dead that is observed in Jewish homes).

As we arrived at the funeral home, a large crowd of mourners had already gathered. After the corpse had been identified and ceremonially cleansed, the time for the actual funeral came. When my departed brother's name was called out loudly over the microphone, Mother wailed terribly. Everybody followed her with tears and wailing. The ladies sobbed, and the men hardly contained their emotions. Shmuel's body was taken out of the funeral home, loaded on a special cart, wrapped in a linen gravecloth, and covered with a *tallit* (prayer shawl).

We followed in a sorrowful procession to the open concrete shelter, where the rabbi read Psalm 91, the one that starts with the words: *"He who dwells in the shelter of the Most High will abide in the shadow of the Almighty."*

The funeral procession continued on toward the newly dug grave. Four men carried the stretcher on their shoulders, and we all accompanied the body to its ultimate resting place. The agonizing laments of my bereaved mother, who pulled her hair out, beat her breast with her clenched fists, and scratched her grief-stricken face, shattered the silence of the cemetery. Father tried in vain to keep his horrible sorrow to himself. He was shocked and distressed and cried uncontrollably.

Another brother of mine, who is several years older than I am, was as strong as a pillar and comforted everybody, especially our parents. I walked beside Father and tried to console him, while all my sisters gathered around my mother, but it was to no avail. Mother cried out to heaven, but the skies were like an expanse of solid brass over her head. From where could she receive the oil of gladness instead of her mourning and the garment of praise instead of this heavy spirit (Isaiah 61:3)? Would my dear mother ever be comforted? Would she ever be willing to listen?

"And I saw in the right hand of Him who sat on the throne a book written inside and on the back, sealed up with seven seals. And I saw a strong angel proclaiming with a loud voice, 'Who is worthy to open the book and to break its seals?' And no one in heaven, or on the earth, or under the earth, was able to open the book, or to look into it. And I began to weep greatly, because no one was found worthy to open the book, or to look into it; And one of the elders said to me, 'Stop weeping; behold, the Lion that is from the tribe of Judah, the Root of David, has overcome so as to open the book and its seven seals'... And they sang a new song, saying, 'Worthy art Thou to take the book and to break its seals; for Thou wast slain, and didst purchase for God with Thy blood men from every tribe and tongue and people and nation.

And Thou hast made them to be a kingdom and priests
to our God; and they will reign upon the earth.'...
'Worthy is the Lamb that was slain
to receive power and riches and wisdom and might
and honor and glory and blessing.'"
(Revelation 5:1–5, 9–10, 12)

I stood silently at the open grave of my oldest brother and looked around me. My distressed mother expressed her grief with painful screams; my father was ready to collapse and fall at any moment; my sisters wept bitterly; and our relatives who gathered to pay the deceased their last respects were in tears.

Terrible questions plagued my mind: How can I tell these beloved people, who pray for the departed's soul to find rest in heaven, that there is no chance for their prayers to be answered? How can I explain to them that a person who did not accept God's forgiveness for his sins through the sacrifice of Yeshua dies in his sins and will be found eternally guilty on Judgment Day?

Then, blasphemous thoughts intermingled with the questions in my mind: What kind of a God is He, anyway, who can send a good, honest person to hell only because he failed to believe in Yeshua? What about all those multitudes of innocent people who never had the opportunity to hear the Gospel of salvation and to be saved? Would a righteous, just God really condemn all these people to everlasting misery?

Suddenly, the truth hit me like a bolt of lightning straight from the throne of God. Because God is holy, righteous, and just, He cannot suffer any sinner to come into His presence and defile it! God's eyes are too pure to behold evil. For that reason, He expelled Adam and Eve from the Garden of Eden after they fell into sin. Anyone who fails to accept God's salvation, for any reason, will have to pay for his own sins, and the wages of sin are death and eternal separation from God.

"If this is really the case," I thought, "then anyone who dies without accepting God's salvation is eternally lost." God has offered us His salvation freely and tells us in no uncertain terms:

"For God so loved the world that He gave His only begotten Son,
that whoever believes in Him should not perish
but have everlasting life" (John 3:16 NKJV).

God gave each and every one of us the free will to accept His salvation or to reject it. We can be compared to a person who is drowning in a swamp. He cannot do anything to pull himself out of the marshy bog; in fact, every movement he makes will only cause him to sink deeper and faster. But, there is someone standing on a solid rock not too far away, who throws a lifeline to him and cries out, "Catch!" Now, it is up to the sinking person to decide whether to grab the lifeline and hold it tightly and be rescued, or to reject the offered salvation and sink in the morass. It does not make much difference whether the person saw the lifeline and rejected it or failed to notice it; in either case, he will drown in the mire! But, the person who consciously rejects God's salvation is actually committing spiritual suicide:

> *"See, I have set before you today life and prosperity,*
> *and death and adversity...*
> *I call heaven and earth to witness against you today,*
> *that I have set before you life and death,*
> *the blessing and the curse.*
> *So choose life in order that you may live,*
> *you and your descendants."*
> (Deuteronomy 30:15, 19)

I raised my eyes, which were full of tears. The sky was clear and blue, and my thoughts carried me far, far away. I thought of God Himself, mourning for His beloved people who had wandered away from Him and had stumbled into multitudes of vain superstitions and man-made traditions. I could imagine the Lord God of Israel sitting in the splendor of His majesty on His throne, watching His people transform His holy Word into an endless series of laws and regulations, which they could never keep despite their best intentions—and all in the name of religion!

It was time to recite the *kaddish* (prayer for the dead) in unison. This prayer, which was written in Aramaic, does not even mention the dead or death. It is a prayer of praise and worship to the Almighty God:

May His great name be magnified and hallowed in the universe, which He has created according to His will, and in which He has raised up His salvation. May He hasten the coming of His Messiah soon in your lifetime, and in the lifetime of all Israel, and let us all say, "Amen!" May His great name be blessed forever and ever! May the name of the Holy One, blessed be He, be blessed and praised and glorified and exalted and uplifted and extolled and revered and honored, above all blessings and songs and praises and consolations that are pronounced in this world, and let us all say, "Amen!" Let there be great peace from heaven and life for us and for all Israel, and let us all say, "Amen!" He who makes peace in His heavenlies, may He in His mercy make peace on us and on all of Israel, and let us all say, "Amen!"

My eyes wandered around, observing those miserable people who believed in a God that they invented for themselves. I understood them so well. They were so pitiful, so hopeless and despairing, that my heart went out to them. In my spirit I embraced every one of them and sought to carry them into the very presence of God, to prove to them the truth in the Messiah. "What do these people really think?" I wondered. "Do they really believe that if they repeat the kaddish enough times, or if they read the right verses from Psalm 119, according to the alphabetical order of the name of the deceased above his grave, that the departed will be privileged to inherit the Garden of Eden? Do they believe that when their day comes, they will have that same privilege?"

I had no idea what my father and my brothers thought deep in their hearts when they raised their voices to say the kaddish. Did they really believe the salvation of Shmuel's soul depended on their faithfulness to say the kaddish every day, every month, and later, every year, on the anniversary of his death? Where did the Jew's faith go wrong? What does the Jew really believe?

I found it extremely difficult to hold my peace and to keep my mouth shut. I wanted to cry out in agony and call this pathetic crowd to return with a sincere heart to the God of their fathers and not to the self-invented religion of Israel, but how would they react? What would my family and all these religious people who gathered here think and say? Here they were, the ones who should represent God! My eyes seemed to penetrate through their outward appearance, and I could see their miserable, sin-stricken hearts through the black cloaks of religion that they wore. I knew that this was how God saw them from His throne on high, but still they refused to accept His salvation. My heart seemed to break with pity and compassion for them. If God in His infinite mercy had not sent Jeff to me, I would have stood here now, as blind as they were to every kind of spiritual truth, lost in my self-delusion!

I suddenly remembered another funeral, that awesome and amazing burial service in the Arizona desert. There, too, bereaved mothers had stood at the open graves of their beloved children— but what a contrast! How different is the sorrow of a person who knows that there is a hope to his future and that God takes those whom He loves unto Himself, in His infinite wisdom and love! How bitter is the sorrow of those who do not have that blessed hope and whose way is hidden from their eyes!

I could not help comparing the mothers. My mother was almost lost in her grief, scratching and beating herself, unable to let go of her son and allow his body to be lowered into the grave. On the other hand, those two mothers in Arizona, whose tragedy was no less severe than that of my mother, sang a song of praise to their loving Lord, realizing with full confidence that their dear ones are alive with their Master and that it was only a matter of time before they would be united again forever.

When the funeral was over, we all returned home to sit on the floor for the shivah. All the mirrors, all the glass windows, and even the television set were covered with blankets because, according to Jewish kabbalistic tradition, reflections would disturb the dead man's soul that was still wandering back and forth in the house, unable to find rest. The family sat on mattresses on the floor for seven days. Neighbors and friends came in and went out without knocking on the door, bringing all kinds of food and drinks.

The rabbi who had conducted the funeral and eulogized my brother with touching words, which he read from a sheet of paper, sat right across from me. Again and again we read Psalms to lead the soul upward to heaven. The rabbi saw to it that all the public prayers were said on time and that the kaddish was said often enough to ensure that the dead man's soul would find its way to paradise. He even tried to comfort the wailing crowd with Torah novelties of his own.

I did not waste my time. Being of an argumentative disposition by nature, I had to give an appropriate answer to the rabbi's every remark. Soon, a heated debate developed between us, and there was not much about which we did not argue. We covered the way of salvation, life after death, the unity and trinity of God, and the Virgin

Birth of the Messiah, the Word of the living God compared to human traditions, and the orthodox Jewish way of life in contrast with that of Messianic Judaism.

I could not ignore one prominent fact. Whenever I brought out any argument from the Bible, the rabbi countered from the sages and the *Talmud* (literally, instruction; the body of Jewish tradition that has been codified). My family could not believe their own ears and remained practically speechless with awe. It was not the same old Jacob they used to know, that scoundrel who once ran away from home, who surprised them all when he came suddenly to his sister's wedding, but who could not wait for his flight back to the United States.

Now it was an altogether different fellow who sat before them, speaking with a genuine conviction and with an authority that came directly from the Word of God, refuting one by one all the claims of a rabbi in Israel. Of course, they tried to hush me every now and then, out of respect for the rabbi's honor, but I could not be silenced. I was like a spring of water, quoting Scriptures *"in season and out of season"* (2 Timothy 4:2), until finally the rabbi warned the family not to read the New Testament, never to raise these subjects at home, and as much as possible not to get into arguments with me about theological matters.

I say then, God has not rejected His people, has He? May it never be! For I too am an Israelite, a descendant of Abraham... (Romans 11:1)

"I am under obligation both to Greeks and to barbarians, both to
the wise and to the foolish. So, for my part, I am eager to preach
the gospel to you also who are in Rome. For I am not ashamed
of the gospel, for it is the power of God for salvation to everyone
who believes, to the Jew first and also to the Greek. For in it the
righteousness of God is revealed from faith to faith; as it is written,
"But the righteous man shall live by faith." (Romans 1:14-17)

Chapter 17

First Steps in the Homeland

Following the confrontation with the rabbi, I felt an urgent need to learn more about the ultraorthodox Jewish way of thinking and living. I could never face the opposition successfully if I did not know them well. I grew a huge beard and joined a famous *yeshiva* (rabbinical school) in Jerusalem. For several months I sat with the rest of the men, listening to their endless debates and sophisticated *pilpul* (intricate reasonings) about ancient, obscure, and irrelevant Talmudic issues. Even the rabbinical students found no relevance for their lives in the material they studied, but they had come to the yeshiva to study the Torah and the Talmud simply for the sake of studying them.

I also noticed that these religious folk esteemed the words of the rabbis and the sages far more than the words of the Scriptures. The most prominent feature here was the absence of anything important. It is true that these men were truly hungry and thirsty for the truth, and they were diligently seeking after it day and night, but their thirst was steadily increasing because they did not have the Water of Life to quench it. They appeared to me as though they were wandering in the desert on a hot summer day, deceived by a mirage, wasting limited energy to chase after this mirage, and ending up exhausted, disillusioned, and thirstier than ever. I saw how their lives were bound by entangling *halakhoth* (traditional regulations of learned men) that dictated each detail of their lives. How different is the spirit of those halakhoth from the Spirit of the Bible! How different is the heavy, unbearable yoke of the halakhoth from the light, easy yoke of the Messiah, the truth of God that sets captives free!

Every religion, in contrast to true faith, is filled with rituals and customs. The religious authorities obscure the divine truth, clothing it with religious garments. They become masters of external commandments, totally ignoring all of God's fulfilled promises regarding the Atonement, the only means for man to come to God and be saved.

How different is the life of faith and true closeness to the Creator from that which is tied with religious chains! I will never forget the *jahrzeit* (death anniversary) of a certain holy rabbi. His disciples went up the Mount of Olives in multitudes in order to pray at his tomb. I was always appalled by this ritual, but since I had accepted Yeshua, it seemed to me sheer idolatry. The modern Jewish concept of the sanctity of the dead stands in complete contradiction to the words of the Torah that consider the dead, and the grave, as the greatest of all uncleanness, which defiles everyone who comes in contact with it. The Torah says clearly:

"The one who touches the corpse of any person shall be unclean for seven days...

This is the law when a man dies in a tent: everyone who comes into the tent and everyone who is in the tent shall be unclean for seven days...

Also, anyone who in the open field touches one who has been slain with the sword or who has died naturally, or a human bone or a grave, shall be unclean for seven days."

(Numbers 19:11, 14, 16)

Contrary to these verses, the *Hasidim* (members of a Jewish sect devoted to the strict observance of the ritual law) ascribe supreme sanctity to the tombs of the righteous and are willing to do almost anything to keep that all-important *mitzvah* (a righteous deed) by making pilgrimages to the tombs of the righteous. We Messianic Jews are perhaps even more sensitive on that point, because we worship a Lord who raised the Messiah victoriously from the dead, leaving an empty tomb behind Him.

When my time came to leave the yeshiva, everyone there marveled at the unexpected and strange step I was taking. Usually, rabbinical students enjoy many privileges, rightfully or not, which they do not relinquish so easily. Yet, here was a student who had come only recently, who did not even have enough time to enjoy the sweet fragrance of the Torah, but who was already deciding to leave.

When they started to ask me questions, I could not keep my secret any longer, and so I told them: "You are studying and meditating upon the pages of the Talmud, like people looking for the hidden treasures of truth. However, the truth cannot be found in the Talmud, only in the Bible, which speaks about the Truth incarnate, about Yeshua HaMashiach!"

I received no response except an ocean of spittle.

Shortly after that occasion, I returned to the enlistment office of the Israeli army, but this time with the opposite purpose from that of my first visit there a dozen years before. Ever since I had become a believer in Yeshua, I had regretted deeply all my mischief in the army and wanted to put things right. Thus, I came again to the army registration office and asked to be reexamined by a medical committee to certify my fitness for active service. The committee invited me for an interview and marveled why a thirty-year-old man would want to join the regular armed forces. "Your file says that you were called up for service in 1970, but half a year later you were released because of maladjustment. What makes you think that now you will do any better?"

"When I was sixteen years old, I was invited to take the first psychometric tests," I replied. "I was still a true patriot then and wanted to volunteer for the paratroopers or the commando unit, as you can see in my records. But soon after that, I ran away from home and left for Eilat. My way of life there altered my whole outlook completely, and I started to think of ways to evade military service. When I was summoned for the first time for the medical exams and received the highest rating, I was glad. Later, however, I learned from some of the other young men in the neighborhood numerous ways to cheat the army. That was how I finally managed to get an early release after only six months of service. Later, I traveled abroad."

"Where have you been?" asked one of the committee members.

"In the United States," I replied.

"And what made you change your mind again?"

"While in the U.S., I started to believe in Yeshua, the Messiah of Israel, who turned me into a Jew in the complete sense of the word. He filled me with love and understanding concerning everything that has to do with the ultimate destiny of Israel, so I came back home. I want to contribute to my country all those things that I did not give her until now and to serve in a unit where I can be most useful to the army!"

One of the members of the committee, the one who wore a kippah, took my service file and pondered it deeply. Then he raised his eyes, scrutinized me from head to foot, and asked, "How did it happen to you, all that story about Yeshu?"

"That's a long story, sir, and I do not wish to go into details. The fact is that while I was reading the Scriptures, I came across passages that I could not explain in any way other than to ascribe them to Yeshua. In the beginning I thought it was nothing but a coincidence, but later I saw more and more passages, each of which added another part to the jigsaw puzzle. Moreover, as I pondered our painful history as a chosen people, I could not close my eyes any longer. The facts spoke for themselves and were louder than all my arguments."

"Did you see any visions?" The psychiatrist of the committee showed some interest. "Well, several supernatural things did happen to me that I considered miracles," I said. "You see, the God of the Bible has never changed. He is alive and well and working in our time exactly the same way He worked in ages past."

"Did it ever occur to you that you might be somewhat unstable?" asked the religious inquisitor. "First you say you were a patriot. Then you changed your way of thinking and became a radical. Now you have converted to Christianity, still another change. How can we be sure that you will not change your mind once again and defect, let's say, to the side of the enemy?"

"That first time, sir, was a passing whim of an adolescent child who was not too smart, who was influenced by the negative peer pressure of the environment in which he lived. However, before I came to believe in Yeshua, I had very difficult inner struggles. I was very well aware of being Jewish, coming from a traditional Sephardi home. As a child I used to frequent the synagogue with my father and study the Tanach like every Jewish child in this country. My stomach turned at the very thought that Yeshua might have been Israel's true Messiah. I knew very well that Israel as a whole had rejected Him then, and that they keep rejecting Him even today. I, too, was well acquainted with all that has happened to us Jews in the last two thousand years of bloody history. Reading our Jewish Scriptures, in which I believed, presented new questions to me for which I had to find the right answers. Various events that took place in my life have made it clear that the truth is unavoidable. God Himself put the choice before me, and I have chosen life.

"Believe me," I went on, "the struggle was not easy, but what happened to me was not a conversion from one religion to another. It was not even a change from one set of dogmas to another. I have received the new life that our Hebrew Bible promises to anyone who believes, and that is an inseparable part of what God wants to give to His people Israel."

"Did you consult with wise men and rabbis before you chose to believe in Yeshu?" asked the religious one.

"Well, to be honest with you, no, I did not. I didn't consult with anybody, because I didn't feel any need to do so. I didn't consult with rabbis because, long before that, I had realized they could not supply adequate, satisfying answers to my questions. Since then, I have had opportunities to speak with many orthodox Jews, and every single one of them has tried to convince me to change my mind and to return to mainstream Judaism. As a matter of fact, they are still trying to do so even today.

"However, when I examined their arguments carefully, I realized how irrelevant they were. They all started from the same point: that "Yeshu" was "a criminal of Israel" or "a bastard son of uncleanness", that He "practiced witchcraft in order to entice Israel with magic formulas (or, with the holy name of God) that He inserted under his skin", that He was "hanged in Jerusalem on Passover Eve and was sentenced to drown in boiling excrement". All those disgusting, sickening stories were concocted by religious people who wanted only to make Yeshua's name hateful to the ordinary, ignorant Jew.

"But, when a Jew is asked to take a good look into the New Covenant, which is the only reliable historical source for the life and ministry of Yeshua, he recoils from it as though from a venomous snake. The Jew forbids himself and his fellow Jews to read the New Covenant and to relate to Yeshua in any way, whether good or bad.

"A devout Jew even avoids calling Him by His true name. He mispronounces it intentionally and calls Him by the abbreviation "Yeshu", which means, "May his name and memory be blotted out!" Yeshua in Hebrew really means "salvation". But, believe me, this does not bother me anymore, because many Jews mispronounce the divine name of God purposely and call Him "Elokim" instead of "Elohim", or "Adoshem" instead of "Adonai", only to avoid using the holy name of God in vain. I consider, therefore, this mispronunciation of Yeshua's name a secret admission of His divinity!

"The Jews are scared to death when they have to cope with the truth, and I am clearly speaking about Yeshua, the Messiah, now. They try to suppress it, to bypass it, and to avoid any meaningful confrontation with it. This is why I could not receive any meaningful answers to my questions from the rabbinical establishment."

The religious committee member then asked, "I have the

impression that you are quite bitter as far as that "rabbinical establishment" is concerned. What do you know about it?"

"I have come here directly from an ultraorthodox yeshiva in Jerusalem, where I spent the last six months. There I studied the Torah and the Talmud in a very concentrated manner until I could make up my mind about it. Let there be no misunderstandings, please; I have no objection whatsoever to the Judaism of the Torah. Quite the contrary! I am a proud Jew; this is how I was born, and this is how I will die. But what aggravates me—and I contend against these with everything within me—are the negative phenomena that are found in established rabbinical Judaism. First of all, I protest against the wicked, hostile attitude of the religious Jews against Yeshua and His followers!"

Again the pious man fired hostile questions at me: "Don't you see that reading that book has caused you to betray your own people and religion? How do you dare even to think that all the rabbis are mistaken and that you alone are right? Is everyone else blind, and you alone can see?"

"Well, sir, first of all I reject your statement that this book caused me to betray my people and my religion. If you had ever read it for yourself, you would have seen with your own eyes that there is absolutely nothing in it that can even imply a call to betray or desert the Jewish people. God forbid! I did not come here requesting to be exempted from army service so that I can escape fulfilling my responsibility to my country and go abroad to study the New Covenant at a Messianic yeshiva. It's exactly the opposite, as a matter of fact. I came here to join the army and to offer myself for my country. Do you call that betrayal? I am of the opinion that the real traitors are those who misuse their religion by refusing to serve in the army or by robbing and exploiting our poor country in every way possible, through "unique allocations" of public funds and many other atrocities!

"As to your second question, my answer is that the rabbis can all be in error. It has happened more than once that the majority was in error and that a few faithful ones were chosen to point out their mistakes to them. The Bible gives many examples where God chose the little remnant. There were only a handful of people in Jeremiah's day who chose to follow God faithfully. I cannot tell you why God chose me out of my entire family, and from the people of Israel, to become *"a light to the nations"* (Isaiah 42:6), but who am I to question God's wisdom and election? I am certainly not ashamed of the Gospel of the Messiah."

"Thank you very much," the psychiatrist abruptly interrupted my flow of words, scribbling something in my file that was in front of him. "You'll receive my answer soon."

I left the place feeling good and with great aspirations. I knew I had given a good testimony about my faith in the Messiah and that I had displayed goodwill and readiness to serve my country. This explains how excited I was to receive, two weeks later, that brown military envelope in the mail. But when I read the few lines that were typed on the white, official form that was folded inside, my eyes suddenly grew dark.

Jacob Damkani, Shalom,

We regret to inform you that the medical committee that investigated your case and reexamined your request to return to military service has come to the conclusion that you are not fit for service in the IDF.

I laid the whole matter in God's hands, and He filled my heart with His peace. I could not understand how and why that medical committee had come to that conclusion. I gathered that God must have other plans for me and that He needed me more in His army. I regretted it then, and I still regret it today, that the right to serve my country as a soldier was denied me. Unfortunately, neither the government nor the army is capable of understanding at this stage what a tremendous and profound change Yeshua can perform in the human heart. Were it not for my faith, I would have stayed abroad and lived happily ever after, like many other Israelis.

Above: Addressing a division of the IDF with the Gospel of Truth.
Only God can open such a door.

Below: Enemies of the Gospel, but beloved of God (Romans 11:28).

Chapter 18

Experiences of Persecution

Because the army did not want me and had given me a final exemption, I began to work as a gardener. Compared to the fortune I had earned in America, it seemed to me that I had returned to the austerity of my childhood. That was all right with me, however.

Now that I had reached the age of thirty, my parents expected me, of course, to get married, raise a family of my own, and make their hearts rejoice with a new grandchild every year. I had other plans, however. I was determined not to waste my time on unimportant matters, but rather to dedicate myself completely to the work of the Gospel. The people of Israel had to know the difference between Yeshu and Yeshua, between mere "Christianity" (so-called Christians who have adopted only the external form of Christianity) and true Messianic Judaism, which keeps the new, and final, covenant of God.

I purchased a pickup truck, gardening tools, and found a job. Twice a week I gardened and did general maintenance work in Holon and Ramat Hasharon, which provided an income that was sufficient for me. All of my siblings except one had completed their studies successfully and had moved out of the house. My parents, my sister who was a kindergarten teacher, and myself were the only ones left. As I did at the age of fourteen, I brought my mother money every week to help provide for the family needs.

After so many years of my absence, everything at home was very much the same as it had been. Mother, who was about sixty at that time, already looked like she was eighty, but she was still strong enough to do all the household work. Father had quit his construction job and worked at the army department store.

Most of my old buddies had married and had children of their own. I talked to many of them about the Messiah, and it hurt me to see how they continued happily to drown, refusing to catch the extended hand of the divine Lifeguard! All those dear friends had shared in forming my character, for better or worse. This was the same character that God later remolded, sanctified, and refined, and has been using ever since for His sake.

A new generation of gangsters had grown up in the neighborhood and, with the exception of several new villas that had sprung up here and there, everything remained more or less the same. I renovated the old, leaking tile roof of my parents' house and slowly entered the everyday routine of life in Israel.

To my surprise, I discovered that there was Messianic life in Israel. Quite a number of Messianic congregations were forming. A Messianic congregation is a group of people who have one essential thing in common: they believe in the Tanach and the New Covenant as the true Word of God. Among a Messianic assembly are Jews who were religious before they were saved, others who were traditional, and even former atheists. Some are not Jewish at all. Among that group are Arab believers who grew up in Islam or traditional Christianity (Roman Catholicism or Greek Orthodox), proselytes who had been nominal "Christians," and even some whose previous beliefs were rooted in eastern Buddhism or Hinduism. Others were saved from the claws of the Jehovah's Witnesses, and still others had been socialists or communists.

Everyone is welcome to attend the meetings of a Messianic congregation. Its doors are open to all, but membership is available only to those who have received God's forgiveness for their sins, as He has offered it in Yeshua the Messiah according to the Holy Scriptures. It does not matter what the background of the person was prior to his salvation or to what religion he belonged by birth. The main issue is that, at a certain point in his life, he came to the conclusion that the God of Israel promised all people a new heart and a new spirit through faith in Yeshua. Such a person can truly confess that he has received God's forgiveness and that he has been born again. Nobody can impose such a faith on another, nor can anyone buy it or sell it for all the silver and gold of this world.

There are at least forty-five Messianic congregations in Israel today, while the number of believers steadily increases. More and more Israelis understand that Yeshua is truly the Messiah. God is still calling the people of Israel—and humanity as a whole—to accept the forgiveness that He offers in the Messiah, to repent, and to turn to Him. The gradual revelation of God to the people of Israel had reached its climax with the first appearance of Yeshua. This does not mean, however, that God has withdrawn from the world since then. It is through the Messianic believers that He calls both Jew and Gentile to Himself today.

I will never forget the uproar that the religious Jews raised in protest against the activity of one of the congregations. Hundreds of angry orthodox yeshiva students demonstrated with indignation one Shabbat morning in front of the meeting hall. Dozens of them later broke into the place, throwing the Bibles and songbooks on the floor. The burning hatred in their eyes was pathetic. "Nazis! Nazis!" they screamed at us with terrible wrath. "The Nazis burnt our bodies, and you come here to burn our souls! Missionaries! Traitors! Converts!"

The riot was horrible indeed. Only after a long struggle did the police manage to evacuate "God's custodians," as they called themselves, from the place and to set guards around it. That day God gave us the opportunity to identify in a very special way with Yeshua and with the persecution He endured for our sakes. We sang praises to the Lord, heard a sermon from the Word of God, prayed for our persecutors, and blessed those who hated and cursed us. Each one of us had his inner struggle, but now I knew—I saw and realized again—what the living Messiah can do in and through us. How I wish the rabbi of that yeshiva, the one who kindled the flames of hatred, could have looked into my heart at that moment to see and experience the power of the Messiah who was living within!

The town was filled with hostile signs and posters, the demonstrations became increasingly more organized, and new events occurred each day. It seemed as if there would be no end to the persecution. The growing hatred escalated to the point of a murder attempt. The religious Jews put pressure on the owner of the congregation's meeting place, and he was compelled to terminate the lease. Being "new" in the country at that time, I found it hard to grasp the magnitude of the religious pressure that was put on the town mayor. Since then, however, all of us have had occasion to see the capabilities of this noisy minority.

The building was not that important to us, however. We began to have open-air meetings in orchards and woods, and we met in the private homes of the assembly members. We continued to grow in our love for God and for our fellow men.

This incident was only one of many. Other congregations have suffered persecution as well. In one of the prayer meetings I attended at the Peniel Congregation in Tiberias, I saw stones being thrown into the meeting hall—and even on the Sabbath, no less! The windows were broken, and it was a miracle that nobody was injured.

In Jerusalem, the congregational hall at the Narkis Street Church was burnt to ashes. These were only a few of the terrible things that the ultraorthodox Jews saw fit to do to other Jews.

Religious violence is ever increasing and is not only expressed against the Messianic public, but also against secular Jews, against members of kibbutzim, and even against other religious Jews who behave differently. It is time that the Sages of the Torah (the highest authority of the Sephardic community) sit together with the Great Ones of the Torah (the Ashkenazim authorities), and discuss together the teachings of Rabbi Gamaliel, who lived in the first century and who said the following words concerning the Messianic Jews:

"And he said to them,
'Men of Israel, take care what you propose to do with these men.
And so in the present case, I say to you,
stay away from these men and let them alone;
for if this plan or action should be of men,
it will be overthrown;
But if it is of God, you will not be able to overthrow them;
or else you may even be found fighting against God.'"
(Acts 5:35, 38–39)

During those days of riots and disorder, when all the media treated us as if we were some mystical cult, I could not help thinking about the persecution that Yeshua's disciples had to endure two thousand years ago. After the Master's crucifixion, the frightened disciples hid themselves behind locked gates in Jerusalem. They were devastated, desperate, and disappointed in Yeshua. As we all know, Yeshua was executed on Passover Eve, and all His disciples' aspirations for a speedy military and political salvation for Israel evaporated. But only three days later, just as He had promised them, He rose again from the dead. During the days between His resurrection and His ascension back to heaven, He showed Himself alive to His disciples on many occasions. He ate in their presence, allowed them to touch His living body, and issued this command:

"And gathering them together,
He commanded them not to leave Jerusalem,
but to wait for what the Father had promised,
'Which,' He said, 'you heard of from Me;
for John baptized with water,

*but you shall be baptized with the Holy Spirit
not many days from now.'"* (Acts 1:4–5)

Yeshua was crucified on Passover Eve, which filled His followers with despair. However, on Shavuot (Pentecost) the circumstances were reversed: the Father's promise was kept and the disciples were filled with the Holy Spirit, with courage and power from on high. For example, just a few hours prior to the Crucifixion, Peter had denied his Lord three times because of his fear of others, especially the chief priests of the Sanhedrin. (See John 18:15–27.) However, on Pentecost, that same Galilean fisherman suddenly stood in the presence of the other disciples and all the Jewish pilgrims present at that time in Jerusalem and gave a powerful sermon (see Acts 2:5, 14–40), in which he boldly proved to them that this was exactly the way things had to be according to the promises of the Old Testament. Yeshua had to die and to pay the penalty for sin in full, in order to pay our debt and to release us from the yoke of sin.

As a result of Peter's sermon, three thousand Jewish people accepted Yeshua, and the first Messianic congregation came into being. This congregation was an integral part of mainstream Judaism at that time. Many Jews believed in Yeshua, and the religious establishment began to worry about the erosion of its authority.

A life-death war was then declared between the truth of God and man-made religion. Actually, it was a new phase in the ancient struggle between God and the powers of darkness. That war, which had begun already in the Garden of Eden, at least here on earth, gathered new momentum now. Similar to the ancient conflict between God's prophet Samuel and the corrupt sons of Eli the priest in the Tanach, the same war was raging in Jerusalem between the believers in Yeshua, whom God filled with His Spirit, and the conservative religious establishment, which held fast to its self-proclaimed authority.

The same Holy Spirit who filled the early disciples with divine strength and enabled them to stand firm against the most severe persecution still gives every individual believer, and every true Messianic congregation, the power needed to do that which is right in the eyes of the Lord and to pursue righteousness and truth out of ardent love for God and for men. When I saw all the demonstrations and riots against the congregation, I felt like stepping forward and crying out clearly to these boisterous young men that they would in

no way be able to hinder or to stop the work of the Spirit, who began
to work in human hearts thousands of years ago. Peter's words on that
ancient day of Shavuot came to mind:

"Men of Israel, listen to these words: Jesus the Nazarene,
a man attested to you by God with miracles and wonders
and signs which God performed through Him in your midst,
just as you yourselves know—
This Man, delivered up by the predetermined plan
and foreknowledge of God, you nailed to a cross
by the hands of godless men and put Him to death.
And God raised Him up again, putting an end to the agony of
death, since it was impossible for Him to be held in its power.
For David says of Him,
'I was always beholding the LORD in my presence;
for He is at my right hand, that I may not be shaken.
Therefore my heart was glad and my tongue exulted;
moreover, my flesh also will abide in hope;
Because Thou wilt not abandon my soul to Hades,
nor allow Thy Holy One to undergo decay.
Thou hast made known to me the ways of life;
Thou wilt make me full of gladness with Thy presence."
[See Psalm 16:8–11]
Brethren, I may confidently say to you
regarding the patriarch David that he both died and was buried,
and his tomb is with us to this day.
And so, because he was a prophet,
he knew that God had sworn to him with an oath
to seat one of his descendants upon his throne,
He looked ahead and spoke of the resurrection of the Christ,
that He was neither abandoned to Hades,
nor did His flesh suffer decay.
This Jesus God raised up again, to which we are all witnesses.
Therefore, having been exalted to the right hand of God,
and having received from the Father the promise of the Holy
Spirit, He has poured forth this which you both see and hear.
For it was not David who ascended into heaven,
but he himself says, "The LORD said to my Lord,
'Sit at my right hand, until I make Thine enemies
a footstool for Thy feet.'" (See Psalm 110:1)

*Therefore let all the house of Israel know for certain
that God has made Him both Lord and Christ—
this Jesus whom you crucified.*" (Acts 2:22–36)

I wondered inwardly, "Would the disciples of this new rabbi
have also repented and been baptized in multitudes, if they had heard
Peter's message today?" I was sure of this one thing: the stronger
the persecution became, the stronger and more loving the Messianic
congregation would become.

However, although I criticize the modern-day religious
establishment, I do not underestimate its tremendous contribution to
the formation of Jewish tradition in the two thousand years of our
dispersion. God knew very well what our needs were as long as we
were exiled from our land and lived in the *Diaspora* (any area outside
of Palestine or modern Israel where Jews have settled), just as He
knows what is best for us today. Now, with the Jews returning home
to Zion, after the Gospel has been preached to the Gentiles around the
globe, the circle has been completed. God has shown us that *"all we
like sheep have gone astray"* (Isaiah 53:6 NKJV)—Jew and Gentile
alike—and that we all need His grace equally: *"For God has shut up
all in disobedience that He might show mercy to all"* (Romans 11:32).
In referring specifically to the Jews, may we all forever remember
this: *"If their rejection be the reconciliation of the world, what will
their acceptance be but life from the dead?"* (Romans 11:15).

I do not wish to create the impression that the Messianic believers
are being assaulted and stoned on every Shabbat in Israel. Neither
do I intend to present the orthodox Jews as ugly and wicked. I have
related this only for the sake of honesty and to bring the truth out
into the light, so that when your own eyes, dear reader, are opened
by the grace of God to behold Him who is the Truth and you decide
to follow Yeshua, there will be no misunderstanding, and everything
will be absolutely clear. I do not want to mislead you to think that
when you accept the Messiah your life will become a bed of roses.
Yeshua Himself predicted that those who follow Him and seek after
godliness will suffer persecution. (See John 15:20 and 2 Timothy
3:12.)

In the meantime, the pressure from my family had grown
stronger. They simply could not understand why I was not trying to
work harder and make more money, to buy myself a house, to marry

a nice Jewish princess, and to behave like any other decent, civilized man. I could not rid myself of the feeling that both my family and my friends from the neighborhood would prefer the old Jacob, the one who chased after skirts and who had an itching palm, rather than Jacob, the messenger of the Messiah!

I began to print tracts based on biblical prophecies and to go out regularly into the streets of Israel distributing the leaflets. As I preached the Gospel without fear or favoritism, I realized that this was a matter of extreme importance for the Jewish people and the glory of God. Wherever I was, and with every person I met, my heart's desire was to magnify and exalt Yeshua, *"the stone which the builders rejected [that] has become the chief corner stone"* (Psalm 118:22). If we are faithful in preaching the Gospel, we will see the fallen tabernacle of David restored again.

My parents noticed that I spent much of my free time in reading the Scriptures and in prayer, or in maintenance work around the house. Gradually, their hearts began to soften toward me. They began to understand that I had not converted to another religion after all, but rather had become a better Jew. It did not take too long before my parents began to read together the New Covenant in Persian that I had presented to them as a gift. This made everything I might have suffered for the sake of spreading the Gospel all worthwhile.

At times we are compared to Nazis by the enemies of the Gospel...

Chapter 19

From Joseph to Joseph

I really enjoyed telling everyone who would listen about Yeshua, which was how I met Joseph one day. Joseph came from a secular home, and like many of the secular *sabras* (native Israelis), he regarded the Tanach only as a historical document that described the ancient history of the people of Israel. He also knew something of modern Bible criticism and was not willing to accept the words simply as they were written. He liked to argue very loudly about almost everything I told him, and I am sure the whole street could hear our lively discussions.

"You cannot convince me," he cried out passionately, "that this Jesus is mentioned in the Tanach! That is nothing but a Christian invention, which considered our "Old Testament" a Christian allegory. The Tanach is a purely Jewish book, free of every Christian doctrine!"

"Of course it is a Jewish book," I replied. "Any Gentile who wants to be saved must accept this Jewish book and the Jewish Messiah it prophesies about. Didn't I tell you that I have not left Judaism and that I have no intention of doing so? I have always believed that there is nothing more ridiculous than the idea that a Jew must "convert" to Christianity in order to believe in the Jewish Messiah of Israel! No, it is these Gentiles who decide to follow Yeshua who adopt a Torah that is strictly Jewish."

Joseph clearly defined Christianity by what he had seen and heard: religious garb, crosses, and organ music. He did not know Yeshua and the new covenant, the only means by which Jews and the whole world can be saved.

"Come on," he replied, "do you mean to tell me that those Christians who worship their idols in their fancy cathedrals to the sound of pipe organs are actually Jews who believe in a Jewish religion? If you imply anything like this, I must conclude that you do not have the faintest idea what it means to be Jewish, and that you do not know anything about Christianity either. These two religions are so far apart from each other that there is no bridge long enough to span the gap between them!"

"I must agree with you about this point, too, Joseph. These two religions are not only totally different, but they also hate each other passionately and are willing to fight one another to the death. By nature, every religion is hostile to its rivals, because each considers itself to be the sole custodian of the divine oracles of God. But, I am not talking to you about either Judaism or Christianity. Yeshua did not come all the way down from heaven, nor did He go all the way to the cross, just to introduce us to a new religion that would eventually rise against its own mother! Yeshua Himself condemned religious rituals that were void of any inner meaning, be it Jewish or non-Jewish. Instead, He taught us that God is a Spirit, and they who truly worship God must do so in spirit and in truth (John 4:23–24)."

"Tell me," Joseph suddenly changed the subject. "Do you *lay tefillin* (put on phylacteries)? Do you keep the Shabbat? What kind of a Jew are you, anyway?"

"Let me answer your question the Jewish way, with another question: Do you do these things yourself? No, you don't, but that doesn't keep you from calling yourself a Jew, does it? You are Jewish because you were born of a Jewish mother, isn't that right? Well, so was I. Can you see? The Jewish rituals don't make us Jews or non-Jews, nor does the cultural legacy we inherited by birth. We were circumcised when we were eight days old. Even the chief rabbi was circumcised when he was eight days old, long before he had any opportunity to keep even one commandment. Nobody asked us during the act of circumcision whether or not we believed in the Jewish religion, true?"

"You told me earlier that the Tanach speaks about Yeshua," said Joseph, changing the subject again. "Can you show me where, please? And do me a favor. Don't start with Isaiah 53."

"As a matter of fact, I did want to talk to you about this extremely important prophecy, but let's talk about something else if you prefer. You are probably familiar with the story of Joseph, the son of Jacob and Rachel."

"Of course! Joseph is my favorite biblical figure. My parents' names are Jacob and Rachel, and so they named me Joseph."

"So, let's review the story of Joseph, and I believe you are about to hear several things that will make your hair stand on end," I challenged him.

"Joseph was the beloved son of Jacob and his favorite wife,

Rachel, and was born in Jacob's old age. Jacob preferred this son above all his other sons and made him a coat of many colors. In other words, he considered that young boy greater than all his older brothers, who noticed that special attitude, of course, and hated their brother for it. Yeshua was also called *"My beloved Son"* (Matthew 3:17) by the Father. He was hated by His Jewish brothers—and still is to this very day."

"Oh, this is just a coincidence!" Joseph laughed. "It doesn't really mean anything." I just laughed, too.

Joseph's curiosity was stirred, and he stopped his arguments for a moment. This gave me the opportunity to proceed.

"Joseph was known as "the dreamer". He had prophetic dreams that revealed to the Jews (his brothers) and to the Gentiles (Pharaoh and his servants) what was going to happen to them in the future. Yeshua was also a prophet, who predicted to His generation what was going to happen.

"Jacob, Joseph's father, sent him to visit his brothers and wish them peace. Although Joseph was well aware of their hostility toward him, he nevertheless obeyed his father and kept his commands. The New Covenant tells us that God the Father sent His beloved Son Yeshua into this world to save His own kindred, the Jews. Yeshua knew what the consequences of that visit would be—that He would be delivered to the Gentiles to be crucified—but He obeyed His heavenly Father anyway, and He did so willingly and lovingly.

"Joseph's brothers seized the opportunity and decided to kill him, but finally they changed their minds and decided to sell him instead to the Gentile Midianites for twenty pieces of silver (Genesis 37:28). The Jewish leaders also sought to kill Yeshua, and when one of His disciples finally betrayed Him to them for thirty pieces of silver, they handed Him over to the Romans.

"Joseph's brothers stripped him of the garment that symbolized authority and dominion and threw him into a pit. Before His Crucifixion, Yeshua was stripped of all His clothes, and afterwards He was buried in the pit of the tomb."

"Hey, I like it!" Joseph got excited. "I've never seen these things this way."

"Just wait. You haven't seen anything yet!" I promised.

"Soon after his arrival in Egypt, Joseph faced a severe temptation and withstood it honorably. The Scriptures tell us that at the very beginning of His public ministry, Yeshua was tempted severely by Satan, but withstood all of those temptations without sin.

Potiphar's wife was furious with Joseph for rejecting her advances. She got even with him by falsely accusing him, although he was not guilty at all. Yeshua, too, was innocently punished for our sins, which He Himself had never committed.

Joseph spent over two years in prison before he was vindicated and raised by Pharaoh to be second in the kingdom. Yeshua spent two nights and three days in the grave before He was raised by God in power and great glory.

Joseph was appointed second to Pharaoh over Egypt. Yeshua was appointed King over the nations, and He sits now on the throne at the right hand of God in heaven, as it is written, *"The LORD says to my Lord: 'Sit at My right hand, until I make Thine enemies a footstool for Thy feet'"* (Psalm 110:1).

Joseph was made the provider, who distributed grain not only to the Egyptians, but also to the entire world that suffered from hunger. Yeshua, as *"the bread of life"* (John 6:48), sustains the whole world with His grace and merciful love.

Joseph's brothers came down to Egypt to buy some food because of the heavy famine that was in Canaan at that time, and finally they appeared before Joseph. The children of Israel starve today spiritually, and those of them who come to Yeshua receive the Bread of Life from Him.

Joseph recognized his brothers, but they did not recognize him. Yeshua knows well all of His Jewish kindred, although their eyes are still blinded so that they do not recognize Him.

Joseph's brothers mistook him for an Egyptian and spoke to him through an interpreter. The Jewish people still treat Yeshua as if He were a Gentile, refuse to call Him by His Jewish name, and fail to recognize Him as their brother.

Joseph treated his brothers roughly until he proved, to his complete satisfaction, that they had repented wholeheartedly. Yeshua is still waiting until His family acknowledges their sin against Him and stop accusing Him for their misfortunes.

Joseph revealed himself to his brothers and told them, *"I am your brother Joseph, whom you sold into Egypt"* (Genesis 45:4). Yeshua will soon reveal His true identity to the house of David, after pouring out on them the Spirit of grace and supplication. Then they will look on Him *"whom they have pierced"* (Zechariah 12:10) and acknowledge that they had sold their brother, their own flesh and blood, to the Gentiles.

Joseph told his brothers not to be grieved or angry with themselves because they had sold him, because God had sent him before them to preserve life (Genesis 45:5). He said to them, *"As for you, you meant evil against me, but God meant it for good in order... to preserve many people alive"* (Genesis 50:20). Likewise, the children of Israel were not aware of what they were doing when they delivered Yeshua to the Romans to be executed. But even on the cross, Yeshua cried out, *"Father, forgive them; for they do not know what they are doing"* (Luke 23:34). God brought good out of this and used the rejection of Yeshua by the Jews to bring about the salvation of the Gentiles.

Joseph invited his brothers to come and live in the land of Goshen because of the famine. Yeshua also reserves places in His kingdom for His people, the Jewish people."

Joseph closed his eyes and thought quietly. I saw that he was bothered. After a few moments of silence, he said, "This is really interesting. I've read the story of Joseph many times, but I never saw this striking similarity between his life and that of Yeshua. I find it quite difficult now to explain it away as merely a coincidence. I could understand if it were only a matter of one or two details, but the way you presented it gives me the impression that the entire story of Joseph and his brothers is a reflection of Yeshua and His attitude toward His Jewish kindred."

At this point my mother came into the room, carrying a tray with two glasses of hot peppermint tea and a plate of cookies. Our conversation obviously had come to an end. At once we descended from the heavenlies and came back down to earth. After some small talk, Joseph left, and I never saw him again.

Afterward, I prayed for him and committed him to the Lord's faithful hands. The Bible says that the Word of God, which we speak to other people, is not given out in vain, but that it will certainly fulfill the purpose for which it was sent.

"Seek the LORD while He may be found;
call upon Him while He is near.

Let the wicked forsake his way,
and the unrighteous man his thoughts;
and let him return to the LORD,
and He will have compassion on him;
and to our God, for He will abundantly pardon.
'For My thoughts are not your thoughts,
neither are your ways My ways,' declares the LORD.
'For as the heavens are higher than the earth,
so are My ways higher than your ways,
and My thoughts than your thoughts.
For as the rain and the snow come down from heaven,
and do not return there without watering the earth,
and making it bear and sprout,
and furnishing seed to the sower and bread to the eater;
So shall My Word be which goes forth from My mouth;
it shall not return to Me empty,
without accomplishing what I desire,
and without succeeding in the matter for which I sent it.'"
(Isaiah 55:6–11)

I believe that the day will come when Joseph will also recognize Yeshua. The people of Israel are God's chosen people, whether they are conscious of that fact or not. They remain God's chosen people even if they refuse and fail to fulfill the task for which they were chosen. The day will surely come when Yeshua will reveal Himself to His people. Then they will accept Him with repentance and remorse: *"In that day a fountain will be opened for the house of David and the inhabitants of Jerusalem, for sin and for impurity"* (Zechariah 13:1). This is the day of which Paul spoke:

"And thus all Israel will be saved; just as it is written,
'The Deliverer will come from Zion.
He will remove ungodliness from Jacob.
This is My covenant with them, when I take away their sins.'"
(Romans 11:26–27)

What a glorious and blessed day awaits us! It is with this day in view that God called, and is still calling, His people to be a kingdom of priests and a holy nation, not to shut themselves away and waste their time on irrelevant relics of the past, but to be a light shining to the world, so that the earth might be filled with *"the knowledge of the LORD as the waters cover the sea"* (Isaiah 11:9). I pray to God that many of the children of Israel will desire to be found faithful to God and to serve the Messiah before He comes as the roaring Lion of Judah *"to judge the living and the dead"* (2 Timothy 4:1).

Come quickly, Lord Jesus!

When they bring you before the synagogues and the rulers and the authorities, do not worry about how or what you are to speak in your defense, or what you are to say; for the Holy Spirit will teach you in that very hour what you ought to say."
(Luke 12:11-12)

Since there are so many misconceptions and lies in the hearts of Israelis concerning Yeshua and the Church, we need to approach them – Israel needs to understand the Gospel of truth and meet true followers of Yeshua!

"Why did nobody ever tell me that a New Covenant was promised to Israel?!" (Jeremiah 31: 31)

So close,
and yet so far -
my kinsmen.

Heart to heart -
conversation about the
true sacrifice,
the Lamb of God,
our Redeemer,
our Lord and Savior!

At the beach. As love and obedience is our drive, we reach the people right where they are.

At times we are rejected. To our deep sorrow some misunderstand Deuteronomy 13, and therefore T-Shirts are torn off our bodies, they spit in our faces, curse, scream and beat us.

However we will not let those very few people stop us from the important task we received directly from God to reach His beloved people with the glorious Gospel of Salvation.
(2 Corinthians 6:4-10)

A Muslim, who came to faith, goes out with us to share the Gospel of Peace - to the Jew first.

"Comfort, O comfort My people," says your God.
"Speak kindly to Jerusalem...
Get yourself up on a high mountain, O Zion, bearer of good news,
Lift up your voice mightily, O Jerusalem, bearer of good news;
Lift it up, do not fear. Say to the cities of Judah, "Here is your God!"
(Isaiah 40:1,2,9)

For Zion's sake I will not keep silent,
And for Jerusalem's sake I will not keep quiet,
Until her righteousness goes forth like brightness,
And her salvation like a torch that is burning. (Isaiah 62:1)

*I have learned that the true comfort has to do
with the presentation of the Gospel.*

Chapter 20

Your people shall be my people and your God, my God

The last two millennia of Jewish history are filled with frightening horror stories about the atrocities that so-called Christians and other anti-Semites have committed against the Jewish people. They began in the very early days of established Christendom, as the teachings of Christ began to take root and spread among heathen nations. Until then, these people had no monotheistic conceptions whatsoever, nor did they have any idea who the God of Israel and His Messiah were.

In the book of Acts in the New Covenant (chapters 10 and 11), we are told that when Yeshua instructed Simon Peter through a vision to go to Caesarea and preach the Gospel to a Gentile family, Peter found it very difficult to believe that he had heard correctly and that this really was the will of God. For him, it was unthinkable to enter into a house of a Gentile—and a Roman, for that matter—and eat with him. Later, he was severely criticized by the rest of the apostles for daring to bring the Gospel of God's salvation to uncircumcised Gentiles. How different is the situation today, when the Gentile Christians marvel at any Jew who finds his way to the Messiah.

Our terrible historical mistake as Jews has been that we have claimed a monopoly on God, as it were, thinking that He belonged only to us. Later, many Gentiles repeated that same error when they accepted the Messiah of Israel by faith, trying deliberately or unwittingly to separate us from Him and to strip Yeshua of all of His Jewishness. By doing so, the Gentiles have deepened the rift that was created at a very early stage between rabbinical and Messianic Judaism.

In addition, many of the idolatrous pagans adopted only the external rites of what they considered a new religion, often integrating and mixing their old pagan rituals with this newly concocted form of Christendom. For example, the worship of the "saints" in the Roman Catholic Church is nothing more than the worship of ancient Greek and Roman pagan deities cloaked in "Christian" garments. The Roman goddess Venus thus became the Virgin Mary, while the rest of the pagan gods became apostles, saints, angels, and patrons. Their statues were placed in cathedrals to be worshipped by the illiterate mobs, who were encouraged by priests and bishops to do so. Every so-called saint was given a special day on the church calendar, which the church at large celebrated. This was also how the traditions associated with Christmas and Easter were established, all of which have little or no scriptural basis whatsoever to support them.

The attitude of some of the church fathers toward the Jews was outrageous. They called the Jews "sons of Satan," "Christ-killers," and "haters of all good things." Priests preached slaughter of the Jews in order to "appease the angry God and reconcile the saints," which were expressions borrowed from the pagan world. Obviously, under such circumstances and in such an atmosphere, Christendom wished to detach itself from Judaism as quickly as possible. Of course, this inclination was mutual.

More than fifteen hundred years of Christian hatred of the Jews passed. Even the Reformation of the sixteenth century did not improve the situation in a meaningful way. The names of the great reformers, including Martin Luther, were associated in the Jewish community with rude, anti-Semitic comments. Many of the Protestant churches inherited from the Catholics their hostile attitude toward the Jews. Although they claimed that the Bible was their only guide in matters of theology, and in spite of the many improvements they made, Protestants retained their distance from Jews, because they, just like their predecessors, believed that God had forsaken His ancient people and had chosen another people instead – the Christian church. This heresy, known as "replacement theology" claims that, under the new covenant in Yeshua, the Church inherited all the blessings promised to the Jews in the Tanach because of the church's faithfulness and obedience to God, while rebellious Israel was left with only the curses of the Law.

Even some of the Christians who saw the truth as it appears in the Scriptures were reluctant to consider the Jews as the chosen people of God, simply on the grounds of God's faithfulness to the patriarchs. These Christians, however, were honest enough to admit that a glorious destiny still awaits the Jews at some time in the future and that they still have an important role to play in the kingdom of God, but only if and when they all convert to Christianity.

Undoubtedly, all such false teachings contain a considerable measure of arrogance and presumption on the part of Gentile

Christians, who consider themselves more righteous, more faithful, and more obedient to God than the wayward Jews. Needless to say, these sentiments of superiority do not find support either in the Bible or in historical reality.

In this context, and for the sake of illustration, I remember the case of Thanus, a young Arab Catholic man whom I met in Jaffa. The many conversations I had with him would have been funny if they were not so sad. Once I visited his home. All the walls were covered with "holy" pictures of the Virgin Mary with baby Jesus in her arms, of Saint George fighting the dragon, a reproduction of Leonardo da Vinci's *The Last Supper*, and a silver crucifix (a representation of Christ on the cross). I could not help thinking about his Jewish religious counterparts, who fill their walls with pictures of rabbis and Jewish "saints." Thanus kept a small cross under the pillow of his bed as a charm against the "evil eye" and for good luck, just like the superstitious charms that Jews keep in their homes. A dusty New Testament, seldom opened, lay on the shelf in his room.

When I spoke with him about the Messiah, Thanus insisted firmly that the Jews must convert to Christianity in order to be saved. I asked him what exactly he meant by the terms "convert to Christianity" and "to be saved." (People may use the same terminology and yet have altogether different meanings in mind, so I wanted to make sure we understood each other correctly.) For him, "to convert" and "to be saved" were synonymous; both meant to join the Roman Catholic Church—in other words, to be a good Catholic, to be baptized by the priest, to attend mass regularly, and to participate in all of the other Catholic rituals.

"Do you really expect a Jew to become a Christian in order to be saved?" I asked. "Yeshua was Jewish, wasn't He? Can you explain to me, Thanus, why a Jew has to change his religion and convert in order to accept his Jewish Messiah?"

"It is true that Jesus was born a Jew," he agreed with me. "But He became a Christian when He was baptized in the Jordan River."

"What is that cross that you have hanging around your neck? Why do you carry it?"

"That is a silly question! I am a Christian, and the cross is the emblem of my religion."

"Did you know that if a person bears the cross only on his neck as a piece of jewelry, instead of carrying it in his life daily, crucifying his own desires and lusts, according to the instructions of Yeshua, the cross will cause death instead of life for him?"

"God forbid!" Thanus quickly made the sign of the cross according to the Catholic custom. "I just wear the cross as my parents and my priest do. All Christians wear crosses and do not think much about it. Anyhow, what is it that makes a Jew like you fascinated with our Christian cross?"

"Thanus, there are many Jews who ask me this same question. They, too, cannot understand why a Jew like me believes in Yeshua, a Man who was hung upon a cross and died shamefully. They would be right if Yeshua had remained in His grave. But, do you remember what happened on the third day?"

"Of course, He rose from the dead!" Thanus boasted with his knowledge.

"And what does that mean to you?" I asked. "Do you know for sure that you have eternal life because Yeshua, who rose from the dead, lives in you? Have you been born again?"

"Of course! I was baptized in the church."

"No, Thanus, I asked you whether or not you were born again. Do you believe that the death and resurrection of Yeshua are your own death and resurrection, too, and that He alone—not the church, not the priest, and not even the Pope himself—can save you and give you true forgiveness of sin?"

Thanus seemed rather confused and embarrassed. He could not tell whether the things that I told him were blunt heresies or the truth of the living God. "Our priest never talked to us about these things," he finally confessed. "We do not believe in such things. This is how the *mujadedin* (Arabic for born-again people) believe."

"This may be what the church says, but what does God say about it? Did you ever read the New Testament?" I asked.

"No, the priest does not allow us to read the New Testament for ourselves. He says that religion is a business for the theologians alone and that only someone who has gone to theological seminary can understand it properly. Every Sunday he explains to us what is written in it, and he even reads to us from the New Testament in Latin."

"You must understand Latin very well then, is that right? Can you understand what the priest is reading?"

"Well, I don't. You see, I'm not such a religious guy. I go to mass only on holidays, and the truth is that since my mother's funeral, I have not gone to mass even on Christmas and Easter. I'm not a religious person, just an ordinary man."

"Do you mean to tell me that even according to your own standards you're not doing your best? If that's true, how can you know where you're going when you die?"

"Nobody can know that." Thanus said meditatively. "If a person leads a good life, prays every day, is baptized, and attends mass regularly, then he has a chance of getting to heaven, and the church may even canonize him as a "saint" many years after his death. If he's bad, he will surely go to hell. But if he's neither a righteous nor a wicked person, he will surely end up in purgatory." (Roman Catholics believe, without scriptural basis, that purgatory is a temporary place where the souls of the dead are purged until they are worthy of heaven.)

"Do you know, Thanus, what the New Testament says about the "new birth"?"

Thanus did not know, which gave me a good opportunity to explain to him the good news of God's salvation through Yeshua the Messiah. Sadly, his prejudices, reservations, and natural inhibitions kept him from giving his life to Yeshua and accepting Him as the Lord of his life. I could only pity him, because this vital relationship with God could have solved so many problems in his life. I discovered it is just as hard for a nominal Christian as it is for a Jew to enter into the kingdom of heaven. Both must accept the lordship of Yeshua and His claim upon their lives.

On one of my trips abroad, I had the chance to sit between an Israeli businessman and a Franciscan monk, who was wearing a thick, brown robe. I remember this incident so clearly because, out of love for my own people as well as out of obedience to the Scripture's instruction to preach the Gospel *"to the Jew first"* (Romans 1:16), I began to speak to the Israeli and introduce the Messiah to him. Somehow I had the feeling that the monk was not a born-again believer. Since the Israeli showed much interest in what I had to say, I decided to illustrate my words with an example to show him that it was not enough to be a "Christian" in order to come into the Kingdom of Heaven. Having already made acquaintance with the monk, I then turned and asked him, "Sir, do you have the confidence that you will go to heaven?"

His answer was very much like that of Thanus: "I sure hope so!"

Next, I asked him, "Let's suppose you're standing at the gates of heaven, and the Lord asks you, 'What makes you think that you can enter?' What would you say to Him?"

The monk's answer was typical: "I did my very best to be good."

"Then, why did Yeshua have to come as a sacrifice, if it is enough for you to 'be good' in order to get into the kingdom?" I made it hard on him.

Just like Thanus, it seemed that he had never asked himself those questions. I opened the Scriptures and asked him to read the following passage:

> *"And you were dead in your trespasses and sins,*
> *In which you formerly walked according to the course of this world, according to the prince of the power of the air,*
> *of the spirit that is now working in the sons of disobedience.*
> *Among them we too all formerly lived in the lusts of our flesh,*
> *indulging the desires of the flesh and of the mind,*
> *and were by nature children of wrath, even as the rest.*
> *But God, being rich in mercy,*
> *because of His great love with which He loved us,*
> *Even when we were dead in our transgressions,*
> *made us alive together with Christ (by grace you have been saved),*
> *And raised us up with Him,*
> *and seated us with Him in the heavenly places, in Christ Jesus,*
> *In order that in the ages to come*
> *He might show the surpassing riches of His grace*
> *in kindness toward us in Christ Jesus.*
> ***For by grace you have been saved through faith;***
> *and that not of yourselves, it is the gift of God;*
> ***Not as a result of works***, *that no one should boast."*

(Ephesians 2:1–9, emphasis added)

I pointed again at the eighth verse: *"For by grace you have been saved through faith; and that not of yourselves, it is the gift of God."* The monk was taken by surprise, as if he had come across this passage for the first time in his life. I used the opportunity to show him some more Scriptures, such as this passage:

"And the witness is this, that God has given us eternal life,
and this life is in His Son.
He who has the Son has the life;
he who does not have the Son of God does not have the life.
These things I have written to you
who believe in the name of the Son of God,
in order that you may know that you have eternal life."
(1 John 5:11–13)

The Israeli businessman, who had listened to my conversation with the monk, seemed amused. I then opened my Bible and showed the Israeli the prophecies in Jeremiah 31 and Ezekiel 36 in which God had promised us Jews a new covenant of forgiveness, a new heart, and a new spirit. I made it clear to him that the whole Messianic faith is based solely on the Tanach, and that anyone who fails to understand this knows neither Yeshua nor the New Testament. The monk served as a living illustration of this truth.

In the face of all the gross anti-Semitism, either concealed or explicit, the phenomenon of Christians who believe in Zionism is like a refreshing breeze in a blazing hot desert. I have already mentioned these Messianic Gentiles who love Israel with all their hearts and who constantly pray for the peace and the prosperity of Israel and Jerusalem. They have recognized the solemn fact that they are in no way any better or superior to any other sinner in the world, Jew or Gentile, and have adopted the words of the apostle Paul on that issue:

"But I am speaking to you who are Gentiles.
For if the root be holy, the branches are too.
But if some of the branches were broken off,
and you, being a wild olive,
were grafted in among them
and became partaker with them of the rich root of the olive tree,
Do not be arrogant toward the branches;
but if you are arrogant,
remember that it is not you who supports the root,
but the root supports you.
You will say then,
'Branches were broken off that I may be grafted in.'
Quite right, they were broken off for their unbelief,
but you stand by your faith.

Do not be conceited, but fear;
For if God did not spare the natural branches,
neither will He spare you.
Behold then the kindness and severity of God;
to those who fell, severity,
but to you, God's kindness,
if you continue in His kindness;
otherwise you also will be cut off.
And they also, if they do not continue in their unbelief,
will be grafted in; for God is able to graft them in again.
For if you were cut off from what is by nature a wild olive tree,
and were grafted contrary to nature into a cultivated olive tree,
how much more shall these who are the natural branches
be grafted into their own olive tree?" (Romans 11:13, 16–24)

Further, we also have this explicit passage:

"Therefore remember, that formerly you, the Gentiles in the
flesh, who are called "Uncircumcision" by the so-called
"Circumcision," which is performed in the flesh by human
hands—
Remember that you were at that time separate from Christ,
excluded from the commonwealth of Israel,
and strangers to the covenants of promise,
having no hope and without God in the world.
But now in Christ Jesus you who formerly were far off
have been brought near by the blood of Christ.
For He Himself is our peace, who made both groups into one,
and broke down the barrier of the dividing wall...
So then you are no longer strangers and aliens,
but you are fellow citizens with the saints,
and are of God's household,
Having been built upon the foundation of the apostles
and prophets, Christ Jesus Himself being the corner stone."
(Ephesians 2:11–14, 19–20)

One can find extreme dedication to the cause of Israel among these Messianic Gentiles, who have truly understood the meaning of the New Covenant's message. Many of them visit Israel frequently.

They donate money, time, and energy for the development of the land. They send their children to work as volunteers in kibbutzim, hospitals, homes for the elderly, and even to serve in the army. They also serve Israel in their own countries, being a very effective pro-Israel lobby for the Zionist cause. For example, many of them pressured the government of the former Soviet Union to release the Jewish "refuseniks" and prisoners. Many people largely owe their liberty and arrival to Israel to these pressures.

Zionist Christian groups do not always agree on all issues. They have controversies about essential matters. However, they are all united in their unrestricted support of Israel's right to exist within her boundaries and in their faith that God's promises to His ancient people are still valid in our day. Together they actively protest against all kinds of international resolutions that condemn Israel.

However, many in the religious establishment in Israel do not approve of the activities of these Zionist Christians and their support for the Jewish state, either because they themselves are anti-Zionists or because they suspect them of having ulterior motives and missionary intentions. The fact is that some who hold key positions in the government are doing their best to hinder them wherever they can. They deny Messianic believers residence in the country as well as refuse to extend the visas of those who are in residence. All in all, they make their lives in Israel miserable.

Sadly, by doing so, the government leaders are cutting off the tree limb on which they are sitting. As we all know, isolated Israel does not have many allies and advocates in the world who love and support her as these Zionist Christians do. I am sure that if the Israeli prime minister were aware of the kind of treatment that has been given to them by the immigration offices, he would implement a change in the policy so that the bond with these allies would be strengthened and built up.

I wholeheartedly believe that the day is drawing near when Isaiah's prophecy regarding the Zionist Christians will literally be fulfilled:

"And nations will come to your light,
and kings to the brightness of your rising...
Then you will see and be radiant,
and your heart will thrill and rejoice;

because the abundance of the sea will be turned to you,
the wealth of the nations will come to you.
...They will bring gold and frankincense,
and will bear good news of the praises of the LORD...
And foreigners will build up your walls,
and their kings will minister to you;
for in My wrath I struck you,
and in My favor I have had compassion on you.
And your gates will be open continually;
they will not be closed day or night,
so that men may bring to you the wealth of the nations,
with their kings led in procession.
For the nation and the kingdom which will not serve you
will perish, and the nations will be utterly ruined....
And the sons of those who afflicted you
will come bowing to you, and all those who despised you
will bow themselves at the soles of your feet;
and they will call you the city of the LORD,
the Zion of the Holy One of Israel." (Isaiah 60:3,5,6,10–12,14)

Our praise and worship throughout Israel open the hearts of many.

Chapter 21

The Rewards of Labor

After several years in my parents' home, the Lord miraculously provided an Arab house for me in the city of Jaffa, not too far from the seashore and the clock tower, and a four-minute walk from where Peter had been given the great vision for the ministry of reconciliation between the Gentiles and the Jews. (See the tenth chapter of Acts.) I never dreamed that God would do this for me, but He knows His children's exact needs, and He is able to supply all of them benevolently and plentifully, in order to enable them to do His will and to fulfill His calling. It still is not the kibbutz of which I had been dreaming, but it serves to illustrate the scriptural principle that says, *"Many are the plans in a man's heart, but the counsel of the LORD, it will stand"* (Proverbs 19:21).

One morning, the telephone rang. Johan, a dear friend from Holland, was on the line. "Jacob!" he exclaimed with his typical enthusiasm, "I am at the Ben-Gurion Airport with a group of twenty friends from abroad. May we come over to see you?"

Johan is one of those people whose charm is irresistible. He will not accept "no" for an answer. Besides, who would want to refuse one who loves the Lord and the Jewish people so much?

Soon I found myself together with these precious friends. After a brief introduction, we began to sing the Lord's praises, and the joy was great. We prayed and read the encouraging Scriptures, and I explained to them the Israeli way of thinking and how to relate the Gospel within the Jewish perspective—from the context of the Old Testament, especially the Torah.

We then prepared bags and filled them with Gospel tracts, which we intended to distribute to the people at the street corners. We stood at the junction of Allenby Street and Rothchild Boulevard, when suddenly I heard a commotion across the street. An elderly orthodox Jew, his white beard waving in the wind, was quaking with excitement, waving his hands, and screaming at the top of his voice, "Oy vey, *Yeeden* (Jews)! Help! Missionaries! Obscenity!"

Within minutes, an aroused, angry mob gathered around one of the young women from our group. She was a Scandinavian who did not know a word of Hebrew besides *shalom*, and who did not have the faintest idea what had caused her to attract so much attention. The hostile crowd fell upon her with clenched fists and eyes blazing with hatred.

"You dirty missionary!"

"Go home, you Nazi pig! You're even worse than the Nazis! The Nazis burnt our bodies, but you're burning our souls!"

"That's all we need here—missionaries!"

As I saw from a distance that they were about to lynch her, I crossed the street at a run, trying to draw the fire to myself.

"Jews!" I shouted above the commotion, "Jews, what on earth are you doing, for heaven's sake? Is there no heart in you? Can't you see that she doesn't understand a word you're saying? Leave her alone and let her go!"

Suddenly the whole mob turned against me. "She's a Christian! She's a missionary! She brings us Jesus!" I heard them complain.

"So what?" I played the innocent. "Is it against the law? Does this offense justify such acts of violence? It doesn't befit Jews to behave like this!"

"But she preaches Yeshu and calls us to believe in Him!" The old man was shaking with indignation.

"Sir, calm down. I don't know what you're talking about. She didn't speak to anyone about Yeshu. His name is Yeshua, and He is the Savior of Israel."

The commotion grew louder, as now the angry crowd began to shout obscenities at me. For them it was so clear: Yeshua belongs to the Gentiles and not to the Jews. This is how the rabbis had taught them, and this is how they think it ought to be.

As the shouting intensified, I continued to cry out loud, "You are doing exactly what your forefathers did to the prophets of old. They stoned them to death then, and today you, their children, will not pay attention to the Word of God. Today, just as then, you continue to create your god in your own image and likeness. Your god allows you to lie, to commit adultery, to steal, and to murder. But this is not the Lord God of Israel! The God of Abraham, Isaac, and Jacob wants to dwell within you by His Holy Spirit, so He sent Yeshua in order to forgive your sins, if you will only believe in Him and repent."

The uproar drew a lot of attention to us, and more people came over out of curiosity to find out what it was all about and asked us for our tracts. This made the mob all the more furious.

"To hell with you and your prophets! This Jesus Christ of yours, curse you and all the prophets!" someone swore, quivering with anger. "We believe only in God, do you hear me? Only in God!"

"Yes, yes! Only in God!" The excited mob caught up with him and continued to boil, everyone adding his own fuel to the bonfire. "We don't need you here, you stinking missionaries! Go, go to your own country! Go tell the Gentiles about your Jesus!"

The heated argument between me and the furious mob of about fifty people, who screamed at me like a choir, went on and on. When I realized that it was practically impossible to talk logic and common sense to so many hotheaded and upset people, I tried to break the siege and go my way. But some of them followed me for several blocks, shouting obscenities at me that echoed all over the place.

"You traitor, troubler of Israel! You sold your soul to the Gentiles! *"Your destroyers and demolishers will come out of your own ranks"* (Isaiah 49:17, author's translation)."

Several religious young men, encouraged by the originator of the uproar, began to hit me hard, trying to snatch my bag of tracts out of my hands. I resisted and held the bag with all my strength. Three young men knocked me down to the ground, while the old man stood above them and gave them orders, "Go on, take that bag from him! Its contents must be burned!"

I curled on the ground, trying to protect my head with the bag that I still tenaciously clung to. Somehow the young men overcame me and managed to pull the bag out of my grasp. They threw all the literature on the sidewalk. Someone lit a match, and within seconds all the tracts caught fire. Then they discovered a New Testament on the pavement. One picked it up, waved it triumphantly above his head, and yelled, "Hey, see what I've got! This is what he wants to bring to us!" He threw it into the fire.

I did not even try to stop them. I knew that even if they incinerated all the books in the world that spoke about Yeshua, they would still be unable to destroy God's truth. *"The good pleasure of the LORD will prosper in His hand"* (Isaiah 53:10). It was only after they had managed to take the tracts away from me and to vent all their fury upon the bundle of papers that they finally let me go.

I got up, bruised and injured. Somebody must have called the police, but when they finally came, the crowd had dispersed. Only one man, who wore a kippah, remained on the spot to enjoy the results of the riot. After a short investigation, the police loaded both of us into the police car and took us to the station.

At the police station, we were both interrogated, and when the policeman was convinced that the young man had been actively involved in the fight and the burning of the tracts, he accepted my complaint against him and opened a criminal file against him, charging him with disturbing the public order and with physical assault.

"But this man is a missionary! He preached Jesus to the people!" the young man insisted.

"We have no law forbidding it in the State of Israel. The distribution of propaganda and advertisement is not against the law, as long as it does not endanger the security of the state or contain pornographic or obscene materials. As I can see here, these leaflets belong to none of these categories."

"But this tract entices people to religious conversion! It offends our religious sentiments."

"If you saw that an offense was being committed," the policeman said patiently, "you should have picked up the phone and called the police. Under no circumstances should you take the law into your own hands and act with violence."

"But I wasn't alone!" The young man tried to vindicate himself. "There were at least fifty people there, and everybody was shouting together. I didn't even know what it was all about!"

"That does not exempt you from responsibility. Do you expect me to believe that you physically attacked a man without even knowing what he did and why you were assaulting him? Come on, I would expect more sense than that from you!"

I genuinely felt sorry for the man. After the statements were taken, and realizing the severity of the penalty he had to pay as a consequence, I turned to the police officer and said, "Listen, I am willing to compromise. If this young man agrees to apologize, to confess his guilt, and to ask for forgiveness, I will be willing to forget all about it and drop the charges."

Two sets of eyes looked at me with surprise. The policeman certainly did not expect to hear such a reaction from me, and the defendant could hardly believe his own ears. The former stared at me with an inquiring look, and the latter blushed and nodded his head.

I looked him straight in the eyes and extended my hand to him. He hesitated and then shook my hand.

We left the room together, and he turned to me and said, "I really appreciate what you have done. I could have gotten into serious trouble. I'm sorry for the whole business."

"Don't mention it, I forgave you long before you even asked me to. Actually, I was not angry at you at all. I think that if I were in your place, I would probably have acted in the same manner. I just wanted you to realize how serious this offense was. God does not neglect or overlook our sins either. He knows that we all deserve the penalty of death for our sin. But still, He loved you and me so much that He was willing to pay the penalty and to carry the punishment for our sins by Himself. For this reason He sent Yeshua to us. You may be happy now for your release, but you still do not know what true happiness is. Wait until you receive total forgiveness for all your sins through the Messiah!" The man smiled, waved his hand, and disappeared down the street.

When I first started my evangelistic work, I experienced many violent incidents, but they have gradually subsided with the passing years. Until recently, many Jews were convinced that there must be some mysterious, monstrous entity that they called "the mission", which spreads its octopus arms out all over the world, especially in our holy land, and thrives on human souls. They thought the only purpose for its existence was to snatch innocent, ignorant Jews and force them to convert to Christianity. This strange idea, which still prevails today among many of the religious Jews, probably originated in the distorted approach of the Catholic Church to the Jewish people during the last two millennia, as they tried to force conversion on the Jews under threats of execution. These methods of compulsion are essentially contrary to the basic principles of the Gospel.

Happily, many Israelis are beginning to realize that we, Messianic Jews, are real Jews and are not in the business of pushing Christianity on anyone. There are many people in the country who, like myself and the Trumpet of Salvation to Israel ministry teams, strongly believe that spreading the truth about Yeshua the Messiah is extremely important, in order to let others know the facts so they can make intelligent choices. The Messianic faith is a matter of personal choice for each individual. One cannot be born into it or impose it on another by force. The word *missionary* actually means a person who has been sent out to accomplish a certain assigned task. However, because of their sad history, the Jews have added negative connotations to this term.

To my regret, the rabbinical establishment continues to use every possible means, including the mass media, which it generally despises, to lead the people astray and to build into them fear and rejection toward anything that has to do with Yeshua Son of David. But God said to them, *"Devise a plan but it will be thwarted; state a proposal, but it will not stand, for God is with us"* (Isaiah 8:10). In His faithfulness, the Lord is opening the eyes of His people to distinguish between the rabbinical religion and the Jewish Messianic faith. The increasing numbers of Israelis who are coming to Yeshua by faith and the Messianic congregations that are rapidly spreading all over the country bear witness to that fact.

The truth is, for every person who curses and attacks us, hoping to kill us and our ministry, there are a thousand Israelis who are willing to listen to the *"words of eternal life"* (John 6:68). In Deuteronomy 13:5–9, Israel was commanded by God to kill anyone who brought other gods into their midst. We need to understand the original source of our attackers' hatred and have compassion on them for their blind belief that Yeshua is a false god and for their distorted attempts to obey God's instructions.

It seems that the circle is closing. The Gospel originated with the Jewish people in the land of Israel and spread from there to the uttermost parts of the earth. Now, with our return to our homeland, the Gospel has returned, too. From this city of Jaffa (or Joppa) the Gospel went forth to the first of the Gentiles, the Roman centurion Cornelius, who lived in Caesarea. (See Acts 10.) Now, almost two thousand years later, it is preached here in Jaffa again.

On another occasion, I was besieged by four ultraorthodox yeshiva students on a main street of downtown Jerusalem. They did not talk much—as a matter of fact, they did not say a word. They just pummeled me with their fists on the back of my head, which made me drop the bag off my shoulder, and then they directed their fists straight to my face. Blood began to gush from my nose and stain my clothes. I began to shout, "Police, police!" and the four disappeared as if swallowed by the earth. I got up gingerly and crossed the street, frustrated and angry with myself for not seizing the rare opportunity to fulfill Yeshua's commandment:

"Blessed are you when men hate you, and ostracize you,
and cast insults at you, and spurn your name as evil,
for the sake of the Son of Man.
Be glad in that day, and leap for joy,
for behold, your reward is great in heaven;
for in the same way their fathers used to treat the prophets. "
(Luke 6:22–23)

"But be on your guard; for they will deliver you to the courts,
and you will be flogged in the synagogues,
and you will stand before governors and kings for My sake,
as a testimony to them. " (Mark 13:9)

Here I had a wonderful opportunity to stand up, injured and beaten as I was, and to testify before the gathering crowd about Yeshua, but I did not. The incident had happened so quickly that the crowd did not understand what had occurred. If only I had taken this chance to stand there and preach the message of salvation, even with my face bleeding profusely! This was the same way the Gospel began to spread in the streets of Jerusalem so many years ago. The prophets, the apostles, and the first disciples paid with their blood for the privilege of being the couriers of the Word of God, and this is probably how the circle will be finally closed in these last days. I often wonder who will be privileged to suffer martyrdom, offering themselves as literal sacrifices on the altar for Israel's spiritual resurrection.

Whenever I remember such incidents, my heart is filled anew with awe and wonder at the magnificent truth of our God:

"But to the degree that you share the sufferings of Christ,
keep on rejoicing; so that also at the revelation of His glory,
you may rejoice with exultation.
If you are reviled for the name of Christ, you are blessed,
because the Spirit of glory and of God rests upon you. "
(1 Peter 4:13–14)

I was blessed beyond words that marvelous day. I was filled with happiness and bliss in the storm. While I stood there, assaulted and bleeding, a wonderful sense of tranquility overwhelmed me, and I could stay quietly in my place without even trying to fight back. I felt embraced in the everlasting arms of my loving, omnipotent Father. It was a peace that was totally independent of any external circumstances, the kind of peace that the world does not know and has never experienced. The extraordinary inner peace, happiness, and divine rest that enveloped my spirit was even far beyond my own understanding. Over the years I have learned that God has a unique spirit of glory and rest in store for those who are being persecuted. This spirit I have not experienced in my prayer closet, in studying the Scriptures, or in worship, but only in the midst of the battle.

I walked slowly to a nearby hospital where I received first aid. It was a very special experience to look defeated, miserable, and trampled, and yet to feel triumphant with a victory of which only the inner man is aware—to be able not to retaliate, but rather to conquer evil with good! Truly, this was the power of the Messiah who works within the spirits of God's redeemed.

Many thoughts bothered me that night. I prayed for those who had attacked me, with the words of Yeshua: *"Father, forgive them; for they do not know what they are doing"* (Luke 23:34). I wasn't angry with them, nor did I hate them. I could see their faces, distorted with wrath, and imagined them returning proudly to their yeshiva, boasting to their friends and the rabbi about catching a missionary and disfiguring him completely. I could also imagine the rabbi praising their bravery and encouraging the other students as well to go out and wage a "holy war" against "those missionaries."

God knew best how to comfort me in my pain. He brought to my mind memories of the Messianic conference, in which I had recently participated, that had brought together Jewish and Arab believers. I thought to myself, *"How great are Thy works, O LORD! Thy thoughts are very deep. A senseless man has no knowledge; nor does a stupid man understand this"* (Psalm 92:5–6). Arabs and Jews, who for so many years have been living in ongoing hostility and distrust, are now being born again, learning how to love and forgive each other, and holding conferences that governments of this world would pay fortunes to be able to sponsor.

In awe, I had witnessed Jews confessing their mistreatment of the Arabs during their military service and asking the Arab believers for forgiveness. Likewise, the Arabs confessed the abysmal hatred that they had developed against the Jews and their natural lust to take revenge and retaliate, and asked the Jewish believers to forgive them.

The Arabs prayed and asked God to put an end to acts of terrorism and violence, and pleaded for the peace of Jerusalem and for the salvation of Israel. We, the Jews, prayed for the Arabs, knowing that they were living "between a rock and a hard place" and asked God to work in the hearts of His people so that they might learn how to treat these strangers with appropriate measures of kindness and mercy. After pouring out our hearts in prayers and supplications, we sang hymns of praise and worship to our Lord, the God of Israel, together. These Arabs knew very well that they were worshipping the God who has chosen Israel out of all the nations.

I lay in bed, my face swollen like an overblown balloon and my eyes masked with dark purplish circles. I prayed, "How long, Lord? We have returned to our country as though saved from the fire. *"Unless the LORD of hosts had left us a few survivors, we would be like Sodom, we would be like Gomorrah"* (Isaiah 1:9). We have made the desert blossom like a rose; we have restored and rebuilt the desolate towns; but what about our hearts? Our souls are still as dry and thirsty as a barren wilderness, and we are panting hungrily for Your presence, O Lord! Please, God, forgive us of our sins and remove that blindness, that veil that causes us to stumble and fall continually.

Where is that light that is supposed to shine brightly in our lives? Not the limelight of fame that fails, not the light of the Hanukkah candles that is nothing but a beautiful tradition. We desire the light of Your presence, Lord! We want to be Your witnesses, bearing Your testimony, not only with our words and by our mere existence, but also by the way we live. Let Your face shine on us, Lord, and on those attackers, too. Cause them to fall at Your feet in true and complete repentance, through faith in Yeshua the Messiah, so that their temple will truly become *"a house of prayer for all the peoples"* (Isaiah 56:7)."

I fell asleep with this prayer still on my lips, knowing that the long-expected day of redemption will surely come and realizing that the blessings of that day will be my eternal reward.

Religion can not bring the answers to the true need of man's heart,
we have to explain to them the difference betwen
biblical and rabbinical Judaism...

"For not knowing about God's righteousness
and seeking to establish their own, they did not subject themselves
to the righteousness of God. For Christ is the end of the law for
righteousness to everyone who believes." (Romans 10:3-4)

Chapter 22

Festivals and Covenants

"Do you, as Messianic Jews, celebrate the feasts of Israel?" People often ask us this question, which puts us constantly on the defensive, as if we have cut ourselves off from Judaism.

We Messianic Jews are an integral part of the Israeli population. Some of us came from secular backgrounds, and others came from religious, even ultraorthodox, families. There are some people among us who live in cities, some in *kibbutzim* (communal farming settlements), and some in *moshavim* (cooperative settlements of small, individual farms). Some served in the Israeli Defense Force, and others did not.

The same diversity applies regarding the Jewish festivals. Some celebrate the *Passover Seder* (order, arrangement for the Passover meal) in the traditional way, while others add explanations of the Messianic symbolism.

If one speaks about "Messianic Jews" as a homogeneous entity, the answer might be more or less in the affirmative: yes, of course, we celebrate the feasts of Israel. We keep the feasts perhaps more carefully than many other Jews. We do not regard them as ancient and outdated rituals; instead, Yeshua HaMashiach, who is the final and ultimate goal of the whole Torah, stands constantly before our eyes, and we see that He is the focal point of each and every festival. All the feasts point to Him; we only have to open our spiritual eyes to see.

Passover is a case in point. Through the years of my stay in the country, I always kept *Pesach* (the Passover) with my family. However, since my mother passed away, the seder has not been the same anymore, and so I attended a Messianic Jewish Pesach seder for the first time. The seder was held in one of the Messianic congregations in the center of the country. I was full of expectation as I arrived at the meeting hall, which was thoroughly cleaned, whitewashed, and decorated with fresh flowers. The tables were magnificently arranged with new silverware, china dishes, crystal wine goblets, and baskets full of square *matzoth* (wafers of unleavened bread eaten especially at the Passover). Slowly the guests walked into the room and took their places at the arranged tables. The leader of the seder and his wife sat at the head of the table, and a beautiful *Hagadah* (a book of traditional readings) was laid at each place setting.

The leader then stood up and said, "The Pesach festival is the feast of our liberation, to commemorate our coming forth out of the slavery of Egypt into the freedom of God's people. The whole household of Israel celebrates the Pesach at this hour, to remember that first Pesach in Egypt. For Messianic Jews, however, there is a double reason to rejoice and celebrate: our eternal Passover Lamb, our Lord Yeshua, the Messiah, was offered for us and redeemed us with His blood from the slavery of sin, the flesh, and the Devil, and brought us out triumphantly into everlasting life in the kingdom of God. *"If therefore the Son shall make you free, you shall be free indeed"* (John 8:36)."

The seder itself was conducted in the traditional manner, as performed in every observant Jewish home. Periodically, the leader stopped the flow in order to expound on one point or another in the light of the new covenant. Instead of washing his hands before reading the hagadah, as is commonly done, we read the narrative of Yeshua as He washed the feet of His disciples at the beginning of the Last Supper, right at this very point in their seder. When saying the traditional blessing over the unleavened bread, the leader explained that this blessing refers to Yeshua Himself, who is *"the living bread that came down out of heaven"* (John 6:51), who was brought *"forth [as] food from the earth"* (Psalm 104:14) when He was raised from the dead.

As our leader said the blessing over the wine, he demonstrated that this blessing spoke of us, the modern-day disciples of Yeshua, who are "the fruit of the True Vine," with this explanation: "Yeshua said to His disciples concerning Himself, *"I am the vine, and you are the branches; he who abides in Me, and I in him, he bears much fruit"* (John 15:5). We, who are also His disciples, are therefore that blessed 'fruit of the Vine.'"

I was most deeply impressed by the traditional *afikoman*. While I was still in my father's home, I had always wondered what the origin and meaning was of that strange practice with its impossible name. Only now, at the Messianic seder, it finally made sense to me.

The three matzoth that were put on the seder table represented not only the three ranks within the Jewish nation—priests, Levites, and Israelites—or the three patriarchs—Abraham, Isaac, and Jacob—but also the three Persons of the Deity—Father, Son, and Holy Spirit. It was the middle *matzah*, the one that represented the Son, that was broken, as a symbol of the Messiah's body that was broken for us on the cross (1 Corinthians 11:24).

A part of this broken matzah is wrapped in a cloth and hidden until the end of the festive meal, while the other piece is restored to its original place between the two other matzoth. Likewise, Yeshua's body was wrapped in a burial linen cloth and temporarily hidden in the grave while, at the same time, He returned to His divine position with the Father and the Spirit. After the meal, the children search for the hidden piece of matzah, and the happy discoverer must bring it to the leader to have it "redeemed." The child is rewarded with a promised gift, which must be presented to him no later than *Shavuot* (Pentecost), even as Yeshua the Messiah was raised victoriously from the tomb, and all who find Him receive from the heavenly Father the gift of the Holy Spirit, with a new heart and a new spirit.

On that night I understood that the complete story of salvation is concealed symbolically in the ancient customs of Passover, which most Jews celebrate year after year without having the slightest clue concerning its profound meaning!

I also liked the ancient prayer formula that was repeated so many times during the ceremony: "I am ready and prepared to fulfill the commandment…for the unification of the name of the Holy One, blessed be He, and His *Shekinah* (Divine Presence), through Him who is hidden and concealed, and in the name of all Israel!" Through this prayer, the whole household of Israel sanctifies and unifies the name of the Father, here called "The Holy One, blessed be He," and the Holy Spirit, "His Shekinah," through "Him who is hidden and concealed," who is none other than the Lord Yeshua the Messiah and who is still concealed from their eyes.

This particular Pesach seder was so impressive for me because I found out that there is something essential missing from the traditional Jewish seder—the Pesach Lamb Himself. Today the Jews actually celebrate only the Feast of the Matzoth (Feast of Unleavened Bread), because they do not have the Pesach at all. As a matter of fact, the whole modern-day seder ceremony came about just to replace that main thing that was missing. Only one who knows Yeshua, the sinless Lamb of God, realizes that the true Pesach Lamb has already been offered, and that what we do today is actually a memorial service to Him who said, *"Do this... in remembrance of Me... as often as you eat this bread and drink the cup"* (1 Corinthians 11:25–26).

Limited space constrains me from going into detail concerning every meaning of the Pesach night in the Messianic Jewish thinking. One thing was made clear, though: Moses delivered us from physical slavery and prepared the way for us to enter into the Promised Land; in comparison, Yeshua saved us from our spiritual servitude to sin and brought us forth into the liberty of the people of God. Yeshua prepared the road for us that leads us safely into the eternal, glorious kingdom of God.

Shavuot (Pentecost) is the feast during which the first fruits were brought into the Temple after the expiration of the fifty days of counting the *omer* (the period of expectancy between Passover and Pentecost). According to rabbinical tradition, Shavuot commemorates the day that the people received the Torah on Mount Sinai. The New Covenant tells us that on this same day, the Holy Spirit came upon the first disciples of Yeshua in Jerusalem. This day is actually the birthday of the early Messianic congregation and the fulfillment of the promised new covenant: *"I will give you a new heart and...a new spirit...and I will put My Spirit within you"* (Ezekiel 36:26–27). On Shavuot, two loaves of bread were traditionally offered to God in the Temple. This offering symbolized the whole Messianic community, which is composed of both Jews and Gentiles.

At *Sukkot* (Feast of Tabernacles or Ingathering), having gathered all his harvest into his barns, the farmer celebrated the harvest with a feast. Unlike the two other festivals of Pesach and Shavuot, the feast of Sukkot has not been fully realized yet. The ultimate fulfillment of it will only occur when Yeshua will come at the sound of the last trumpet to gather His elect unto Himself and take them to heaven. (Will this be the last *shofar*, or ram's horn trumpet, blown at the end of Yom Kippur?) Then it will truly be the Feast of the Ingathering. All the nations who will survive the last great war and will remain in the world after that event, will come up annually to Jerusalem to worship the Lord God of Hosts and celebrate the feast of Sukkot, according to the prophecy of Zechariah (chapter 14).

In this context, I must mention Yom Kippur, with its detailed description in Leviticus 16. There is a vast difference between Yom Kippur as it is celebrated today, according to the Yoma section of the Talmud, and the biblical Day of Atonement. Today, there is no temple and no sacrifice; therefore, the people of Israel have no atonement, since there is no real atonement without the shedding of blood (Hebrews 9:22). The substitute that the rabbis have concocted, according to which "prayer and penitence and righteous alms remove the evil decree," explicitly expresses how great their frustration is because of that fact.

Only one who knows Yeshua realizes that the ultimate, final, perfect atonement has already been made, once and for all. Because Yeshua, through His sacrificial death, tore down the veil that separates us from Holy of Holies and the presence of God, He has secured everlasting salvation for all who trust in Him. The Messianic Jews are sure that their names are eternally inscribed and sealed forever in the Lamb's Book of Life, while all the rest of the Jews just wish one another *"Gemar hatimah tovah"* (May your name be inscribed in the Book of Life), putting all their trust in their prayer and fasting, which, according to the Torah, cannot remove sin.

I am often asked, concerning the *Sabbath*, if Messianic Jews observe the Shabbat to keep it holy, according to the *Halachah* (the collective body of Jewish religious laws derived from the Written and Oral Torah). Here, too, the answer may be in the positive and the negative at the same time. We do keep the Sabbath holy unto the Lord, but we do not regard the rabbinical traditional prohibitions as binding. Yeshua called Himself *"Lord of the Sabbath"* (Matthew 12:8); thus, He is not enslaved by the traditional Shabbat regulations, and neither are we. It is true that we have the privilege to rest on that holy day from all the labors of this world and rejoice in the Lord our God, but what if this involves traveling? I am sure that even Moses himself, if he lived with us today, would go by car to the congregational hall and back home, if it were necessary. If rejoicing in the Sabbath rest involves healing suffering people or accommodating visitors who come from far away, then we do it willingly unto the Lord. In the long run, every one of us has to give an account for his deeds and failures before the Lord alone. After all, *"these are* [the festivals and] *the appointed times of the LORD"* (Leviticus 23:37) and not our own. I deeply desire that the church would lay aside the Christmas Santas and Easter eggs and would embrace and celebrate these God-appointed commemorations.

So much more could be said about these wonderfully symbolic holy days. In the same way that these feasts, which the Lord has commanded us to observe, point so clearly to the Messiah, so also do the three covenants that He made with us. When we look at each of the covenants, we can see Yeshua in all of them. Let's look first at the covenant God made with Abraham.

The Abrahamic Covenant

"Now the LORD said to Abram,
'Go forth from your country, and from your relatives
and from your father's house, to the land which I will show you;
And I will make you a great nation, and I will bless you,
and make your name great; and so you shall be a blessing;
And I will bless those who bless you,
and the ones who curse you I will curse.
And in you all the families of the earth shall be blessed.'"
(Genesis 12:1–3)

It is important to note that this passage contains three unconditional promises:

1. **The promise concerning the land:** God promised to show Abraham the land that He promised to give to his descendants as an everlasting inheritance.

2. **The promise regarding the seed:** God promised Abraham offspring.

3. **The promise about the blessing:** God promised that Abraham's descendants would be a blessing to all the families of the earth.

Truly, in Yeshua the Messiah, the spiritual children of Abraham—all the true believers, both Jewish and Gentile—have become a blessing to all the families of the earth.

But what, in fact, is a covenant? To begin with, a covenant is a binding agreement made between two or more parties. After God gave Abraham these promises, He sealed them with two covenants, "the covenant between the parts" (see Genesis 15) and the "covenant of circumcision" (see Genesis 17). In both cases, He gave Abraham several unconditional promises. Abraham did not have to do anything in order to make God keep those promises, except to bring the animals for the sacrifice and to circumcise all the males in his household. But, one thing was essential in both cases: in order to make a covenant, blood must be shed. Every covenant with God must involve blood.

In biblical times, covenants such as peace treaties, defense agreements, and brotherhood pacts were also made between people. Every covenant involved a feast and a meal that was an inseparable part of the celebration. Each party presented his conditions, and at the signing of the covenant, blood had to be shed, which validated it and made it binding for both sides. For this reason, when a circumcised man converts to Judaism, "covenant blood" must still be drawn from him.

The Sinai Covenant

At the foot of Mount Sinai, Moses made a covenant with God for Israel. We read this about it:

> *"And he sent young men of the sons of Israel,*
> *and they offered burnt offerings and sacrificed young bulls*
> *as peace offerings to the LORD.*
> *And Moses took half of the blood and put it in basins,*
> *and the other half of the blood he sprinkled on the altar.*
> *Then he took the book of the covenant*
> *and read it in the hearing of the people;*
> *and they said, 'All that the LORD has spoken, we will do,*
> *and we will be obedient!'*
> *So Moses took the blood and sprinkled it on the people,*
> *and said, 'Behold the blood of the covenant,*
> *which the LORD has made with you in accordance*
> *with all these words.'"* (Exodus 24:5–8)

God made an unconditional covenant with Abraham, who was only required to exercise faith, for Abraham *"believed in the LORD; and He reckoned it to him as righteousness"* (Genesis 15:6). In contrast, the covenant made at Sinai had a very important condition attached to it: uncompromising, total obedience to God's Torah.

"Now, it shall be, if you will diligently obey the LORD your God,
being careful to do all His commandments
which I command you today,
the LORD your God
will set you high above all the nations of the earth.?
But it shall come about,
if you will not obey the LORD your God,
to observe to do all His commandments and His statutes
with which I charge you today,
then all these curses shall come upon you and overtake you."
(Deuteronomy 28:1,15)

The condition God posed in the Sinai covenant was therefore
one of total obedience to the Torah, to keep it to the letter; not just
the parts of it that we find attractive or easy to handle, not only those
that seem logical and that make sense to us, but each and every one of
them. God said that He would put under His curse every person who
failed to keep His commandments and statutes literally, to the most
minute detail.

"Cursed is he who does not confirm the words of this law by
doing them. And all the people shall say, 'Amen.'"
(Deuteronomy 27:26)

Now, is there one single person in the whole world who can truly
testify about himself that he has always kept every single aspect of
the Torah, literally and in full, without failing or sinning even once
in all his life? If there is one, then that person makes God a liar,
because the Scriptures declare that *"there is no man who does not*
sin" (1 Kings 8:46) and *"there is not a righteous man on earth who*
continually does good and who never sins" (Ecclesiastes 7:20). In
other words, every single person has failed miserably in keeping the
Torah.

The people of Israel still consider themselves bound to God by
the covenant of Sinai. But in God's eyes, this covenant was broken
by Israel even before it was made. Moses was still on his way down
from the top of the mountain with the tablets of the covenant in his
hands, while the people were dancing wildly and lewdly around
the golden calf, which they had demanded Aaron to make for them

because of their impatience with Moses. Thus, they broke the first commandment, which forbade idolatry! Was this only a one-time failure, an exceptional lapse in the history of the Jewish people? Or, was there a period in the history of our ancient people during which we did not fall into worshipping idols, gods made of wood and stone, gold and silver, materialism and religion, until we were forced to be exiled from our land because of "idolatry, incest, and bloodshed"?

One may be misled into thinking that God intentionally mixes Himself up with a problem that seems to have no solution. On the one hand, in the covenant that He made with our father Abraham, He promised to make us a blessing to all the families of the earth and called us to be a light to the Gentiles. On the other hand, He gave us a Torah of righteousness and truth that none of us can keep, thus putting us under His curse. However, there is a way out of that dilemma, because God never intended to curse us. He never forsook His covenant people of Israel. Even before He exiled us from our own land, even before He allowed His first Temple to be destroyed, He already promised us through the prophet Jeremiah that He was going to visit His people again by making a new covenant with them.

The New Covenant

As we have already seen, the new covenant is not a Christian invention at all. It is a promise that God made to His people, because the people, not God, broke the Sinai covenant.

" 'Behold, days are coming,' declares the LORD,
'when I will make a new covenant with the house of Israel
and with the house of Judah,
Not like the covenant which I made with their fathers
in the day I took them by the hand
to bring them out of the land of Egypt,
My covenant which they broke,
although I was a husband to them,' declares the LORD.
'But this is the covenant which I will make with the house of
Israel after those days,' declares the LORD,
'I will put my law within them,
and on their heart I will write it;

and I will be their God, and they shall be My people.
And they shall not teach again,
each man his neighbor and each man his brother, saying,
'Know the LORD,' for they shall all know Me,
from the least of them to the greatest of them,' declares the
LORD, 'for I will forgive their iniquity,
and their sin I will remember no more.'" (Jeremiah 31:31–34)

Obviously, God promised that He was going to make and seal a new covenant between Himself and His people, the house of Israel and the house of Judah, to replace the covenant of Sinai that had been broken. God stated very clearly that it was the people of Israel who had broken His covenant, although God had kept it as a faithful husband. However, when one of the parties breaks a covenant, the second party is released from any obligation he previously had in connection with that solemn agreement. Therefore, God did not promise Israel that He was going to renew the old covenant, which could not be kept anyway because of its impossible conditions. Instead, He promised to make an altogether new covenant, validated by His own faithfulness and love.

The Sinai covenant was made on a basis that was not only shaky, but actually impossible. No man has ever been able to keep the Torah wholly and without fail. This was also the reason why God provided a way out through the sacrificial system. All the claims of the modern-day Jew, that he can approach God himself without any need for a mediator, are utterly false and show a lack of basic understanding regarding the office of the priesthood. Notice God's promise in Jeremiah: *"For I will forgive their iniquity, and their sin I will remember no more."* How could God promise us forgiveness and remission of sins without first providing the sacrifice? According to the Scriptures, there must be a sacrifice to cleanse sinners:

"So Moses took the blood and sprinkled it on the people,
and said, 'Behold the blood of the covenant,
which the LORD has made with you in accordance
with all these words.'" (Exodus 24:8)

"Therefore even the first covenant
was not inaugurated without blood.

For when every commandment had been spoken
by Moses to all the people according to the Law,
he took the blood of the calves and the goats,
with water and scarlet wool and hyssop,
and sprinkled both the book itself and all the people,
Saying, 'This is the blood of the covenant
which God commanded you.'
And in the same way he sprinkled both the tabernacle
and all the vessels of the ministry with the blood.
And according to the Law, one may almost say,
all things are cleansed with blood,
and without shedding of blood there is no forgiveness."
(Hebrews 9:18–22)

"As for you also, because of the blood of My covenant with you,
I have set your prisoners free from the waterless pit".
(Zechariah 9:11)

This is why our people pray and ask God to regard their petitions and supplications as if they had offered their sacrifices according to the Torah. However, God does not ask us to replace our sacrifices with prayers, because such a substitution is not acceptable to Him. All He asks us to do is to accept His covenant, which He has sealed with the blood of the eternal, spotless Lamb of God, the everlastingly satisfactory Sacrifice. God does not demand anything from us except that we accept by faith what He so graciously provided for us through His new covenant—a new heart and a new spirit, which will lead us to follow Him out of a love that stems from His love and forgiveness of our sins. All these blessings are fulfilled in the new covenant, through the death and resurrection of Yeshua the Messiah, because His blood was *"shed for many for the remission of sins"* (Matthew 26:28 NKJV).

The tragedy of the people of Israel throughout the millennia of their existence may be traced back to this principle. We have considered the receiving of the Torah a sign of our uniqueness as a nation before God, but we failed to see that we have actually been called to be an army of evangelists, *"a kingdom of priests and a holy nation"* (Exodus 19:6), to bear the testimony of God to the world. In Yeshua the Messiah, God actually fulfilled His promise that the people of Israel would become a blessing to all the families of the earth and a light to the Gentiles. The fact that many Gentiles twisted and distorted the Word of God does not negate this fulfillment; it only points again to the sinful nature of man. Haven't we Jews also perverted the truths of Moses and the prophets by misinterpreting them as closed yeshivas, ultraorthodox communes, and special privileges?

God is not limited to man's ways, however. He gave this world the new covenant, sealed with the blood of the Messiah, exactly as He had promised. We Jews have left it to the Christians to do the work that was originally assigned to us, because it was they who translated our Hebrew Bible into more than fourteen hundred languages and dialects and made it available to practically every literate person around the globe. We must realize that God did not choose us because we were any better or any holier than others. It would be far better for us if we stopped thinking that there was one truth for the Jews and a different one for the rest of the world, or that there are different plans of salvation for Jews and for Gentiles. Quite the contrary, the truth of God is singular, it is eternal and absolute, and it is valid and good for the whole of humanity.

God created us all in His image and in His likeness, and He wants to save all men equally. Yeshua is the Way, the Truth, and the Life. Instead of forcing the Gentiles to go through the whole complicated ordeal of conversion to Judaism, we should teach them what God taught us through Abraham, who *"believed in the LORD; and He reckoned it to him as righteousness"* (Genesis 15:6). We must remember that God first made a covenant with Abram, when he was still uncircumcised, and that the important consideration for God has always been the condition of a person's heart, not his outward appearance.

Chapter 23

O Michael, Michael!

One morning, without any previous notice, Michael rang my doorbell. I had not heard from him since I had left America and was quite surprised that he had managed to locate me. Directly in front of me stood that young man who was once sent by his parents to Jerusalem to be ordained as a rabbi, but who rather preferred the sweet vanities of nightclubs and pubs. He was the same person who practiced karate with his friend back in Brooklyn to retaliate against the aggressive Gentiles. Michael, who had become wealthy in his own right, succeeded in surprising me exactly the way I had when I knocked on his door and caught him off guard fifteen years earlier. Now, my dear friend had come to Israel for one purpose: to try to speak sense to me, convince me to forsake all this nonsense about Yeshua and Messianism, and bring me back to the warm bosom of rabbinical Judaism—at least, as he understood it.

"I want you to come with me to a certain yeshiva in Jerusalem," he pleaded with me. "Come, speak to a learned rabbi, and explain why you believe that Jesus is the Messiah. Open your Bible before him, and show him all those prophecies you once showed me. I want to see his reaction to all those claims of yours. I want to see how he will answer your arguments, in which you present Messianic Judaism as true Judaism."

I remembered all the heated arguments we had engaged in. Michael, who had known the old Jacob quite well, was impressed by the profound change in me, but he still refused to admit that it came about because of my newfound faith in Yeshua. He found it difficult to believe that I had discovered peace and joy beyond description in the everlasting inheritance of the Lord God of Israel through His Messiah—and without bowing down before the rabbis about whom he heard day and night from his religious parents.

Years had passed since those debates, but Michael obviously could not forget the things he had heard from me concerning the faith. Could it be that my testimony had stirred something in his troubled heart? Maybe he wanted to ease his conscience and prove to himself, through a learned rabbi, that I was wrong.

"Do you want me to duel with a rabbi?" I asked enthusiastically. "What an interesting idea!" Michael looked bewildered. He obviously had expected me to react differently—to shrink back from my position and to be afraid to hear other opinions.

"Now, if the rabbi succeeds in convincing you to return to Judaism the way all the people of Israel understand it, would you be willing to relinquish your faith in Christ and admit that you made a mistake? Would you admit that all this Jesus business was nothing but folly?" he asked with bewilderment.

I replied, "First, I want to remind you that not all the people of Israel accept Judaism the way the rabbis present it. However, I definitely promise you—and you can have this in writing—that if the rabbi convinces me beyond doubt that rabbinical Judaism is correct and that Messianic Judaism is wrong, I will certainly confess my mistake. Moreover, I also pledge to publish an open letter in the daily paper and confess my grievous error that I have misled many, so that those Israelis who have already come to the faith will renounce that faith and return to rabbinical Judaism. I think this is quite a fair deal, don't you?"

Afraid that I might change my mind, Michael exclaimed, "Let's not waste any time! We'll go to the yeshiva right away."

Getting into the elegant Mercedes that he had rented when he arrived in Israel, we were soon on the highway to Jerusalem. Michael parked the car not far from the yeshiva, which was located within walking distance of Meah Shaarim, the most ultraorthodox neighborhood in Jerusalem. The walls of the neglected buildings were covered with layers upon layers of printed posters, which warned the public against breaking the Shabbat, against "immoral" women who expose their necks or ankles, and against the neighboring rabbi and his court. Other posters encouraged the faithful to come in multitudes to revival meetings or to wage holy wars against the crooked elections to the *Knesset* (the Israeli parliament), the defilement of television, the soul-snatching missionaries, and whatever else someone felt was unclean.

Michael and I had engaged in small talk while we traveled. I could not understand what made Michael, who was a very rich man now, want to take me to that rabbi. Was he really so concerned about the eternal destiny of my soul, or was he hearing the still, small voice of God calling, "My son, where are you?"

Suddenly Michael pulled two white kippahs out of his pocket, put one of them on his head, and handed the other one to me. He said, "I hope you don't mind wearing this, do you?"

I looked him straight in the eye and replied, "Michael, if I believed that this is all it takes to be a kosher Jew, I would even put a *streimel* (fur hat of the ultraorthodox) on my head. But, I'm sorry, I am not willing to pretend and wear a disguise!"

Quite surprised and disappointed at my reluctance to cooperate, Michael stuffed the kippah back into his pocket and asked apologetically, "What do we have to do to look different from the Gentiles?" I kept quiet and gave him a look that spoke for itself. He understood it very well.

We entered through a large iron gate, upon which was inscribed, *"This is the gate of the LORD; the righteous will enter through it"* (Psalm 118:20). Out in the large courtyard there were small groups of yeshiva students who were busy in vain conversations. Michael, who was wearing a tailored three-piece suit of the latest New York fashion and an elegant kippah, entered the yeshiva as if it were his own property. Having spent his childhood and youth in Brooklyn yeshivas helped him to feel at home here as well. Although he had retired from the religious arena at a rather early stage in his life, he had enough confidence to believe that since I had already repented and believed in God and despised the vanities of this world, I would find my rightful place within the yeshiva walls quite easily.

Michael could not understand the fact that I was living in the secular world and looked very much like the rest of the world, but that I still maintained a way of life that was altogether different from worldly ways. What baffled Michael the most was how one could resist all the temptations lying in wait around every corner without withdrawing to the communes. Monks and hermits withdraw into their monasteries, and orthodox Jews hide from the hostile world in yeshivas and communities of their own. Michael wondered how a man, who was accustomed to the pleasures of this world, could repent and not look any different outwardly.

We slowly crossed the broad yeshiva hall. The students sat in pairs, face-to-face, rocking their bodies rhythmically back and forth while leaning over their large Talmudic commentaries. Every issue was thoroughly examined from every possible angle, and when they finally reached their conclusions, they were sure that it was by the merit of the rabbis and their students that this world still exists.

Michael seemed tense as we stood at the door of the rabbi's office. He smiled at me and then knocked gently. From behind the door, we immediately heard the rabbi's voice inviting us in. We entered with solemn expressions on our faces. The rabbi was very courteous, as he motioned to us with a broad gesture to be seated. His table was loaded with papers, and the walls were hidden behind huge bookshelves, bearing hundreds of imposing volumes of sacred literature. Michael and I sat facing the rabbi and exchanged amused glances. Twenty years had passed since we had turned our backs on the Jewish religious establishment, and now we found ourselves together again in a Jerusalem yeshiva under peculiar circumstances. Frankly, I did not know what to expect. I imagined that a heated argument might develop. It might well be that the rabbi, after giving me a piece of his mind, would summon all the students to curse me and throw me down the stairs. I was really prepared for the worst.

"Honorable Rabbi," Michael started in surprisingly fluent Hebrew with a heavy New York accent, "Jacob is a dear friend of mine, and right now he believes in Jesus Christ. I brought him here so that you might talk common sense to him. Perhaps you can lead him back to Judaism."

"Certainly! It is a very great *mitzvah* (a righteous deed) to restore an erring Jew to his original roots." The room was oppressively quiet. The rabbi lifted his eyes as he gave me a look of sympathy and understanding. Then, with a note of authority, as if he knew my heart and recognized my convictions even better than I did, he said "Tell me, what makes you think that the Gentile New Testament tells the truth, and our Jewish Tanach does not?"

"Honorable Rabbi," I replied modestly, "allow me to correct your statement, please. First, I do not believe that the New Testament, as you call it, is "Gentile" or that it belongs only to the Gentiles; I believe that the New Covenant is a sacred Jewish book, exactly like our Jewish Tanach. Neither do I believe that the New Covenant is more truthful than our Jewish Tanach. Why do we have to contrast them and put them one against the other? They are complimentary pieces of sacred literature, equally inspired as the Word of the living God!"

That was provocation indeed, and the rabbi's reaction to it was something to behold! His eyes hardened, and his whole manner of speech changed. "How dare you even compare our holy Torah, which was given to Moses on Mount Sinai, with that unclean, despicable New Testament! How dare you claim it is a Jewish book! Do your ears hear what your mouth is saying?"

"I am sorry, sir," I answered, "I agree with you that the holy Torah was given to Moses on Mount Sinai, and I do not deny one single letter of it. But please let me defend the New Covenant. It is neither unclean nor despicable. It may be written in a simpler language than the Tanach, but God used that method in order to make His message clear and understandable to everyone around the world. However, the New Covenant was not given in order to change the Tanach or to replace it, God forbid, but rather to prove the faithfulness of our Lord, the God of Israel, who had promised us the Messiah and who fulfilled His promise.

"Allow me, Rabbi, to ask you a question. Have you ever looked into the New Covenant? Do you have any idea what is written in it?"

"Of course not!" The rabbi was horrified, as if I had suggested to him to eat a ham and cheese sandwich on a Yom Kippur that fell on a Shabbat. "I have never defiled myself with such impurity. It is an unclean, despicable book, which was written to teach the Gentiles how awful and terrible was the crime of the Jews who rejected Jesus, their Messiah. Jesus and that book He wrote were the main cause of all our trouble and sufferings in this world. In the name of that man, the Gentiles have butchered us for the last two thousand years. Every Jew who reads that book does it at the risk of his own life!"

The tiresome conversation went on and on. I do not remember all the details, but the arguments grew more and more violent. I only remember quoting a long series of prophecies referring to the Messiah, who was to come first as the Lamb of God that takes away the sins of the world, and later to return as the Lion of Judah. But, as usual with an ultraorthodox Jew, one can hardly use the Tanach against the writings of the sages, because the power and the authority of the rabbinic commentaries is more highly esteemed by them than those of the Tanach. We could agree that several biblical passages did speak about a suffering Messiah, but according to the rabbi, nobody can know today who this *Mashiach Ben Yosef* (Messiah, son of Joseph) is.

I asked, "Then, how will we know Him when He comes?" The rabbi had a prepared answer for that. *Maimonides* (also known as

Rambam, a twelfth century Jewish philosopher) was the only and final authority—at least, for him—in the matter of the Messiah's identification. The rabbi took from his bookshelf the impressive volume of Rambam's *Mishnah Torah—Hayad Hahazakah*, opened it expertly to the right chapter, and started chanting aloud from the *"Rules of the Kings"*:

"And when a king from the house of David shall rise up, meditating upon the Torah and doing works of righteousness like David his father, according to the written and the oral Torah, and will compel the entire people of Israel to walk in it and to hold fast to it, and will fight the battles of the Lord—then he is potentially the Messiah.

And if He has done all these things successfully, and builds the Temple in its appointed place, and returns the exiled of Israel—then He is the Messiah for certain."

I tried vigorously to explain to the rabbi the vast difference between Rambam's description and the true Messiah as described in the Scriptures. The theory of the sages distinguished and separated between two Messiahs. One is Mashiach Ben Yosef, who will have to come first and die in war, and then Mashiach Ben David will come victoriously as the conquering King. According to this theory, there must be two different Messianic figures, while the Tanach actually speaks only of one Messiah who has to come twice: first, He will come in order to atone for the people with His death, thereby saving them from eternal damnation, and to open wide the gates of salvation for the Gentiles by His resurrection; later, He will come for the second time as the victorious King of kings. The Tanach does not imply the possibility of two Messiahs, just as there is no biblical evidence for the opinion that the Messiah will come when the entire people of Israel will keep two Shabbats properly!

"On the contrary, honorable Rabbi," I exclaimed, "Yeshua alone is the answer to all the biblical requirements concerning Mashiach Ben Yosef, because the husband of Miryam (Mary), His mother, was called Yosef, and also because He resembles the righteous Yosef, the son of Jacob our father, in his entire biography. He is also expected to fulfill all the prophecies concerning Mashiach Ben David when He returns soon in the clouds of heaven with great honor and glory, to establish God's kingdom upon earth."

I noticed that when I expounded on the prophecies about the

Messiah the rabbi's interest was aroused, and he listened to my conversation more and more attentively. Gradually, he stopped interrupting me so aggressively.

Finally, the rabbi asked me whether or not I was willing to attend the values seminar for new penitents (the religious term for those secular people who want to become orthodox), where I would receive the answers to all my questions. He failed to notice that I had not asked him a single question.

"Sure, Rabbi," I said, "but I will do it only under one condition, that the yeshiva pay for my stay and cover all my expenses there, because I am not willing to spend one *agorah* (penny) on such a seminar."

The rabbi looked a little offended by my insolent demand, but the only chance he still had to bring me back to my senses probably appealed to him so much that he was willing to accept my condition. Thus, I went to Netanya to the hotel where the seminar took place.

This seminar was a classic example of the intense brainwashing methods applied by those who endeavor to convince their poor, ignorant victims. About two hundred people—many of them knowing very little about religion in general, or Judaism in particular—were there, listening attentively to a marathon of lectures from early in the morning until late at night. Air Force pilots, artists, doctors, and university professors—all of them with the prefix "ex"—went up to the platform and told the eager, credulous audience how the keeping of the commandments of the Torah had completely changed their lives. Others related exciting experiences that had occurred in séances and other spiritualistic phenomena. It seemed that they were fascinated with the occult so much that they did not realize they were dealing with demonic powers. The deeper they penetrated into the esoteric, the more they gained the sympathy of the excited crowd. Most of the lectures were no more than a campaign of systematic intimidation and threats of the horrors of hell, which those who continued in their secular lifestyles could expect. I agreed wholeheartedly with some of the things that were said, since no one had to prove to me the existence of God and Satan, or of heaven and hell. Still, I rebelled with all my might against the pressures that were applied and the methods of brainwashing that I witnessed. Throughout this tiresome seminar, the Bible was not opened once, and nobody referred to it, even indirectly.

The psychological peer pressure applied to the people was immense. In the corridors, religious articles were sold, such as bottles of "holy water" from the faucets of the *Baba Sali* (a Sephardi rabbi rumored to have miraculous powers), sacred portraits of great rabbis, cassettes of famous rabbis, and music of religious soloists and choirs, black velvet kippahs, prayer shawls, and *tzitzith*. Those followers bought them all!

On the last evening of that long week, most of the attendees walked to the platform and related their experiences of the week. They tearfully pledged to keep the commandments, and especially those of Shabbat and *kashruth* (Jewish kosher dietary laws). At the end, only another kibbutznik dissident and I were left behind in the entire auditorium.

I sat there, thinking what would happen in the near future to many of the people who were present in the auditorium that night. Many of them would try their best to keep the rabbinical commandments and traditions, but soon enough they would realize how incompetent and unable they were to appease God by works. On my evangelistic outreaches, I have met with many "seminar graduates" who were frustrated and disillusioned, wondering where they had gone wrong, how they had failed to keep this or that commandment, and why they had to keep it properly anyway. However, they were repeatedly told not to express doubts or ask questions. Some had been commanded to divorce their spouses who did not follow in their penitence. They broke off all relations with their own children and even refused to visit their parents and eat at their "defiled" tables, thus breaking God's positive commandment to *"honor your father and your mother, that your days may be prolonged in the land which the LORD your God gives you"* (Exodus 20:12).

Meanwhile, the seminar leader, Rabbi Peretz himself, came over to me and asked me why I persisted in my rebellion and refused to come to the platform to confess and renounce my sins in public and to repent in front of the encouraging mob.

I did not respond. How could I express what was in my heart?

Rabbi Peretz looked at me as if he could read my thoughts and asked me, "Why don't you talk to Rabbi Yitzak Amnon at the end of the meeting?"

Rabbi Amnon, "the Great Lion," only found time to meet with me at two o'clock in the morning. We sat together with several other rabbis, and at their request I began to expound to them the principles of the Messianic faith, based on the Torah and the Prophets, relating to the need of the human heart to find forgiveness for sins and reconciliation with the Holy God. That far, they agreed with me wholeheartedly and were even encouraged. But the moment I began to quote the Scriptures dealing with the Messiah, the atmosphere suddenly became gloomy and depressing. Needless to say, they unanimously rejected the New Covenant in no uncertain terms.

"I don't have to read it!" Rabbi Amnon said with determination. "My forefathers decided to discredit it, and that is good enough for me. Moreover, my ancestors received the Torah at Sinai and passed it on faithfully from generation to generation until this very day. From whom did you receive the New Covenant? Was it from your fathers or from the Gentiles?"

"The New Covenant was written by my Jewish forefathers," I replied. "They also brought the message of God's salvation to the four corners of the earth." It is true that Jeff, the one who told me that message for the first time, was not Jewish, but I did not receive the new heart and the new spirit that I have within me from Jeff, nor from my fathers or my forefathers, but from the Lord God of Israel Himself.

I remembered that our Jewish ancestors were failing, sinful human beings like the rest of us. More than once in biblical days they had missed the mark and misled the whole people to live in error. Likewise, they are doing the same today. *Say to the house of Israel, Thus says the Lord GOD, 'Will you defile yourselves after the manner of your fathers, and play the harlot after their detestable things?'* (Ezekiel 20:30).

I continued: "What do you expect me to do, gentlemen, to treat my forefathers and the ancient rabbis with reverence and sanctity, just because they preceded me historically? Do you want me to sanctify their words above the Word of the living God? The religious and spiritual leaders of Israel rejected the true prophets whenever they brought a divine message from God. Isn't it possible that when Yeshua came, of whom it was said, *"Behold, your King is coming to you; He is just and endowed with salvation, humble, and mounted on a donkey, even on a colt, the foal of a donkey"* (Zechariah 9:9), that they rejected Him, too, because he did not fit their popular yet unbiblical expectations?" I looked directly into the rabbis' eyes and asked, "What is it about Yeshua that you reject? Exactly what sin did He commit to deserve such passionate hatred from you? When will you finally learn to see Him in His true light?

"Now, as in ancient days, religious leaders wait for some imaginary, unidentifiable "Jewish" Messiah, who is supposed to save the people of Israel from their servitude to the unclean Gentiles, while God makes it clear that He desires to save His people first from the defilement of their unclean, sinful hearts. Whom should I believe, then? Should I obey my forefathers and the rabbinical sages, or God's Holy Word?

"When will that glorious day come when you rabbis will finally recognize the divine truth and lay your own glory and vain prestige at the foot of the Messiah's cross? When will you stop accusing Yeshua and blaming Him for all your tribulations and cry out loudly with the whole household of Israel, *"Blessed is he who comes in the name of the LORD!"* (Psalm 118:26 NKJV)?"

It was an exciting night, but sad. At dawn we said goodbye to each other and went our separate ways. The rabbis insisted that my interpretation was not valid because I rejected the oral traditions of the Jewish sages, the rabbinic regulations that they regarded as sacred. Thus, they held fast to their convictions that I had adopted Christianity, which was, according to them, a Gentile religion. I, on the other hand, was convinced that it was they who had traded the original faith of the Bible for a man-made and therefore false religion.

But, despite the heated arguments, the atmosphere had been civilized and dignified. I must also admit that for the first time I had a confrontation with rabbis who respected my views and even wished me well at the end of the conversation. My heart's desire is that the Word of God, which they heard from me so abundantly, will truly speak to their hearts!

Chapter 24

Lion of Stone, Lion of Judah

Now, as I look back at the many years of my service in God's Kingdom and His growing vineyard in Israel, I can only marvel at the long distance traveled by the boy from Kiryat Shmonah. He had grown from the thoughts of vengeance and wrath against the Gentiles he had harbored while at Tel-Hai's stone monument of the roaring lion, becoming a man with words of comfort and salvation in his mouth, to the people of Israel first, and also to the Gentiles.

This intense sense of mission did not come from myself. I did not ask for it, nor did I seek the ministry of an evangelist. Neither was it the fruit of my feverish imagination. The truth is that I would not be able to keep at it for one single day if I were not living the fully satisfying life at the feet of *"the Lion... of Judah"* (Revelation 5:5), the Lord Yeshua, my Redeemer.

The days have passed, so have the years,
Since that very early childhood.
I went up then to Tel-Hai
To see my youth there.
Am I all alone here, in my native land?
No, my brother,
You are not alone at all
In the Jewish struggle for survival.

On Memorial Day
They come here, all of them,
To raise their flags.
First at half-mast, and then up on high.
Somebody speaks of the blood of the fallen,
And everybody sheds tears.
Then, when the mourning is over,
The dancers whirl around in circles.
Later, everything returns to normal,

And, like all the rest of the nations,
We continue to serve our own gods:
No longer the Baal and the Ashtaroth,
Or idols made by human hands,
But rather man and God's creation,
And the precious native land,
Because the Lord,
Who gave this land to us,
Became an incredible myth long ago.

At the feet of the stony lion,
Fathers prepare their children
To surrender their lives to the country—
To fall, to die, the victims of war!
No, my brother, you are not alone
In the Jewish struggle for survival!

By blood and fire Judah fell;
This was predestined by God.
And He brings us back, year after year.
But the people of Israel cannot see.
God calls us continually,
But we have no answer.

Since my early childhood
I was brought up on the love for Trumpeldor.
I prepared my blood, and the fire of my soul,
For the existence of the Jewish people.

But God hid His face from me,
And, like everyone else, I asked myself,
"What does it mean to be a Jew?"
The answer that I received
Was a message from on high:
The blood was shed; the covenant cut;
Eternal peace with God is made.
No longer stony lion, dead,
The Lion of Judah still lives!
In Him eternal life is found.
To Him be all the honor, praise, and glory! Jacob Damkani

The way has been long and troublesome, full of obstacles and failures, suffering and stumbling blocks, sins and victories. My life is not easy, even today. The Messiah never promised us a rose garden, did He? Anyone who thinks that Yeshua gave us a Torah that is easier to keep than that of Moses simply does not know the truth. But, I would not trade it for the whole world. If you are born again, you know exactly what I mean.

Within the whirlwinds and the storms of this world, when I pass through the deep floods of water or walk through the fires of affliction and persecution, I have the firm promise of God that He will never leave me or forsake me (Hebrews 13:5), and He will be with me always, even to the ends of the earth (Matthew 28:20). If I stumble and fall, He is always there to extend His strong, mighty arm to me and to establish my feet on the solid Rock again. God has always been faithful to keep His promises (Hebrews 10:23), although I have often failed Him.

At times, when I close my eyes in meditative contemplation, I can see before my eyes, floating from the distant past as from a different world, a picture of a father and his son. I see a twelve-year-old boy standing near his father at the synagogue of the Persian and Iraqi Jews in Kiryat Shmonah. And I see the father bending over his son and pointing lovingly at the place in the prayer book where the cantor is reading. The young lad finds it difficult to follow the fast reading of the worshippers, but he does his best not to put his father to shame publicly, God forbid. He learns from his father what being Jewish is all about and is proud of his Jewishness.

Then, suddenly, the scene changes. It is a beautiful spring day, during a festive celebration at a large Messianic conference in a convention hall on Mount Carmel. Again I see this boy, many years older, at the side of his aging father. The preacher stands behind the pulpit and reads from the Scriptures into the microphone. The son holds a book in his hand—it is not the Sephardi Siddur (prayer book), but rather the Bible, the Word of the living God—and follows the reader with his finger pointing to the text, showing his father what being a Messianic Jew is all about, and he is proud of his Jewishness!

Israel, unlike any other nation, is bound to its religion, yet it is striving to recover its identity, one that no longer seems clear because it is in dire need of restoration of the definition of what it means to be a Jew. Until this day, however, the Israeli government has not been able to define who is to be called a Jew. Thus, most Israelis have only a sense of national pride, and only the common threat against national security unites the people together. Yet, most have no real bond with their Jewish heritage, because the God of the Scriptures is still ignored and forgotten, while the traditions of man are reverenced.

The man that I have become, with my new heart and spirit that have been transformed by the living God, no longer asks, "Why me, Lord? Why was I born a Jew?" I now know that God's design for my life is far more perfect than anything I could ever imagine for myself. I now dream of the day when all of my people and all the peoples of the world will discover their true Jewish roots, as I have. To that end I gladly offer my life as a living sacrifice (Romans 12:1). My prayer is that Jews of all confessions—orthodox and conservative, reformed and secular, Hassidic and Messianic—will be able to sing and dance together, gladly drawing the living water from the everlasting wells of salvation!

This does not mean that we should stop lighting the Shabbat candles, or reciting the *kiddush* (prayer of sanctification) over the wine and bread, or cease from building a booth on Sukkot. Neither does it say that now we can start eating leavened bread on Passover or break the Shabbat in public, or stop fasting on Yom Kippur. On the contrary, we should certainly continue to draw water from the springs of Judaism. We should keep the festivals according to the sanctified traditions of our fathers, inasmuch as they do not contradict the Word of God and as long as we know that these are not the means of our eternal salvation. God alone is our Savior, and He has provided His salvation to us, not based on human traditions, but through the atoning death and resurrection of His Son, Yeshua the Messiah.

If I have managed to present a faithful and accurate account, testifying to all the marvelous things that the King of Kings and the Lord of Lords has done in my life—let that be my reward. All the praise and the glory be to God and to His Messiah forever and ever, Amen!

Epilogue

"To the Jew First..."

Dear readers, especially my fellow Jews, whatever religious ideology you belong to, I want to clarify that everything written in this book was brought forth with much love and true concern to bring the truth to light. I have done my very best to support the Messianic faith with quotations from the Word of God, but perhaps the most significant Scripture I could share with you is this:

> *"For I am not ashamed of the gospel,*
> *for it is the power of God for salvation to everyone who believes,*
> *to the Jew first and also to the Greek."* (Romans 1:16)

All the evidence shown here is but a tiny drop in the bucket, drawn out of the vast ocean of God's Word. Everybody, great or small, is welcome to drink of that fresh and living Water of Life, and drink until his burning thirst for the truth is quenched, because it was not designated for the wise and the learned only, nor just for possessors of esoteric knowledge—it is here for you and for me, available upon request.

I do not have any delusions, dear reader, that the reading of this book alone will make a Messianic believer of you. I do not underestimate your intelligence, and I know that much more than this is needed. All I wanted to achieve in writing this book was to introduce to you the Person whom I love most, the Messiah of Israel, Yeshua of Nazareth. He freed me from the slavery of sin and into the wonderful freedom of being a child of God. I simply wanted to bear witness to the wonderful things that God has brought into my life. I do not pretend to know all the answers to all the questions. But this one thing I do know: God knows the answers very well!

If you still have any questions, any doubts, or thoughts that give you no rest (and I am sure you do), I want to encourage you to turn to the Word of God, to both the Tanach and the New Covenant. There you will surely find all the answers to all your questions. There you will also come to know our God and His salvation better.

Yeshua the Messiah said,
"Come to Me, all who are weary and heavy-laden,
and I will give you rest.
Take My yoke upon you, and learn from Me,
for I am gentle and humble in heart;
and you shall find rest for your souls.
For My yoke is easy, and My load is light." (Matthew 11:28–30)

Turn, then, to God with all your questions, doubts, and problems, and especially with the burden of your sins. He knows you thoroughly—all your pretenses, your sins, your shortcomings, and your needs. He is no respecter of persons. You might be the son of a king or the illegitimate child of a prostitute—He loves you just the same. He does not care whether your father was a rabbi or a Christian minister, the general manager of a large enterprise or an unemployed alcoholic, a dignified professor or a convicted prisoner. God created you, and He desires, through the promise of the new birth, to be your heavenly Father. Thus, He sent His only begotten Son into this world so that you might be saved. He knows you far better than you will ever know yourself—and He still loves you anyway, more than anyone else in this universe will ever be able to love you.

Right now, perhaps you might want to close your eyes for a moment, think about the things that you have read, and even pray. Just think of the miracles that Yeshua is able to perform in the life of every individual, no matter who he is. He could be a great and mighty king like David, or a despised and hated tax collector like Matthew Ben Levi, the publican and apostle. Just think what God can and wants to do in the lives of ordinary people like us—not too righteous, not too bright—if we will only let Him take over our lives and use them according to His blessed will.

I know well that this is a difficult decision to make, to capitulate and surrender to the divine truth. Your religious way of life until now (or, alternately, the profanity and hedonistic secularity that have been your guidelines) will stand in the way of your making the right decisions concerning your life. But, remember, God does not care at all about your religious convictions, whatever they are, or about the traditions in which you were educated. He desires to have your heart and nothing short of that!

What do you think God will do with this heart of yours, once you give it to Him? He will look at it, examine it well, and come to the inevitable conclusion that *"the heart is more deceitful than all else and is desperately sick; who can understand it?"* (Jeremiah 17:9). Then He will remove that rotten, sinful heart from your bosom, throw it into the garbage dump, and replace it with a brand new one, as He promised through the prophet Ezekiel:

*"Moreover, I will give you a **new heart**
and put a **new spirit** within you;
and I will remove the heart of stone from your flesh
and give you a heart of flesh."* (Ezekiel 36:26)

This is the new birth of which I wrote in this book. It is offered to you as a free gift by the grace of God, and it is yours for the asking. It will be a new beginning, the opening of a new page in your life.

This may be your very first confrontation with the issue of Yeshua HaMashiach, or maybe somebody has already introduced Him to you in the past. You might have read something about Him or even met with some Messianic believers before. If this is the case, I would like at this point to suggest a prayer. You do not have to say it if you do not mean it earnestly. There is no magic power in the words of this prayer, and if your heart does not say it with a deep inner conviction, it will cause no change in your life.

If you have never known Yeshua before, and by reading this book you would like to meet Him and be assured of His veracity, please say the following prayer in your own words:

God and Father, the God of Abraham, Isaac, and Jacob,
Until this day I knew nothing about the truth of Your Torah, nor was I aware of Your great love for me. In the light of Your Word, Your truth has become clear to me. You are holy, and I am thoroughly unclean. I cannot vindicate myself in any way. I want to accept by faith the forgiveness of sins that You have promised me.
But I find it extremely difficult, and I don't have to tell You why. You know so well the way I was brought up, and how I was indoctrinated concerning Yeshua.
Lord, I want to be the human being that You expect me to be. Help me through Your Holy Spirit to do what I cannot do with my own strength. Reveal to me the truth of the eternal sacrifice

of Yeshua the Messiah, who died as a substitution for my sin and who rose again to justify me before You. Help me to accept Him as my Messiah by faith. Work this change in my heart, Lord. Amen

It may be that you have not been exposed to hostile doctrines about Yeshua. You may have come in touch with the Messianic movement in the past by reading a tract or a book you received in the street, and the things that you have been reading are clear and self-evident to you. You agree with the divine truth and are willing to accept it without prejudice and bias. It is clear to you that God has one way of salvation for the whole world, for Jews and Gentiles alike, and you can understand why Yeshua had to come first as the Lamb of God to take away the sin of the world, that He will return as the Lion of Judah in the near future, and that then His feet will stand on the Mount of Olives in Jerusalem. You can see from the Scriptures that, in the eyes of God, you are a lost sinner who desperately needs His forgiveness, and you are willing to ask for it and be born again through sincere repentance. If that is the case, please pray the following prayer in your own words:

O God of Israel,
I come to You now, just as I am, and accept by faith the sacrifice of Yeshua, who rose from the dead on the third day, and of whom You have testified in the Torah, the Prophets, and the Psalms that He might be my Atonement for the remission of my sins. I believe with all my heart that by His blood You have removed my sins from me, that You have cleansed me, justified me, and sanctified me, and that You have given me a pure heart and a new spirit.
I thank You, Lord, for Your loving gifts of eternal life through Yeshua and the guidance of the Holy Spirit. Help me now to follow in the footsteps of Yeshua and to be His faithful disciple, so that I can bear much fruit for Your glory. Amen!

Even if you do not feel like praying at all, that's all right. The day will come when you will change your mind, because I am sure that someday you will eventually want to communicate with your beloved Savior, and this is what prayer is all about, isn't it?

If you have chosen the first prayer, I would recommend that you start reading the New Covenant and visit a Messianic congregation that is near your home. There you will find loving believers who will help you with all your questions.

If you have chosen the second option as the prayer of your heart, you can be assured right here and now that all your sins have truly been forgiven, that the heavy burden of your sin, which you carried on your heart until this day (even if you were not aware of its existence), has been lifted away for good, and it can no longer bother your conscience. Now you can taste of the wonderful, abundant life that the Lord has provided for you through the new covenant that He has made with you.

One of the most prominent evidences of the new birth is the wonderful joy and happiness that will fill your heart to overflowing. The peace of God that passes all understanding will overwhelm you even in the midst of the storm. You will experience the love of God within your heart through the Holy Spirit given to you. Springs of living water will break forth out of your heart in songs of praise and worship to the living God, turning you into a living temple, a sanctuary for His Holy Spirit. You will find in yourself the desire to do that which is right and acceptable in the eyes of the Lord, and you will begin to see the world and this life from God's point of view.

Other clear signs in the life of the newborn child of God are a tremendous hunger for the Word of God and the development of a special sensitivity regarding those things that do not please the Lord, which should be avoided. You will also discover on such occasions that the Spirit points to those things that must be done. As a matter of fact, if we diligently keep ourselves busy doing to others whatever we would like them to do unto us, then we will find no time to do what is wrong.

You will have a new desire to meet and have fellowship with your brothers and sisters in the faith, although their external appearance might not necessarily be appealing to you. I am certain you will find at least some things in common with them: the shared desires to worship the Lord together and to commit yourselves to His service. These people will certainly encourage you in your steps of faith. They will pray with you and for you, lovingly pointing out various sins that may be a snare to you, and lead you safely on the narrow way that leads to a closer relationship with your heavenly Father.

As a true believer, you will also have a deep desire to share your faith with others. You can expect that your friends will misunderstand you and interpret the step that you have taken as an act of religious conversion. When you begin to follow Yeshua, there might be some who will reject you and abhor you with disgust. This is very painful and insulting, indeed, but do not let this rejection trouble your spirit or rob you of the joy of your salvation. Do not allow these pressures to discourage you from following Yeshua or make you change your mind. Remember, you have made the best decision possible. You have chosen to follow the one and only true and living God, the Creator of the universe, who stands on your side against all odds.

Welcome, then, to the universal Messianic congregation that embraces all the families of the earth and that reflects His divine light throughout the world. Now you know what it means to be a true, completed Jew (or Gentile). Blessed is the man who is not offended by Yeshua.

I thank you for devoting some of your precious time to read this book. But if you wish to read the New Covenant or any other material about this subject, I will be delighted to provide you with the appropriate materials. Also, if you want to visit or join a local Messianic assembly or to meet Messianic believers, I will be more than happy to help you meet the believers who live close to you.

In any case, I want to hear your response and your opinions—even your reservations—concerning this book. The best way to contact me is through my Israeli address, telephone, fax, E-mail, or home page, all of which are given in the front of this book on the copyright page. Life with the Messiah is an inexhaustible source of joy and encouragement, and I would appreciate the opportunity of sharing that abundant life with you.

> *"Let us know, let us follow on to know Jehovah: his going forth is sure as the morning; and he will come unto us as the rain, as the latter rain that watereth the earth."* (Hosea 6:3)

Wherever you go with your life,
may the God of Abraham, Isaac and
Jacob bless you richly!
Jacob Damkani

A Word to the Believer

Up to 1948 we could say, *"The wild dove had its nests, the fox its cave, mankind its country, Israel, but a grave"*. Israel has returned from the grave and the ashes of Germany to her homeland, but she has returned as dry bones.

Israel, unlike any other nation, is bound to her religion. Yet she is striving to recover her identity, one that no longer seems clear, because she is in dire need of defining what it means to be a Jew. Until this day the Israeli government has not been able to define who is to be called a Jew. Thus, most Israelis have only a sense of national pride and the common threat against national security, which unite the people.

Israel today, as in most of her history, is full of man-made laws and traditions, which are revered, while the God of the Scriptures is ignored. However, as believers we should never forget that everything that we hold dear to our heart – everything we are willing to die and to live for, the Word of God, Old and New Testaments, the prophets and the apostles, our Lord and Savior Himself – has come to us through the Jewish people. We should also never forget that 2,000 years ago, it was Israel that painfully gave birth to the Church.

Now after 2,000 years: Are the Jewish people enemies or friends? For the Church and thus for many Christians, this question is a stumbling block. However, the Word of God clearly states that, *"From the standpoint of the gospel they are enemies for your sake, but from the standpoint of God's choice they are beloved for the sake of the fathers; for the gift and the calling of God are irrevocable."* (Romans 11:28-29)

"God has not rejected His people, has He? May it never be!" (Romans 11:1) All throughout the Bible it is very clear that God's heart towards the Jewish people is one of love and compassion. Although they have been unfaithful to Him, He remains faithful to His everlasting covenant which He made with their forefathers.

"Thus says the LORD of hosts: I am jealous for Zion with great jealousy, and I am jealous for her with great wrath. Thus says the LORD: I will return to Zion, and will dwell in the midst of Jerusalem." (Zechariah 8)

It is such a tragedy that most believers do not realize that the second coming of our Lord is closely associated with Israel even as it was with His first coming. Beloved of God, Yeshua did not arrive unexpectedly; He was promised to Israel in great detail. There are 660 prophesies in the Scriptures, 330 of them are about Yeshua. Of those 330 prophesies there are 109 which tell of His first coming and 221 prophecies which tell of His second coming.

The Lord Himself spoke of His second coming 21 times and we are called over 50 times to be ready for His second coming. With all that in mind, the Kingdom of God is mentioned in the Bible over 100 times.

When the Lord was asked by His disciples *"...Lord, do You at this time restore the kingdom to Israel? And He said to them, it is not for you to know the times or the seasons, which the Father has put in His own authority"* (Acts 1). First of all, let us realize that the Lord does not take away the Kingdom from Israel, but He brings to their attention the fact that the time and the season of their Kingdom to come is in the hand of the Father.

As a born again believer, have you come to terms with the fact that the entire Bible and all of its promises relate to Israel? Please, I beg of you to take every promise of God and embrace it, lean on it, apply it into your life, let your soul rest in it – but please put it back in its place as it all belongs to Israel as a nation. Did you ever think about God's final salvation and redemption and the promised new heaven and earth? Did you realize that it is all connected with Israel, the people God chose for Himself? God has bound them to their Promised Land, and when He returns, He will return to Zion. *"For I say unto you (Jerusalem, the Jewish people), ye shall not see me henceforth, till ye shall say, blessed is He that cometh in the name of the Lord"* (Matthew 23:39).

The time has come for us to realize that no-one knows the day or the hour of the coming of our Lord, but we are certainly called to recognize the season in which the Lord is to arrive. Now is the time for all true believers to come to terms with the fact that God did not bring the Jewish people back to their Promised Land just to have another nation on the face of the earth. The Lord is preparing the platform for His second coming; Israel is the timetable and the fig tree of God, which we must observe for the signs of the time. The return of the Jewish people to their Promised Land is one of the clear signs, which we are called to recognize. There is another in Zechariah 12:3, *"And in that day I will make Jerusalem a burdensome stone for all peoples. All who lift it shall be slashed, and all the nations of the earth will be gathered against it."*

It is said that the United Nations is spending two-thirds of its time trying to deal with Israel. Yes, Jerusalem is like a "thorn in the side" of the world. Perhaps one of the most powerful signs of the time is the fact that for the first time since the time of the book of Acts, over 150,000 Jews worldwide are born again and are calling on the name of the Lord, Yeshua.

To my deep sorrow, many well-meaning believers fall into the trap of two major streams of erroneous teaching.

1.   Replacement theology –

Doctrine that teaches that the God of Israel has forsaken Israel and replaced them with the Church as if Israel is no longer the people of God and there is no future purpose or plan for them. If that were true, all the prophets, as well as the apostles, would be liars! If that were true then the entire Word of God would be one big lie! God forbid! If God were not true to His everlasting covenant with Abraham, Isaac, Jacob and David, then what hope or assurance do the Gentile believers have in such a fickle God? If God breaks His everlasting covenant with His people Israel, what makes you so sure that this very same God will keep His covenant and promises to you?

2.   Satan, the father of all lies, has spread the second major lie, which throughout the Church is connected with Romans 11:26: *"all Israel shall be saved."*

Because of this promise, many well-meaning believers have come to believe the lie, which has penetrated the heart of the Church that there is no need to proclaim the Gospel to the Jews, because after all – *"all Israel shall be saved"*. However this great promise is only to the Jewish people who are alive at the coming day of the Lord.

This promise is related to the three most important chapters in the entire Bible, Romans 9, 10 and 11, in which we see Paul's heart-cry to build confidence in the heart of the reader. The apostle wants to bring the reader to an understanding that God has not forsaken His people, Israel. God is a trustworthy God, He will surely fulfill

His promises to Israel and therefore, you as a believer can trust your entire life into His loving and faithful hands. So whether you eat or drink, live or die, you should obey the God of Israel and do all things to His glory.

Paul wants the reader to be sure that God in His perfect timing will surely restore the Kingdom to Israel. In Romans 9, 10 and 11 he defends God's loyalty and faithfulness to His covenant people: *"...don't doubt the God of Israel, in due time He will surely fulfill His promises to His people, the Deliverer will return to Zion; He will remove ungodliness from Jacob."* Paul is simply referring to the coming day of the Lord, described in Daniel 7, Zechariah 12 and 14, when Israel as a nation will look upon Him whom they have pierced, when there will be a great national repentance and thus all Israel shall be saved.

However as much as Israel is God's covenant people, a chosen nation, nevertheless when it comes to salvation *"...there is no distinction between Jew and Greek: For the same Lord is Lord of all, and is rich unto all that call upon him."* (Romans 10:12) The only way to be saved for the Jew as for the Gentile is to call on the name of Yeshua.

But here we must prayerfully consider this scriptural question: *"How then shall they call upon Him, in whom they have not believed? And how shall they believe in Him whom they have not heard? And how shall they hear without a preacher?"* (Romans 10:14)

As born again believers we are commanded to take the Gospel message to all the world (Mark 16:15) – to the Jew first and also to the Gentile: *"For I am not ashamed of the gospel of Christ, for it is the power of God unto salvation to everyone who believes, to the Jew first and also to the Greek."* (Romans 1:16)

Paul knew the importance of the Jewish people in the eyes of God so much so that he commanded to take the Gospel to the Jew first, not because they are better, more holy or more beautiful, but because, *"... if the casting away of them is the reconciling of the world, what shall the receiving of them be, but life from the dead?"* (Romans 11:15)

Beloved of God, I am confident in the Holy Spirit that God's time has come for the believers from the nations, to be instruments in the hand of God and a true answer to the heart-cry of the Lord who is calling the Gentile believers to provoke Israel to jealousy.

"First the Lord spoke through Moses, *"I will provoke you to jealousy with that which is no nation, with a nation void of understanding will I anger you."* Then through Paul, *"I say then, have they stumbled that they should fall? God forbid: But rather through their fall salvation is come unto the Gentiles, for to provoke them to jealousy..."* (Romans 10 and 11). Oh, how I long for the day in which all true believers will come to realize that it is only because Israel has stumbled over the stone which the Lord laid in Zion (Isaiah 28:16), only because Israel rejected Yeshua "the stone" in Psalm 118:22, that salvation has come to the Gentiles in order to provoke Israel to jealousy. So Paul is asking: *"Has Israel stumbled over the stone which God laid in Zion in order to fall?"* And he quickly answers, *"God forbid: Israel has stumbled over the stone in order for the Gentiles to be blessed and enter into the promised salvation and thus provoke Israel to jealousy. "For God hath shut up all unto disobedience, that he might have mercy upon all!"*

Dear believer, consider now this marvelous truth: The Lord has commissioned us to take the Gospel unto the uttermost parts of the earth. Now that the Gospel has reached the four corners of the earth and God is gathering His covenant people back to their Promised Land as dry bones, God asks the Son of Man to prophesy, *"And He said to me, Prophesy to the Spirit, prophesy, son of man, and say to the Spirit, so says the Lord Jehovah: Come from the four winds, O Spirit, and breathe on these dead ones so that they may live."* (Ezekiel 37)

The Jewish people are still dead in their sin and God is pushing them into the corner as He did in the time of the judges, only this time not by the Ammonites, Edomites or Moabites, but by their Moslem neighbors. Now most of the world stands against Israel and she feels so lonely, she is in great despair and losing all hope. As Israel is coming to the end of her rope, could it be that now it is not Gideon, Deborah or Samson who are to be God's spokesmen, but you, the Gentile believers, who are called to provoke the Jews to jealousy? Could it be that finally after 2,000 years the time has come for you to take part in what God so much wants to accomplish?

Could it be that now God calls you, the Gentile believers, to come from the four winds, to breathe on these dead ones so that they may put their faith and trust in the rock of their salvation and come to life? Could it be that the time has come for the Gentile believers to provoke Israel to jealousy, to breathe the promised Spirit into the dry bones by proclaiming the Gospel *"to the Jew first"*? May we finally understand that if we deny the need of Israel's conversion, we undermine the foundation of our own salvation!

Beloved of God, Israel as a nation always seems to be standing at a crossroad. As long as they continue to turn their back on Yeshua, they will continue to make the wrong turn. The time has come for us to rise together as one, the Jewish and the Gentile believers, the one new man! We of God's household can help Israel to make the right turn at this time in her history.

God no longer has Moses, Samuel, Jeremiah, Paul, Peter, or John to work with Him on earth, but He has you, born of His Spirit, whoever and wherever you are. By the grace, mercy and the calling of God on my life, I founded "Trumpet of Salvation to Israel". This ministry is made up of Jewish and Gentile believers, who are united in heart and spirit to blow the trumpet in Zion.

For 30 years the Lord has used "Trumpet of Salvation to Israel" to teach, encourage, challenge and mobilize Jewish and Gentile believers to present the Jewish Gospel to the Jewish people in a Jewish way. By God's grace we disciple many Israelis who come to faith, teach them the basic principles in their new found faith and establish them in the truth of God. We help them understand that their life now is about God and His kingdom. We encourage them and help them to withstand the pressure from family and the religious orthodox. We then help them to find a Messianic congregation which is suitable for them and thus help to build the Messianic Jewish believing community in Israel.

After almost 40 years, "Trumpet of Salvation to Israel" is coming to a new junction in the Lord's ministry among His covenant people. Now more than ever we need you to be a partner in the work of the Lord in Israel. Please take time to pray, meditate and think on what you have read. Please remember it is HIS STORY, which He wants to complete and it is a great privilege and a duty for us to take part in accomplishing His will on earth. Beloved of God, Israel is in great need of you, so she can move from Sinai to Zion, so she can enter into the better covenant – the New Covenant.

Trumpet of Salvation to Israel is in great need of you to

accomplish God's heart desire. This is the call of God on your life – to help provoke the Jews to jealousy, calling them back to their almighty God, introducing them to Yeshua in His Jewish context.

I'd like to leave you with a quotation from Charles Spurgeon, which sums up the motivation of my heart for the mission to which God has called each and every one of us:

"If you are eager for real joy, such as you may think over and sleep upon, I am persuaded that no joy of growing wealthy, no joy of increasing knowledge, no joy of influence over your fellow creatures, no joy of any other sort, can ever be compared with the rapture of saving a soul from death and helping to restore our lost family to our great Father's house."

In the name of our Lord, Yeshua, I am calling you to please pray and ask if you should take part in accomplishing the will of God at this most important time in the history of Israel. Please write or call us – we would love to hear from you. For more information or any questions or comments you might have about the vital work of "Trumpet of Salvation to Israel" or about the book which you just finished reading, please do not hesitate and write to our address in Israel provided on the copyright page at the front of this book. I am looking forward to hearing from you! Praise Him forevermore! Bow down before Him! Worship, adore and obey Him!

With all of His love, faithfulness and grace, which are at work within you, take a greater step of love and faith, serve Him wherever you are and live your life to His glory.

I pray that you may be able to joyfully proclaim with Yeshua,

"I must be about My Father's business." (Luke 2:49)

Because He lives! Jacob Damkani

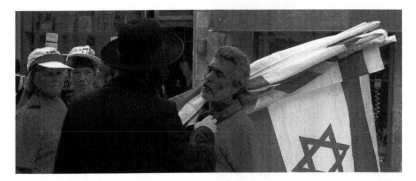

Glossary

Adon Olam - The Master of the Universe, a strictly metrical hymn in the Jewish liturgy written in lines of eight syllables

Afikoman - The three matzoth that are put on the Seder table represented the three ranks within the Jewish nation—priests, Levites, and Israelites—or the three patriarchs—Abraham, Isaac, and Jacob. It was the middle matzoh, the one that represented the Son, that was broken, as a symbol of the Messiah's body that was broken for us on the cross

Agorah – penny

Aleynu or Aleinu leshabei'ach – it is our obligation or duty to praise God, a Jewish prayer found in the siddur

Amidah – the Standing Prayer, also called the Shmoneh Esreh (the Eighteen), in reference to the original number of constituent blessings: there are now nineteen, is the central prayer of the Jewish liturgy

Aron Hakodesh – the Holy Ark

Ashkenazim – European Jews

Baba Sali – a Sephardi rabbi rumored to have miraculous powers

Bamah – podium

Bar Mitzvah – the initiatory ceremony recognizing a Jewish boy as a Bar Mitzvah: a son of the divine law

Brit Hadashah – New Testament

Challah, challot – a special bread for Shabbat

Chutzpah – egotism, nerve

Cocosine – a white, greasy substitute for margarine, made of coconut oil

Counting of the Omer or Sefirat HaOmer – an important verbal counting of each of the forty-nine days between the Jewish holidays of Passover and Shavuot as stated in Leviticus 23:15–16

Crucifix – a representation of Christ on the cross

Diaspora – any area outside of Palestine or modern Israel where Jews have settled

Eretz Yisrael – Land of Israel

Falafel – spicy fried patties of ground vegetables such as chick peas or fava beans

Ganuvin – Yiddish for thieves

Gehenna or Gehenom – hell

Gemar hatimah tovah – may your name be inscribed in the Book of Life

Goy, Goyim – Gentile, Gentiles

Haftarah – the weekly reading from the Prophets

Hagadah – the readings on Passover Night

Halachah, Halakhoth – the collective body of Jewish religious laws derived from the Written and Oral Torah, traditional regulations of learned men

Hanoar HaOved – Working Youth, now politically associated with the Labour Party

Hashomer HaTzair – Young Guard, the left-wing youth movement

Hasidim – members of a Jewish sect devoted to the strict observance of the ritual law

HaTikvah – The Hope, a Jewish poem by Naftali Herz Imber 1878, and the national anthem of Israel. The romantic anthem's theme reflects the Jews' 2,000-year-old hope of returning to the Land of Israel, restoring it, and reclaiming it as a sovereign nation; it was adopted as an anthem in 1897.

Hazan – the worship leader in the synagogue

Jahrzeit – death anniversary

Julian calendar – introduced in Rome in 46 B.C. establishing the 12 month year of 365 days with each fourth year having 366 days and the months each having 31 or 30 days except for February, which has 28 or in leap years 29 days. The Gregorian calendar, a slight modification of the leap year rules of the Julian calendar (which does not pertain to this calculation), was introduced in 1582 and adopted in Great Britain and the American colonies in 1752.

Kabbalah – mystical Jewish philosophies

Kaddish – a hymn of praises to God found in Jewish prayer services. The central theme of it is the magnification and sanctification of God's name. The term "Kaddish" is often used to refer specifically to "The Mourner's Kaddish", said as part of the mourning rituals at funerals, and for 11 months after the death of a close relative. When mention is made of "saying Kaddish", this unambiguously refers to the rituals of mourning. Mourners say Kaddish to show that despite the loss they still praise God.

Karet – meant in Hebrew "death by heaven"

Kashruth – Jewish kosher dietary laws

Katyusha – missiles fired at us from across the border of Lebanon

Kibbutz, kibbutzim – a communal farm or settlement in Israel

Kiddush – traditional prayer of sanctification, over the *yay'in* and *challah*, wine and Sabbath bread.

Kippah, yarmulke – head covering like a beanie or a skullcap

Kiryat Shmonah – the Town of the Eight

Knesset – the Israeli parliament

Kosher – ritually fit for use

Lag b'Omer – holiday on the 33rd day of the Counting of the Omer

(Lay) Tefillin – put on phylacteries

Magen Avraham – Defender of Abraham

Maimonides – Moses ben Maimon, also known as Rambam, a twelfth century Jewish philosopher

Mashiach Ben Yosef – Messiah, son of Joseph

Mashiach Ben David – Messiah, son of David

Matzah, matzoth – wafers of unleavened bread eaten at Passover

Messiah – saviour or liberator of a group of people, often referred to as "King Messiah" is to be a human leader, physically descended from the paternal Davidic line through King David and King Solomon. In Christianity, the Messiah is called the Christ, translating the Hebrew word of the same meaning

Messianic Jew – Messianic Judaism believes that Jesus is the Jewish Messiah and the Son of God, and that the Hebrew Bible, Old Testament and New Testament are all authoritative Scriptures.

Mikveh – a ritual bath

Minim – apostates, and also the initials of the Hebrew phrase for "believers in Jesus of Nazareth"

Mishnah – study by repetition. It is the first major written redaction of the Jewish oral traditions known as the *Oral Torah*, by Judah the Prince at the beginning of the third century, in a time when, according to the Talmud, the persecution of the Jews and the passage of time raised the possibility that the details of the oral traditions of the Pharisees from the Second Temple period (536 BCE – 70 CE) would be forgotten.

Missionary – someone sent to proclaim the Good News. In Israel, it is considered something immoral to do.

Mitzvah, mitzvahs, mizvoth – a righteous deed, a commandment of the Jewish law; a meritorious deed or a charitable act.

Moshav – agricultural settlement

Mujadedin – Arabic for born-again people

Neshamah – can mean both, "soul" or "spirit".

Sefirat HaOmer – counting of the Omer is an important verbal counting of each of the forty-nine days between the Jewish holidays of Passover and Shavuot as stated in Leviticus 23:15–16

Oseh Shalom – Maker of Peace

Passover Seder – order, arrangement for the Passover meal

Pesach – the Passover

Pilpul – intricate reasonings

Rambam — Moses ben Maimon, also known as Maimonides, a twelfth century Jewish philosopher

Rambam's Mishnah Torah—Hayad Hahazakah

Rosh Hashanah – Jewish New Year, today celebrated at the time of the Feast of Trumpets

Sabbath, Shabbat – the holy Sabbath, the seventh day of the week.

Sabra, Sabras – native Israeli

Sephardim – Jews from the Mediterranean and the Middle East

Shalom – peace

Shavuah, Shavuot, shavuim – week, weeks

Shavuot – Pentecost

Shekinah – Divine Presence

Shir Hakavod – hymn of Glory

Shivah – the traditional seven-day period of mourning for the dead that is observed in Jewish homes

Shofar – ram's horn trumpet

Siddur – Jewish prayer book

Streimel – fur hat of the ultraorthodox

Sukkot – Feast of Tabernacles

Tachanun – supplication, petition

Tallit – prayer shawl

Talmud – literally, instruction; the body of Jewish tradition that has been codified

Tanach – Old Testament

Tashlich – symbolically throwing away our sins into its water

Tefillin – phylacteries or amulets, small leather boxes containing slips inscribed with scriptural passages and traditionally worn on the arm and head by Jewish men during morning prayers

Tel-Hai – Living Hill

The Last Supper – the final meal that Jesus shared with his Apostles in Jerusalem before his crucifixion

Torah – the scrolls of the Pentateuch, the five books of Moses

Tzitzith, tzitsiyot – specially knotted ritual fringes, or tassels, worn in antiquity by Israelites and today by observant Jews and Samaritans. Tzitzit are attached to the four corners of the tallit (prayer shawl) and tallit katan (everyday undergarment).

Yamim Noraim – the ten "days of awe" before Yom Kippur

Yay'in – wine

Yeeden – Jews, Yiddish

Yehoshua Ben Nun – Joshua, son of Nun

Yeshiva – rabbinical school

Yeshu – a "play" on Yeshua's correct name, acronym standing for Yimmach Shemo Ve-zikro—May his name and memory be blotted out.

Yeshu'ah – salvation

Yeshua Ben David – Jesus, son of David

Yeshua HaMashiach – Jesus the Messiah; literally from the Hebrew, "Salvation, the Anointed One"; more commonly translated, "Savior, the Messiah"

Yeshua – Jesus

Yom Kippur – the Day of Atonement

Yored – emigrant

Zohar – mystical Jewish philosophies

Please contact us:
Trumpet of Salvation to Israel
P.O. Box 3565
Tel Aviv 6103402 Israel
Elisheva@TrumpetofSalvation.org
www.TrumpetofSalvation.org